Minor Transpacific

ASIAN AMERICA
A series edited by Gordon H. Chang

Minor Transpacific

Triangulating American, Japanese, and Korean Fictions

David S. Roh

STANFORD UNIVERSITY PRESS

STANFORD, CALIFORNIA

STANFORD UNIVERSITY PRESS
Stanford, California

Chapter 1 is a revised version of an article titled "Scientific Management in Younghill Kang's *East Goes West*: The Japanese and American Construction of Korean Labor," originally published in *MELUS: Multi-Ethnic Literatures of the United States* 37, no. 1 (2012): 83–104. Reprinted with permission.

Chapter 2 is a revised version of an article titled "Kaneshiro Kazuki's *GO* and the American Racializing of Zainichi Koreans," originally published in *Verge: Studies in Global Asia* 2, no. 2 (2016). Reprinted with permission.

Printed in the United States of America on acid-free, archival-quality paper

Library of Congress Cataloging-in-Publication Data
Names: Roh, David S., 1978– author.
Title: Minor transpacific : triangulating American, Japanese, and Korean-fictions / David S. Roh.
Other titles: Asian America.
Description: Stanford, California : Stanford University Press, 2021. | Series: Asian America | Includes bibliographical references and index.
Identifiers: LCCN 2020051469 (print) | LCCN 2020051470 (ebook) | ISBN 9781503611764 (cloth) | ISBN 9781503628007 (paperback) | ISBN 9781503628014 (epub)
Subjects: LCSH: American fiction—Korean American authors—History and criticism. | Japanese fiction—Korean authors—History and criticism. | Imperialism in literature. | United States—In literature. | Japan—In literature. | Korea—In literature.
Classification: LCC PS153.K67 R64 2021 (print) | LCC PS153.K67 (ebook) |
  DDC 810.9/8957—dc23
LC record available at https://lccn.loc.gov/2020051469
LC ebook record available at https://lccn.loc.gov/2020051470

Cover design: Rob Ehle
Typeset by Kevin Barrett Kane in 11/14 Adobe Garamond Pro

For Tae-yang

Contents

Preface

This is a story of instant noodles.

In the early 1970s, two immigrants arrived separately in Los Angeles's Koreatown, where they met, married, and began a family. Part of an influx, thanks to the 1965 Immigration Act, their presence added to Koreatown's steady growth, as well as its requisite array of grocery stores, beauty salons, and restaurants. But after a mugging near their apartment, our immigrant couple headed south to Orange County, infant son in tow, seeking less crime and more opportunities. However, the move came with the disadvantage of distancing them from the goods and services that tied them to their ethnic heritage. So they made do with what was available nearby, buying Japanese foodstuffs in lieu of Korean. As a result, while our young immigrant couple spent long hours at work, their latchkey children—a daughter had since joined the family—ended up sustaining themselves on a bad diet of television and Japanese instant noodles: Sapporo Ichiban in its iconically red and white packaging.

I confess: to this day, despite years of counterprogramming, I still prefer Sapporo Ichiban over the now widely available array of Korean instant noodles.

Japan has always loomed large in Korea, America, and Korean America. In my mind, its presence registered on multiple levels. For one, there was my largely conventional understanding of Japan from a post-1970s American childhood—high-end electronics, campy popular culture, and economic menace signified by the proliferation of Hondas and Toyotas threading the freeway. Yet when Japanese and Japanese Americans were vilified in popular media and the press, I recoiled; even then I intuited that there were few distinctions between Asian Americans in the broader American imaginary. On another level, there was a household unease—hostile comments muttered by my parents that I cannot recall in detail, but enough to have wormed their way into my subconscious. I vaguely recalled that my grandparents spoke Japanese—always mentioned in passing, whispered between breaths, but not something I ever witnessed. I had only the haziest picture of colonial Japan, yet it was ever present, even if I couldn't fully articulate it.

Three vignettes come to mind. The first is embarrassingly juvenile. One day on the school playground, two classmates, as elementary students are wont to do, accosted me and asked if I liked (that is, "liked liked") the only other Asian American student in our class. My mind raced. Panicked, I exclaimed no, I didn't like her, because, because—she's Japanese! I registered confusion on their faces, their hopes for racial romance dashed, and they left me to dwell in my own befuddlement: Why had I chosen her ethnicity as the reason for my objection?

The second informs the first. Upon graduating from college and before embarking on a year of teaching English in the Japan Exchange and Teaching Program, I was taken aside by my father, who sternly admonished me in no uncertain terms that I was forbidden to bring home a Japanese partner. My understanding of colonial Korea was abstract, but in my father's mind its contours were sharply defined, despite his having been born after liberation. His scars were intergenerational legacies, and here, he reminded me, they were mine as well.

With the third story, our time line compresses. After nearly a year living and working in Japan, I stumbled upon a new Korean restaurant in town and met the proprietor. After exchanging pleasantries in Korean, I asked him about his travels, and how often he visited *hanguk* (South Korea), a name that I had always associated with the entirety of Korea. He answered that he'd never been there because he was not able. Confused, I asked him why, and he explained that he couldn't travel to South Korea because he held North Korean citizenship. I was dumbstruck; it was my first encounter with a North Korean. After recovering from my initial shock, I thanked him for opening the restaurant and promised to return soon. I left, deeply embarrassed and unmoored by my reaction. The restaurateur had spoken Korean with a slight Japanese inflection (my American accent was likely equally disconcerting to him), so while he was technically North Korean, he hadn't been born there—he was as much Japanese as I was American. Yet in this third national space, while we both self-identified as ethnically Korean, we still anchored ourselves according to national allegiances that had little to do with our realities as racialized subjects—I as an Asian American, and he as Zainichi (Resident Korean in Japan). Only in this third national site as diasporic subjects could we have had an encounter that foregrounded the politics of *both* our homelands and our destination countries simultaneously, a dizzying moment that destabilized my understanding of citizenship, race, and ethnicity. I had no point of reference for comprehending that encounter as an Asian American; and I had no way of articulating the dialogue occurring along so many intersecting racial and political lines.

I make these confessions not to seek absolution but to underscore how much Korean America was and is tied to Japan and yet how little vocabulary was available to me and would be available, even as I was coming to study and understand Asian America, for the complexities of its tangled web of colonial history in our present critical discourse. The first vignette belongs to Asian America, the second to Korean America, and the third to a nebulous, undefined space that I had yet to come to terms with. But in all three, sharply defined borders were transgressed by more complexities than I could count. In a way, this book is an attempt to build an ontology to work through an encounter that has continued to haunt me. With national borders becoming more porous and global flows of bodies increasing, the need for ethnic literary criticism to incorporate multiple sites will only escalate.

I come to this work at a fortuitous time. There has long been interest in Asian American studies among Asian scholars. In Japan, for example, the *Asian American Literature Association Journal* specializes in Asian American literary studies, and scholars in Korea have long had an interest in Asian American studies, recently leading to a formal relationship between the American Studies Association of Korea and the Association for Asian American Studies. However, there appears to be less enthusiasm among Asian studies scholars based in the West, for reasons I detail in the Introduction. What *has* gained traction among Asian studies scholars is Zainichi studies, with the publication of pioneering works such as *Zainichi* (University of California Press, 2008), *Diaspora without Homeland* (University of California Press, 2009), *Lamentation as History* (Stanford University Press, 2005), and recent anthologies in translation such as *Into the Light* (University of Hawaii Press, 2010) and *Zainichi Literature* (University of California Press, 2018). Yet in Asian American studies circles, there are few, if any, discussions of Zainichi literature. It is my hope that as an interloper with hybrid tastes and interests due to a confluence of circumstances, migration patterns, and pure accident, I have written a book that can serve as one of many steps toward connecting these bodies of knowledge.

Acknowledgments

This book has been in the making, in one form or another, for nearly two decades, during which time it has been shaped by countless conversations with friends and colleagues over desultory walks and overpriced coffee.

I'm grateful to friends and colleagues who took the time to read through various portions of this book in its more protean stages and to offer feedback over the years, including Song Hyewon, Haruko Iwasaki, Delores Phillips, the late Imtiaz Habib, Scott Black, Jeremy Rosen, Cindi Textor, Kya Mangrum, Diana Leong, Vince Cheng, Kimberly Jue, Mamiko Suzuki, and Wes Sasaki-Uemura. My colleagues at the University of Utah have gone out of their way to support me and my work. Dianne Harris and Barry Weller stewarded my arrival and acclimation to Salt Lake City, and colleagues such as Howard Horwitz, Craig Dworkin, Anne Jamison, Matt Potolsky, Michael Mejia, Kathryn Stockton, Vince Pecora, Angela Smith, Matt Basso, Paisley Rekdal, Kate Coles, Janet Theiss, and Kent Ono were generous with their hospitality and institutional knowledge. In addition, department administrators Shawn Adrian, Marc Hoenig, Gail Sitton, and Gerri Mackey cannot go unrecognized. Special thanks go to Emily Anderson for checking my math. Friends and colleagues Edmund Fong, Annie Fukushima, Lulu Alberto, Lisa Swanstrom, Rebekah Cummings, Lizzie Callaway, Erin Beeghly, and Josh Rivkin kept me in good company and mirth. I'd like to especially thank Victor Bascara and Christopher Hanscom for serving as external readers for a manuscript workshop hosted by the University of Utah College of Humanities.

Iterations of various chapters were shared at the generous invitation of
Erin Suzuki, Todd Henry, and Ari Heinrich at the University of California San Diego's Department of Literature; Leo Ching and Aimee Kwon at
Duke's Department of Asian and Middle Eastern Studies; David Kang at
the University of Southern California Korean Studies Institute; Julia Lee
and Ed Park at Loyola Marymount University's English Department; Joe
Jeon and Julia H. Lee at UC Irvine's Center for Critical Korean Studies
and Department of Asian American Studies; and Anne Cheng at Princeton
University's Program in American Studies. Portions were also delivered at
the American Studies Association of Korea and the Association for Asian
American Studies Conference, where I benefited from the feedback and fel-
lowship of Jim Lee, Sonia Kim, Anita Mannur, Jennifer Ho, Chris Fan,
Robert Ku, Nadia Kim, and Jinah Kim.

I must thank my editor Margo Irvin and series editor Gordon Chang,
who championed this book as it wended through the review and production process. Jessica Ling has likewise been instrumental in the book's advancement to the final stages of publication. Several anonymous readers
provided detailed and sharp feedback in their reports—the book is all the
better for their largesse.

Institutional support afforded me the time to bring my project to completion: the IIE Fulbright Commission, the University of Utah Research
Council and College of Humanities, and the National Humanities Center.
Additional thanks go to Hotei Toshihiro for sponsoring my residency at
Waseda University, and to the Japan Exchange and Teaching Program for
introducing me to Japanese language and culture, leading to a life-changing
year in Okazaki City, Aichi-ken.

The largest portion of my gratitude I've reserved for my family. This book
is the direct result of the intrepid travels of my parents, Noh Chan Yong and
Kim Young Hee, whose story I obliquely chronicle. Emily has gone from
little sister to go-to consultant on all things. I couldn't have made the mad
dash to the finish line without Kendra, my partner and biggest cheerleader,
whose unwavering support propped me up when my spirits flagged. Finally,
I write this at the dawn of the life of our son, Noah Tae-yang Roh, for
whom the voyage is only beginning—I pray that he has a horizon boundless
beyond my poor imagination.

Note on Translation

Translating Zainichi Korean fiction presents unique challenges. While the texts discussed in this book are written in Japanese, some take place in English and others in Korean—and sometimes a combination of the two—which creates two or three layers of linguistic displacement. Where Korean words are phonetically represented in Zainichi novels, I have elected to preserve their transcription followed by an English translation. Korean and Japanese names are presented in their original order (surname first), except for Korean American and Japanese American figures, whose names follow Western conventions. Moreover, Korean names phonetically presented in Japanese are preserved, rather than given in a direct Korean-to-English romanization. Korean words conform to the McCune-Reischauer system.

Minor Transpacific

Triangulating Fictions

> Neither the Japanese Government nor, so far as is known, the
> Korean Government has taken any definite position in regard
> to solution of the Korean minority problem in Japan.
>
> —Supreme Command for Allied Powers, "Status of Koreans in Japan,"
> Confidential Memorandum

> Zainichi—rootless like tumbleweed, deprived of the protective
> carapace of "nation," fighting among themselves even when in a foreign
> country, the country to which they should return split in two. In the
> popular mind, they were nothing short of "the dregs of history."
>
> —Kang Sang-jung, "Memories of a Zainichi Childhood"

> To imagine otherwise is not about imagining as the other,
> but rather, is about imagining the other differently.
>
> —Kandice Chuh, *Imagine Otherwise*

WALK BY THE Japanese Embassy in Seoul, South Korea, and one might notice a striking display. A statue of a young woman wearing a traditional Korean dress (Korean: *chŏgori*) faces the embassy, expressionless, hands in her lap, and feet bare (figure 1). Erected in 2011, the statue has become a flash point of controversy over the issue of comfort women (K: *wianbu*; J: *ianfu*), who were forcibly conscripted by the Japanese Empire during World War II to serve as sex slaves for soldiers on military bases. For many Koreans, the Japanese government's slow response and reluctance to acknowledge its crimes has been a sore point; clearly, the statue was installed to provoke a response. Predictably, Korean-Japanese relations soured considerably afterwards, with nationalists on both sides of the Yellow Sea expressing outrage.

It is less clear why comfort women monuments have appeared in the United States—Palisades Park, New Jersey; Westbury, New York; Glendale, California; Southfield, Michigan; Fairfax, Virginia; Atlanta, Georgia; and most recently, San Francisco, California.[1] In contrast to the statue in Seoul, her sisters in America are usually located in less prominent arenas. The Glendale statue is nestled behind a senior community center building and a public park, within walking distance to the Glendale Galleria shopping mall (figure 2); the Southfield statue stands guard outside the Korean Cultural Center; and the Fairfax memorial is rather remote—as well as being more abstract—seated behind a large federal building, hundreds of yards away from public view on a grassy slope (figure 3). While the reaction has not been nearly as vociferous as it was in Japan, the statues have caused some first-generation Japanese Americans to lodge complaints and file a lawsuit demanding their removal.[2]

The odds of a comfort woman statue appearing in Japan are slim; in 2012, a small-scale version of the statue was displayed at an art exhibit at Tokyo Metropolitan Art Museum but was quickly taken down because of complaints.[3] However, should one walk around the antiwar memorial Peace Park in Hiroshima, Japan, one might stumble upon a shaded, discreet area devoted to the Korean victims of the atomic bomb (figure 4), which has its own tortured and complicated history.[4]

How do we read the statues' placements?[5] Memorials installed in Hiroshima and Seoul make some intuitive sense; California, Michigan, and Virginia are less intelligible. A Japan-Korea national binary offers the easiest path for reading these memorials. It is not difficult to understand the transpacific travels of the comfort women memorial as an extension of grievances against Japan by South Korea—first the provocative installation of the statue in front of the Japanese Embassy, and then efforts calling attention to the issue abroad in partner nations through similar pieces.[6] Likewise, the Hiroshima memorial to the Korean victims could be understood as part of the antiwar, universalist message undergirding the broader mission of the Peace Park.

But scratch the surface and questions begin to arise. For instance, understanding the role of the Korean memorial at Hiroshima in Japanese history is anything but simple. As Lisa Yoneyama notes in her seminal *Hiroshima Traces*, the Peace Park is evidence a collective and discursive "memory work"—in this case serving as a vehicle for Japan's national consciousness to come to terms with the war. Of significance is the Korean memorial's

FIGURE 1 Comfort woman statue in front of the Japanese embassy in Seoul, South Korea. Photograph by author.

FIGURE 2 Comfort woman statue, Glendale, California, USA. Photograph by author.

FIGURE 3 Comfort woman memorial, Fairfax, Virginia, USA. Photograph by author.

FIGURE 4 Memorial to Korean victims of the atomic bomb, Hiroshima Peace Memorial Park, Japan. Note that the inscription specifies only *kankokujin* (South Korean). Photograph by author.

placement beyond the main section of the park and behind a small river, which some read as a sign of continued Korean marginalization.[7] Yet one could instead read the memorial, as Yoneyama does, as a mobilization of Korean bodies for a postwar reconstruction of national Japaneseness,[8] just as Korean bodies were once exploited for Japan's imperial project.[9] Similarly, the memorial in Fairfax, Virginia, is not only a diasporic Korean effort to author international history but also an attempt to galvanize Asian American politics. Why, for example, did the Korean American community appeal to Congressperson Mike Honda, a *sansei* (third-generation Japanese American) representing Silicon Valley's Fifteenth District, to sponsor a resolution explicitly condemning Japan's exploitation of comfort women?[10] Did they calculate that Representative Honda would sympathize with this abject alterity created by the state because of the time he spent in the Japanese internment camps? Or was there some other obscured factor at play?[11]

If we expand our framing to include tertiary sites, a more comprehensive picture may come into view. In a Korea-Japan narrative, the sizable Korean American community leverages political capital to install comfort women statues to pressure Japan on behalf of South Korea, but there is little room, say, to consider the United States' function as a third national space, or to understand an Asian American domestic agenda in ways that account for internal tensions and disparate histories. In a similar vein, according to Yoneyama, the Hiroshima memorial to the Korean victims was a gross miscalculation relying on the same Korea-Japan binary;[12] it acknowledged only South Korean victims with its memorialization and failed to account for how that would be received by its domestic Korean population who might have defined themselves in relation to many other dimensions, including North Korean and burgeoning Zainichi (Resident Korean in Japan) identities.[13] In a way, the memorial continues colonial-era policies that mobilized Korean bodies for the Japanese national project, now as part of a postwar reconstruction of *yamato damashii* (Japanese spirit) that is oblivious to the emergence of a Zainichi body politic.

Given a binaristic paradigm, these memorials are syllepsistically read "past" each other; but a solution may lie in building a transpacific framework flexible enough to account for expanded readings. Yet disciplinary boundaries have few accommodations for an Asian and Asian American studies dialogue. The comfort woman statues in Glendale are unreadable (or incompletely read) in an Asian American context; and the national narrative of the Hiroshima memorial is illegible to the Zainichi, who have no place in a monoethnic national identity. How are we to account for these transpacific exchanges across multiple sites that do not neatly conform to well-worn disciplinary grooves?

Minor Transpacific interrogates how minority literary traditions engage with each other through intermediary national sites, on two intersecting lines.[14] First, working within transpacific studies, this book acknowledges shortcomings in existing frameworks of empire, race, and minor diasporic literatures and asks how Asian American studies can incorporate a "minor transnationalism" that accounts for tertiary national sites.[15] Korean American literature in particular is a rich site for the study of imperial Japan's legacy in Asian America, which, for historical and political reasons, has been verboten; this book expressly exposes and complicates those disincentives. Similarly, while Japanese fiction falls under the purview of Asian studies, neglecting American racial discourse results in an incomplete and two-dimensional picture. Second, comparing Zainichi and Korean American fiction requires scholars to challenge axioms in both Asian and Asian American studies and to build a model that avoids both an essentialist ethno-nationalism and domestic pan-Asian Americanism. For example, a Zainichi literary tradition accounting for American political and cultural interventions must extend beyond a Korea-Japan dualism; and Korean American literature grappling with the legacy of Japanese imperialism has to negotiate tensions within a pan-Asian American political alliance.[16] A transpacific interminority study, then, resolves how Asian American scholars looking beyond domestic literature might detect American racial and cultural discourse in diasporic communities abroad; and conversely, how Asian studies scholars might uncover connections to minority fictions in the United States. In both cases, this book challenges inconvenient historical and disciplinary barriers in the service of building a more expansive—and interesting—critical discourse.

Mediated, Minor, and Transpacific

What is the intellectual justification for a comparative study of Korean diasporic literatures? After all, Koreans' respective traditions in the United States and Japan are quite dissimilar, as are their present legal and cultural conditions. Put another way, what connects the two bodies of literature other than a shared (and essentialist) ethnic heritage and history? As a possible answer, my study extends beyond shared and divergent ethnic histories to the tensions that these diasporic literatures reflect. Zainichi Korean and Korean American fiction are the end points; this project works backwards to uncover how they reflect and refract a triangulation of multiple national actors, transits, and sites, thereby revealing previously neglected questions and highlighting new critical directions. The ties between these literatures are the myriad imperial forms that have appeared in both and persist even into the present.

A structured approach connecting seemingly disparate bodies of culture and discourse requires some refinement—a mediated minor transpacific. The "mediated minor" modifier widens the transpacific lens to shift focus from binary to ternary relationships. More importantly, "mediated" requires recognizing that a subject's passage through one or more sites leaves that subject indelibly marked—and that this transitional period demands a full accounting. And "minor" requires recognizing the marginalization and objectification of the subject and at the same time reorients the frame to displace the major. Collectively, this theoretical triptych allows consideration of—to borrow from Lisa Lowe—the intimacies of imperial ambitions and capital modernity.[17]

To ground my articulation of a mediated minor transpacific—that is, the interweaving of Korean, Japanese, and American politico-cultural discourse in minor literatures—we must first understand the critical shift toward an interdisciplinary transnational and transpacific dialogue. The tension between the fields of Asian American and Asian (and area) studies is well documented, and their reluctance to engage one another is perhaps a legacy of their historic alignments—area studies with national intelligence, and ethnic studies with 1960s student activism.[18] Consequently, write Janet Hoskins and Viet Thanh Nguyen, there is a structural disincentive for Asian American studies to turn eastward: "The Asian American movement was a reaction against the political order that had given birth to area studies and American studies, and while Asian American studies has sought to be included in American studies, it has had a tense relationship with area studies, particularly Asian studies. This reflects Asian American studies' hesitation in turning toward and across the Pacific."[19] The cumulative effect was that much early Asian American literary criticism tended to focus on the United States as the main site of cultural and political formation—particularly with respect to social justice and racial inclusion—and to gloss over intermediary Asian spaces.

Calls for a corrective engagement, as mentioned above, began to grow louder in the 1990s.[20] A desire to "claim America" and to legitimate and self-define "Asian American" as a racial identity with the attendant rights and privileges of citizenship had led to a strongly binarized dynamic in which Asia was perceived as the distant homeland, while America was destination and destiny.[21] Now Asian American studies began to shift away from domestic-oriented criticism, and critics including Lisa Lowe, Susan Koshy, Kandice Chuh, and Laura Hyun Yi Kang broadened its scope to investigate Asian American literature as a site of theoretical discourse.[22]

Part of that theoretical turn has been a transnational and transpacific shift in Asian American studies, in tandem with a parallel trend in Asian studies, which I categorize as occurring in three areas. The first is a recognition of economic and migratory flows as a starting point for expanding our theory of Asian American studies. It begins with Lisa Lowe and Elaine Kim's critical intervention in a special issue of *positions*. According to the authors, "Both the racialized, gendered character of Asian immigrant labor within the emergence of U.S. capitalism and the U.S. colonial modes of development and exploitation in Asia indicate that U.S. capital has historically accumulated and profited through the differentiation of labor, rather than through its homogenization; in the global expansion of the capitalist mode, the racial and gendered character of labor has been further exaggerated, refined, and built into the regime itself."[23]

If labor and its attendant structures constitute one of the primary engines driving racialization of Asian Americans, we should recognize and acknowledge that theory must account for an influx of new immigrants who face very different historical, cultural, and legal contexts and that that makeup will inexorably alter projected and self-determined forms of race. Part of the solution, Lowe and Kim contend, is to open channels between Asian and Asian American studies.[24] Their argument is an extension of Lowe's *Immigrant Acts*, which posits that Asian American studies needs to avoid reifying metanarratives of intergenerational conflict and filial relations because such practices can mask issues of class, gender, and national diversities.[25] Instead, Asian American studies must be reconfigured to account for heterogeneity, hybridity, and multiplicity.[26] At the root of her thesis is the recognition that migration patterns driven by labor and capital require an epistemological awareness that can account for the contesting of racialization.

The second trend of transpacific studies is a focus on an aesthetic argument for the intertextual and discursive relationship between Asia and America through generative literatures. In *Transpacific Displacement*, Yunte Huang traces how American modernists such as Herman Melville, Ezra Pound, and Ernest Fenollosa imagined (or imaged) Asia as the site of their literary travels, arguing that their translation of Asia belies a bidirectional relationship. That is, in constructing Asia as the Other, writers such as Pound simultaneously destabilize and refract American literature.[27] Similarly, Josephine Park explores that refraction in a narrower context; she notes that Asian American writers used American Orientalism to "write back" against the political alliances that structured it and to contest its restrictive characterization of Asian Americans: "To return to Orientalist literature as an instigator for Asian American literature is to examine anew a political and aesthetic response—one which has long been deemed a case of simple rejection—as a crucial point of contact which defined a literary movement."[28] Park likewise draws upon modernists such as Fenollosa, Pound, and Whitman to highlight how American Orientalism had a hand in constructing Asian American poetics; it is a theory of Asian American literature that shows the ties between modernist American and Asia American poetry, even if they are politically antithetical. In other words, American Orientalism was integral to the construction of Asian American literature, and this means the critic must pay attention to the American formation (or deformation) of Asia as aesthetic method.

The third trend—and the most germane to this study—explicitly decenters the state and the colonizer-colonized binary. Such an enterprise requires critical commentary on the state of the disciplines.[29] There is wide recognition of the inherent instability and fluidity of Asian American racial identity, and the need for a framework that can adequately account for globalization, multiplicity, hybridity, and the decline of the nation-state. Yet at the same time, transpacific studies has arrived at a point when the rising economic threat of Asia is having the countereffect of hardening national boundaries. It is important, therefore, for those working in Asian or Asian American studies to acknowledge that they cannot help but be influenced by institutional networks of power that define the parameters of their work.[30] Kandice Chuh and Karen Shimakawa offer a countermeasure in *Orientations*—a decentralized approach to transpacific studies that revels in multiplicity and a recognition of the shaping structures of power: "This volume does not finally focus on disciplinarity itself, but instead maps multiple iterations of Asianness as epistemological objects in their relationships to specific disciplinary and institutional areas and practices."[31] That is, cognizance of how "Asian" and "Asian American" are constructs of various institutions, practices, and discourses that are historically and regionally specific foregrounds the scaffold rather than the object.[32] While today this may appear self-evident—obvious, even—one has to recall the previous iteration of Asian American studies (resisting structural racism and claiming America) to completely appreciate the turn. Becoming defined by a discourse of powerlessness, writes Chuh, can have deleterious effects; the strongly political origins of Asian American studies as a field heralded its institutionalization, but for Asian American studies as a methodology and theory, defining the field solely along these parameters is severely limiting.[33]

This work follows in the steps of recent scholarship in both Asian and Asian American studies. In the field of Asian studies, scholars have made an impression in their respective subfields with multilingual studies traversing multiple national sites.[34] Of particular interest to my study is the integration of critical race theory in Japanese imperial studies to articulate how race and racialization were used within a unique historical, material, and political context, in what Christopher Hanscom and Dennis Washburn call the "affect of race" and Takashi Fujitani terms "polite racism."[35] However, I am sensitive to the stumbling block of blithely projecting a largely Americanized theorization of race onto Asian studies without qualification. For example, working within the Japanese language reveals that there is no one-to-one correlation between relevant Japanese and English terms. In Japanese, "race" could roughly be translated as *minzoku* (民族) or *jinshu* (人種), but these could also mean "ethnicity" or a "people," depending on the context. There is less of a sharp delineation between definitions, which is reflective of the overlapping histories of race, ethnicity, and nationality in an East Asian setting. Instead of attempting to reconcile or "translate" the difference, it may be more productive to frame these nuances of race as a point of negotiation, reflective of the gap between disciplines.

In Asian American studies, transpacific work has reached critical mass, with several scholars explicitly writing against the grain of convention by integrating Asian texts or situating minority gender formation in transnational contexts. In *Chinese Literature without Borders*, King-Kok Cheung adopts an "interlingual and bidirectional interpretive strategy" to amplify "voices muffled on either shore."[36] Her "extending Asian Americanist critique to Asia," she writes, "would have been unthinkable, if not roundly censured, in Asian American literary circles in the 1970s and 1980s, when American nativity and Anglophone writing were key to the formation of the field."[37] Likewise, Denise Cruz's *Transpacific Femininities* triangulates multiple sites informing the constitution of a writing and racialized Filipina body, since the "transpacific femininities," she argues, "are influenced by the contact between the Philippines and the United States, Spain, and Japan. . . . They draw from a long history of colonial contact in the Philippines."[38] Focusing on South America, Ana Paulina Lee's study of Chinese-Brazilian material culture puts forward a theory of "circumoceanic memory" to capture the complex networks of trade, human trafficking, and labor that define Chinese racialization in Brazilian and Portuguese contexts. That is not to say they worked seamlessly in concert to produce the "coolie." Rather, "Brazilian cultural production as well as Qing diplomatic writings contradictorily produced ideas about Chinese laborers as both the colonizing settler and the newly enslaved population; the figure of the Chinese migrant laborer would both fulfill the dreams of expansionism via immigration/colonization and serve as the necessarily disposable collateral for nation building."[39] Lee's study follows how the coolie as cultural construct would eventually enter the American lexicon, where it would continue to evolve. All three examples of transpacific scholarship pull from multiple sites and discourses to make connections across disciplinary boundaries to illuminate new critical terrains and create new bodies of knowledge. Collectively, they make a strong argument for a longitudinal approach to Asian American studies that includes international sources and contexts.

Let us return to Korean diasporic literatures—the subject of this study. As I have written, the scholarly precedents for multilingual, transpacific literary study have been advanced by pioneers in the field, who, according to Cheung, recognize Asian American literature as social text, "a textual world contiguous with the one we inhabit"; moreover, the transnational turn is the logical result of that social text only being "fully legible in both national and transnational contexts."[40] That is, widen our focus, and rich sites of critical inquiry come into view. Writing specifically about the potential for Asian American studies to engage with Japanese studies, Rika

Nakamura detects immense potential but stresses the need for a robust theoretical framework that would avoid replicating old world paradigms: "To facilitate such a comparative study scheme . . . what is also called for, I believe, is the conversation between Asian American studies in Japan and Japan-based Asian and Japanese studies. After all, they are the experts in the areas of Japanese colonial and ethno-racial minority studies. . . . In so doing, Asian American studies in Japan can assemble a comparative framework for looking at issues such as Japan-based ethno-racial minority experiences constructed within the discursive contexts of Japan and Asian America."[41] In short, a comprehensive understanding of both Asian and Asian American texts occurs only through a comparative, discursive engagement activating historical, cultural, and political knowledge. Writing from the other side, Ueki Teruyo of the Japan-based Asian American Literature Association likewise notes that Japanese scholars' intersecting with Asian American studies can be "liberating" and generative; by shifting away from an "Euro-centric or Anglo-centric vision" they can both "[relocate] the image of America in a multi-ethnic, multicultural perspective" and address their neglected "relationships with Asia, which has been so near to Japan in geography but so far in recognition."[42] That is to say, not only do efforts to bridge fields stem from a sincere intellectual interest, but with respect to race and ethnic studies, it would be politically irresponsible not to engage in them. To return to the question posed at the beginning of this section, my comparative study of Korean American and Zainichi fiction stems not from an ethnic essentialism but from the premise that it is *only through their literary conversation* that both can be completely understood.

If there is a single organizing principle in this study, it is a discursive *triangulation* of texts, nations, and empire. A mediated minor transpacific is, admittedly, this critic's construct for comprehending a body of work that fails to neatly conform to existing disciplinary and national traditions. However, triangulation is also the result of minor literatures that emerge in the gaps, the inchoate and nebulous spaces between defined forms of national identity and empire—an emergent third space.[43] Moreover, there may be a multiplicity of triangulations, overlapping or intersecting only at specific points.[44] *Minor Transpacific* articulates a theory of minor texts, pulling from the three modes of transpacific studies enumerated above— the juridical and cultural constructions of race; the intertextual flows of the Pacific in multiple languages; and a decentering of the colonial metropole through an emphasis on sites, transits, and discourse.[45] First, I examine the cultural interventions in forming Korean American and Zainichi minorities and interrogate the role of Japanese imperialism in the formation of an Asian American political identity to complicate the narrative of a pan-Asian America. At the same time, I reveal how American military legal infrastructure, racial discourse, and Asian American culture shape the Zainichi. Second, a multilingual and multidisciplinary exploration of minor literatures (English, Japanese, and some Korean) brings together disparate histories and revisits disciplinary axioms in Asian and Asian American studies. That is, I read Zainichi and Korean American fiction as both object and site of disciplinary and linguistic syllepsis to reveal critical gaps. Third, I decenter the West as the primary lens through which to view the East;[46] instead, I focus on minor traditions engaging with one another through their respective imperial sites.[47] While the tendency is for critics to focus on the primary site's relationship with the minority body (the United States and Asian Americans, or Japan and the Zainichi), what is needed instead is an articulation of gradations and temporalities of mediating empires in minor transpacific texts. As I will show, the specter of the Japanese Empire haunts Korean American fiction, and so does the specter of America's external and internal imperial ambitions haunt Zainichi literature.

A History of Displacement

Labor and temporality nuance my definition of the Korean diaspora—the displacement of Korean bodies to Japan and the US by political and economic determinants. Labor defines the parameters of displacement and the character of the community narrative. That is, forced labor creates a structural longing for a return home, and voluntary exile in search of labor entails the construction of home. Temporality is useful for comparative purposes, for these two populations, in the US and in Japan, do not align perfectly, nor do they develop at the same rate—Korean America, in general, is defined largely by its first and second generations, whereas Zainichi Koreans are deep into their third and at the dawn of their fourth generation. Correcting for generational difference is not only useful but necessary for articulating both populations' respective trajectories. While they may have histories that are quite dissimilar, they are inextricably intertwined; my brief sketch of their makeup serves only to explain the form of their respective minoritized subjectivities, which I posit were not built in isolation but enfolded within each other through tertiary mediating sites.

While Zainichi Koreans have a substantially more robust history of migration to Japan than Korean Americans do to the US, it is only recently that a domestic identity fusing together Japanese and Korean has emerged. John Lie, in his definitive *Zainichi*, declares that the twenty-first century is the first period to witness "the rise of the post-Zainichi generation: ethnic Koreans who are ready to embrace their Japaneseness, including Japanese citizenship. The rise of assimilation, naturalization, and Japanization paradoxically generated the assertion of postcolonial identity, primarily as Korean Japanese."[48] That is not to say that the Zainichi intellectual and literary community did not spend considerable time wrestling with the question of Zainichi identity. Indeed, much of the literature by Zainichi Koreans grapples with several interrelated, recurring themes: citizenship, colonialism, Korean ethno-nationalism, legislative alienation, racism, language, and passing. Moreover, since Zainichi Koreans came to Japan largely involuntarily, the very question of whether their movement can be called migration has been contestable within the Zainichi Korean community for decades. The term *Zainichi* reflects the politics of their conditional acceptance in Japanese society. Yasunori Fukuoka points out that "the terminology is symbolic. Whatever the legal status of each member of the Korean minority, and however permanently they may in fact be living in Japan, at the conceptual level they are still viewed as mere temporary residents by most members of Japanese society, whether unconsciously or by some mechanism of collective subjectivity."[49] While in the United States, Korean residents who have gained citizenship are commonly referred to as "Korean Americans," with the emphasis on *Americans* functioning as a noun and *Korean* as an adjective, *zainichi kankokujin* (Resident South Koreans in Japan) or *zainichi chōsenjin* (Resident North Korean in Japan) puts the focus on *Koreans* as the noun, highlighting difference. They are semantically speaking, if not in sentiment, perpetual foreigners.[50]

The history of Korean immigration to Japan provides a partial explanation for themes dominant in Zainichi literature. Beginning with a series of diplomatic and militaristic maneuvers, Japan annexed Korea in 1910 and began funneling its agricultural resources to the colonial center.[51] This caused a mass emigration of Koreans looking for work in Japan and China, but the circumstances upon their arrival were grim. Despite discrimination, ghettoization, and violent upheavals—such as the aftermath of the Great Kanto Earthquake of 1923, when over six thousand Koreans were killed by the police and mass mobs—they continued to arrive, sometimes as students but mostly as laborers. By 1938, about eight hundred thousand Koreans were living and working in Japan.[52] World War II saw an explosion of growth with the involuntary immigration and labor of even more Koreans, including a large contingent of women forced into prostitution as "comfort women," ostensibly to boost morale among Japanese troops. It is estimated that by 1945 there were 2.3 million Koreans living in Japan.[53]

In the early 1940s, Japanese rulers in Korea launched a campaign, dubbed "Japan and Korea as One" (*naisen ittai*), to make loyal subjects out of the Koreans. This also involved the prohibition of the Korean language and the forced adoption of Japanese names. Because of fundamental cultural conflicts regarding issues of kinship and naming (*tsumei*), as well as the presupposition of racial superiority, the campaign largely failed to capture the hearts and minds of the Koreans. On the contrary, "The majority of Koreans emerged from the colonial experience with deep-rooted anger toward Japan and fierce patriotism and nationalism."[54] When Japan surrendered in 1945, Koreans in Japan and colonial Korea celebrated their liberation but quickly found themselves in a state of limbo. With both Korea and Japan in ruins, up to three-fourths of Zainichi initially repatriated, but six hundred thousand remained behind.[55]

For those who remained, life in Japan was not easy. Koreans in Japan, who during the colonial period had been technically considered citizens of the empire, were suddenly without citizenship and essentially stateless. The Allied occupying forces, concerned mainly with rebuilding Japan, left the question of their rights and legal status up to the state, which wanted nothing to do with them. The instability of the Korean peninsula added to the confusion, particularly with the division between North and South after the Korean War, which was reflected by a division in Japan among the Zainichi. Eventually, with the normalization of relations between Japan and South Korea in 1965, Zainichi Koreans were given the option of claiming South Korean citizenship, an offer that left those who remained ideologically aligned with the North without a state; it was not until 1982 that non–South Korean Zainichi could apply for "general permanent resident" status.[56] Moreover, integrating into Japanese society came with a fierce pressure to assimilate; and permanent alien status meant that Zainichi were not allowed to take part in electoral politics or access social welfare benefits and that they were openly discriminated against in public and private sectors. Also attendant were humiliating exercises such as ward registration of alien residents, including mandatory fingerprinting at fourteen years of age, which intimated to many Zainichi the presumption of an inherent criminality (see chapter 2). Only in 1991, after intense activism, did the government grant a "special permanent resident" status to all Zainichi Koreans that broadened access to rights such as medical and welfare benefits.[57] No wonder, then, that much early discourse in Zainichi circles centered on ideas of assimilation as betrayal and Japan as only a temporary home.

The story of Koreans in America is quite different. If there is one commonality between Korean immigration to Japan and the United States, it is labor: "The Korean is the pick of all Orientals as a workman. I have worked Chinese, Japanese, and Koreans during the past seven years, and I have not the slightest hesitation in saying that the Korean is decidedly the best."[58] Such were the perceptions of some that led to the exporting of Korean labor from the parochial peninsula to the Hawaiian Islands. The first group of Korean immigrants to the United States landed in 1888,[59] shortly after Korea was forced to open its ports and establish diplomatic relations with the United States.[60] However, since their numbers were small, most do not regard Korean immigration to have begun until the first shipload of laborers arrived in Hawaii in 1903.[61] The "second wave" occurred shortly after the cessation of hostilities in the Korean War. They consisted mainly of orphaned children, exchange students, and war brides of American GIs.[62] The final and current "third wave" came as the result of the Immigration Act and Naturalization Act of 1965.[63] The 2010 census reported 1.7 million Korean immigrants in the US,[64] and a Pew Research study estimated an increase to 1.82 million in 2015.[65]

Evident in these criminally brief overviews of multifaceted histories is the fact that Zainichi and Korean Americans occupy very different positions in the diasporic time line. In tying together Zainichi and Korean American literary histories, I resist the temptation to essentialize based on ethnicity; instead, their histories are threaded together by a shared memory of a Korea that no longer exists, one that has been indelibly altered by, and filtered through, US and Japanese interventions. Finally, these histories detail the groundwork for convergence of both Korean America and Zainichi Japan, for the ethno-national discourse of both groups eventually gives way to an emergent racial discourse involving national, international, and domestic minoritization.

The Structural Formation of Zainichi in Japan

Japan is viewed as a homogeneous country, but as John Lie and others have noted, that is in part due to an ideology of monoethnicity, a holdover of its colonial ambitions. In truth, Japan is home to the indigenous Ainu and Okinawans, ethnic Koreans, and an increasing number of Brazilian, Chinese, Filipino, and Vietnamese. Still, the myth of monoethnicity persists, which, coupled with a colonizer-colonized binary, occludes reading Zainichi literature as anything but active resistance to a Japanese identity or ambivalence between Korean and Japanese identities. Instead, I propose to interrogate the either/or binary with a triumvirate of Korean, Japanese, and American shaping forces. The US in particular functions as an intermediary structural force in the shaping of Zainichi subjectivity, as Melissa Wender notes in her pioneering *Lamentation as History*: "The relationship between Japan and Korea . . . has long been triangulated by the 'west' generally and the United States specifically. We must be careful, then, not to overlook the equally important influence on Zainichi Koreans of that country more usually thought of as imperialist, both culturally and politically: the United States. It does not loom as large or as negatively as Japan itself, but as for other residents of the islands, *it is a towering presence*."[66] Despite her assertion of the importance of understanding the West and the United States in particular as a shaping influence in Zainichi subjectivity, I have not encountered any major study exploring the triangulation of which she writes. Part of the reason, perhaps, is that the US's presence in the racializing of Zainichi is overshadowed by its militaristic violence—most notably the atomic bomb. In the wake of that catastrophic force, however, lies a stark emptiness and vacuum that affords Zainichi room enough to begin to construct a subjectivity that is neither Korean nor Japanese. For a narrative illustration of that absence, I turn to Kim Sok-pom's short story "A Tale of Empty Dreams" (*Kyomutan*).

For the majority in Japan, August 14, 1945, was seared into collective memory as tragedy, but for the Korean minority it was cause for celebration.

The Zainichi rejoiced to see their oppressors humbled, and they reclaimed their independence and sovereignty.[67] However, "A Tale of Empty Dreams" intimates an ambivalence that underscores the fact that there will be no simple return to a pristine ethno-nationalist identity, for Zainichi Koreans have been raced as both Korean and Japanese in contradictory ways.[68] With liberation, they did not simply default to a precolonial identity; rather, a confluence of elements, including the ideation of a precolonial Korea, local activism, and the presence of the United States, wrought a heterogeneous diasporicity.

Kim Sok-pom, elder statesman and Zainichi intellectual, reconstructs the moment of liberation. As one of the vanguard Zainichi writers, he seems anachronistic in his politics and at times impractical; he rejects Japanese, South Korean, and North Korean labels. In a newspaper interview, he once remarked, "Why will I have to choose the citizenship [of either South or North Korea]? There is no way I will become a citizen of the [North Korean] People's Republic. I'll opt for being a stateless person."[69] Kim refuses to acknowledge that Korea has been divided and exists as two separate nations, and he refers to it somewhat nostalgically as *chōsen*.[70] In addition, he declines to select Japan as his official residence and lives as a stateless being who will stay permanently in exile until the day Korea reunifies. Even in his writing, Kim performs a kind of political protest with his unique blend of Japanese and Korean syntax. As Wender points out, he believes that Zainichi writers "should resist linguistic assimilation by making certain that their language has a 'Korean flavor.' [He] also stresses that their language should be in some way unique, if they are to avoid becoming Japanized in the process of writing in Japanese. . . . They should resist the Japanese language, at least in part because it was 'the language of extremely invasive rulers in Asia, not only in the political sense, but morally as well.'"[71] From his statements on Korea-Japan politics and his philosophy on language, Kim appears to identify as a prewar, stateless Korean (*chōsenjin*) and resists becoming Japanese. But even so, he is not without conflict in his struggle to retain and construct his Zainichi subjecthood.

In "A Tale of Empty Dreams," Kim channels that patriotic ethno-nationalism through an encounter on a city train. While the rest of Japan sits in stunned silence after the emperor's announcement of surrender, our narrator finds it difficult to refrain from a public outburst of joy. In contrast, the city train is heavy with the silence of its passengers, with the exception of the convulsive weeping of a despondent rider. Meanwhile, Kim's nineteen-year-old proxy darkly revels in their desperation—he hopes to catch a glimpse of a group of military generals committing ritual suicide outside the imperial palace to atone for their losing the war. Riding on the train, surrounded by the city ruins, he imagines how compatriots in Korea must be celebrating: "I was as nervous as a hedgehog in the dead calm. My countrymen would've thrown up their fists and sprung from villages, towns, and fields in Korea— they would've hugged, sobbed, danced, and run at full gallop, bursting with joy. And they would've planted a flag on the mountain summit while crying, "Korean Independence! Mansei!" My distant friends in Seoul appeared to me, tears streaming down their faces. I would've cried. I would've cried my heart out."[72] Yet Kim's protagonist does not run through the streets declaring victory, nor does he harangue the despondent populace. Instead, he joins the Japanese in their silence—his ebullience is confined to interior monologue. On the one hand, he is torn that he cannot join his friends in Seoul, who are surely celebrating. Instead, he plans to hike a local mountain in Japan so that he can shout "Mansei!" at the top of his lungs, but that serves only to further isolate him and does nothing to mitigate his present reticence. Despite liberation, Kim restrains himself because he does not default to a pre-colonial Korean subjectivity; he finds himself caught between. He wonders to himself, "But where in Japan, which is neither Korea nor Seoul, can I raise that cry?" (203). Since he occupies a nebulous space between nations, he can neither comfortably actualize his Korean patriotism nor completely share in the melancholy of the Japanese.

Kim further illustrates his narrator's internal conflict when a young woman enters the train. Flushed from running for the train, she sits opposite of the narrator. While she hangs her head in silence, he surreptitiously notes her clothes and posture, and speculates on her livelihood. Kim sympathizes, for she is obviously distraught; also, she is attractive and he cannot keep his eyes off her. When she raises her head, he marvels at her beauty. "I wished that the girl who lowered her eyes would show her face again" (204). His attraction to her is distinctively coded as Japanese; he savors the "white nape of the neck between her rounded shoulders, which had been wrapped in an indigo paisley print kimono."[73] However, politics violently reasserts itself. Kim suddenly remembers that he is not Japanese: "When I realized the consequences of my Korean self mistakenly reacting to the tears that had fallen as though I were of the same race, I panicked" (206–7). His attraction to her is precluded by the fact that he is Korean. "But what connection does this really have with me? My people's enmity that lies within me is too great for any sympathizing with her" (207). His confusion stems from his being framed in a Korean-Japanese binary; he abruptly jumps from attraction to a repulsion based on national politics.

It is only in his vision of a great void that he can transcend national boundaries. Now that both nations have been equally decimated, Japan by defeat and Korea by colonization, Kim feels they can finally "stand on the same level" (207). At the end of the text, he envisions a "bright emptiness" wrought by natural disaster. Only on this blank canvas can he construct an identity that does not tear him apart. Living as a Korean in Japan rends him because he cannot truly feel at home, but it is also apparent that he has internalized Japanese culture to such an extent that he would not feel at home in Korea either. Regardless of Kim's self-perception of being completely Korean, his narrative intimates a complexity that his narrator cannot completely articulate. His ambivalence and equivocation are present throughout the text, particularly in the closing line: "And I see a bright extinction. The Genkai Sea [that separates Japan from the Korean peninsula] is split in two and a surge of water rises up toward heaven. And the spray at its mountain-like tip is transformed into a rainbow by the glittering ocean sun beneath which this erasure lies" (207). The emptiness under the "midsummer ocean sun" is where his Zainichi identity lives. His politics may be in Korea and his body in Japan, but his consciousness occupies the space between, under the ocean sun, surrounded by nothing.

The empty space between is of particular interest in this study. It is an absence, inchoate and undefined, but also an allusion to the literal and figurative violence of the atomic bomb. Korean citizenship returns only once Japan has surrendered, and becoming "foreign" once again enables the narrator to imagine being on an equal footing with the Japanese. The central point of tension lies in a binary system, with only an either/or Korean-Japanese duality. Kim's narrator seemingly rejects both in favor of a constructed identity cobbled together with elements from both spaces. It is a space that is created by the presence of the United States—its military intervention and the terrible human cost, but also its legal interventions that redefined Koreans as either liberated people or Japanese citizens. As I argue in more depth in chapter 2, Zainichi subjectivity has been coeval with a complicated, fraught relationship among Korean, Japanese, and American states, particularly the military juridical system.

Asian America and the Japanese Empire

In *Model Minority Imperialism*, Victor Bascara argues that Asian American studies must confront the legacy of American imperialism, lest it unwittingly forge ahead, unaware that its disciplinary narrative of multicultural liberalism may be subsumed by advanced capitalism's flexibility. The solution, he posits, is to "make U.S. imperialism reappear"; moreover, Asian American culture has to recognize how it is "both manifestation and a critique of U.S. global hegemony."[74] Likewise, *Minor Transpacific* attempts to make Japanese imperialism "reappear" and show how Asian America is both critique and manifestation of a tertiary imperial presence. My focus is on Korean American fiction, but the Japanese presence sometimes appears across a spectrum of Asian American literature. Yet commentary from Asian American critics is conspicuously absent; it is, perhaps, a lagging consequence of the early social justice–oriented origins of Asian American studies, which relied on the mobilization of a pan-Asian American identity to consolidate political power. While this was necessary and critical to the formation of Asian American studies, even as early Asian American writers grappled with the subject of the legacy of inter-Asian hostility, violence, and trauma, there was a peculiar reluctance to engage in criticism that could run counter to advancements in domestic minority subject formation.[75] In a way, an odd parallel could be drawn between Asian America and Japan's colonial project of creating a pan-Asian identity in service to a political project. Of course, these are *not* the same, and Japan's policy of racial inclusion was duplicitous at best, but both have a similarly muting effect that represses a more sophisticated consideration of Asian American fictions speaking to a contrapuntal transpacific, rather than solely domestic, discourse. Broadly speaking, Japan as discursive site and racial construct serves several functions in Asian American literature—as an exoticized projection, as a threat, a colonial power, and finally, in Korean American fiction, as a both rival and sympathetic immigrant community.

Here I enumerate several conspicuous instances of Japan complicating Asian American racialization, illustrative of a constant presence that calls for theorizing. Even in the earliest instantiations of Asian American literature, Japan's presence makes itself known as a desirable point of reference or comparison. The autobiographical *Leaves from the Mental Portfolio of an Eurasian*

(1909) by Sui Sin Far (Edith Eaton) recounts a brief courtship the narrator has with a White American suitor, who encourages her to deny her Chinese heritage and pass herself as Japanese. "You shall do just as you please, my darling. But—but—consider a moment. Wouldn't it just be a little pleasanter for us if, after we are married, we allowed it to be presumed that you were—er—Japanese? So many of my friends have inquired of me if that is not your nationality. They would be so charmed to meet a little Japanese lady."[76] Insulted by the suggestion, the narrator rejects her suitor's marriage proposal, but the episode evinces an awareness of a racial hierarchy that is more than merely an aside. In fact, Sui Sin Far's sister, Winnifred Eaton, would actually embrace the suitor's suggestion, adopting the nonsensical nom de plume Onoto Watanna and writing a series of Orientalizing vignettes about her life in Japan, where every scene abounds with cherry blossoms and rickshaws. Critics hail Sui Sin Far as an early harbinger of Asian American literature, but there is little commentary on the fetishization of Japan at the cost of a Chinese American self. It is a far cry from a cohesive, unified Asian American identity—the question is, how did Japan as imperial force and Western Japanophilia affect that identity's eventual formation?

World War II brought an obvious development, as both Japan and Japanese America were vilified with the same cruel, broad brushstroke. Hisaye Yamamoto's *Seventeen Syllables* chronicles postwar Japanese American subjectivity through a series of vignettes. In "Wilshire Bus," Esther boards a bus and encounters a belligerent passenger who harasses an elderly Chinese couple with racist comments. From her window seat, Esther recalls seeing an Asian American on the street and initially taking him for a kindred spirit, only to realize that he did not view her the same way: "Briefly, there bobbled on her memory the face of an elderly Oriental man whom she had once seen from a streetcar on her way home from work. . . . The old man was on a concrete island at Seventh and Broadway, waiting for his streetcar. She had looked down on him benignly as a fellow Oriental, from her seat by the window, then been suddenly thrown for a loop by the legend on a large lapel button on his jacket. I AM KOREAN, said the button."[77] Critics read this scene as a moment of political and racial division, as the presumably Korean man differentiates himself from Japanese Americans to avoid racial discrimination. Koreans, as colonial subjects, were technically Japanese citizens; there was some early discussion that Executive Order 9066 would have included them as Japanese subjects. The elderly Korean man's declaration of his non-Japaneseness is multivalent; it is both a declaration against racial persecution at the expense of Japanese Americans as Asian Americans, and a political act resisting the Japanese Empire's subsuming of his ethnicity. Esther's encounter with him occurs after the war and after internment, yet he is still compelled to distinguish himself; and her ambivalence regarding the encounter speaks to the complexities of his betrayal.

Jessica Hagedorn's *Dogeaters* meditates on the thorny relationship between the United States as colonial center and the Philippines in a post-colonial deconstruction of the nation-state. Yet at certain points in her postmodern rendering, the legacy of Japanese imperialism asserts itself, most notably in the form of commodities. Two minor characters, Romeo Rosales and Trinidad, work in the service industry and voraciously consume American films, images of which saturate their dreams. Romeo pines for stardom, and Trinidad fuels his aspirations with her earnings working at SPORTEX, a signifier of capital modernity. While Hagedorn reserves her most acerbic passages for American and Spanish colonialism, a key exchange between Romeo and Trinidad reveals the terrible symmetry between political and economic imperialism. Trinidad mentions to a large sale she made to the "*Hapon*," at which Romeo seethes: "'You deserve a bonus and a raise for waiting on those Japs,' he grumbles. His father, grandfather, and uncle were all tortured by the Japanese soldiers during the war, a fact Romeo has never forgotten."[78] Oblivious to his resentment, Trinidad plows ahead, telling him "about her plan to study conversational Japanese under Mrs. Ala-cran's sponsorship, so she can sell more goods to the hordes of the Japanese tourists who shop at SPORTEX."[79] Romeo's fevered dreams of stardom are indirectly funded by the largesse of Japanese tourists, a fact that he does not seem to appreciate. Romeo and Trinidad are eventually crushed by the gears of political machinery, but their pursuit of modernity had no chance of success to begin with, for they were merely conduits for former colonial powers to continue exchanging capital.

Korean American fiction in particular has a complex relationship to Japan that typifies my concern. Susan Choi's *The Foreign Student* exemplifies some of those complexities, which have gone utterly unremarked. Centering on the romance between Chang "Chuck" Ahn, a university student from Korea, and Katherine, a southern scion, Choi's novel meditates on the loss and formation of home in the two Souths (Korea and America). At one point, Chang's alienation results in his escaping to Chicago from Sewanee, Tennessee, for a summer between school sessions. There he gravitates toward the local Japanese immigrant community, where he finds a sense of belonging. His fluency due to having lived through the colonial period as a child affords him solace in a hostile America, where both Japanese and Korean are seen as equally abject. Yet his easy integration is not without its complications, for it was his father's self-serving instincts that imparted his Japanese to him: "His childhood Japanese lessons had all been aimed toward the year he would be sent to boarding school in Osaka. . . . 'Collaboration is outweighed by opportunity,' his father would lecture him. 'Take the police. They have the power now, but when the Japanese leave, what do they have? The hatred of the people, and ignorance. We'll have the knowledge.'"[80] He is trained to become a collaborator so that he can fill the power vacuum once the Japanese flee Korea, yet when the war breaks out, he is unburdened by any national allegiance; then, once he moves to the United States, his relationship to Japan and Japanese transforms once again, to a racial solidarity. The US's imperial and racial politics transform his relationship to Japan twice over.[81]

These episodes of conspicuous hostility toward, ambivalence toward, and solidarity with the Japanese and the Japanese state in Asian American fiction deserve scrutiny. The legacy of Japanese imperialism in Asian American fiction is absorbed into a broader geopolitical narrative between the United States and Japan, but it needs to be made opaque and visible, and that can only occur through a transpacific study that decenters not only the West and the metropole but Asian American studies as well.

The aforementioned texts are by no means exhaustive, nor are they necessarily representative of all Asian American or Zainichi fiction, but they do evince how appearances by vestiges of Japanese imperialism are numerous and conspicuous enough to bear revisiting; likewise, American racial and political forces haunt the periphery of Zainichi literature, intimating a connection that demands examination. My point is that the historical legacy of Asian American studies being born of a necessary alliance among Asian ethnicities in the United States effectively renders imperial Japan inarticulable in Asian American criticism. Part of the reason may be that Japanese America was a galvanizing political force in rectifying the injustices of Executive Order 9066 and the World War II internment camps. These political considerations have blunted the initiative to theorize the Japanese imperial presence in Asian American literature. Similarly, Zainichi literature, usually the domain of area studies, does not instinctively turn to critical race theory pervasive in American and ethnic studies; consequently, moments of divergence and parallels in racial formation are missed. Critically, and to the detriment of the fields, the same syllepsistic mistakes are being committed time and again. This book, through a mediated minor transpacific, seeks to make visible those connections.

The next five chapters present several conduits through which these conversations take place. Each chapter centers on an institution or institutional by-product. Chapter 1 typifies how the specter of colonialism shadows Korean American fiction by tracing, in Younghill Kang's work, colonial *labor* practices from Japan to the United States. I frame *East Goes West*'s critique of American capitalism as part of an expansive discussion of colonial labor and manufacturing techniques. While much of the scholarly discourse on Kang's novel focuses on its critique of American cultural materialism, I concentrate on the mechanism driving it, "Taylorism," to link modern industrialism in America with colonial modernity in the Japanese Empire. Kang's critique of race within a stratified economic system, I argue, echoes his early experiences with imperial Japan.

Chapter 2 turns to a Japanese-language novel, Kaneshiro Kazuki's *GO*, to theorize how Zainichi literature betrays an awareness of Asian American subject formation. I show how Kaneshiro integrates American racial discourse, particularly African American and Korean American, through *culture* to reconceptualize Zainichi identity in Japan. Specifically, *GO* incorporates Asian American discourse to conceptualize a mode of "transpacific cultural mediation"—that is, American culture and Korean America functioning as mediating spaces for Zainichi identity negotiation in Japan.

Chapter 3, in concert with chapter 1, makes visible how Japanese colonial *trauma* haunts contemporary Korean American fiction by examining Chang-rae Lee's *A Gesture Life* and Ronyoung Kim's *Clay Walls*. I explore how these texts grapple with the legacy of colonialism, which both interrupts and shapes Korean American literary formation. Furthermore, I argue that that influence extends to nearly all Korean American literature: in other words, Korean America is intimately intertwined with Japanese America, and the two cannot be considered in isolation.

Chapter 4, focusing on Yi Yang-ji's *Yuhi*, a semiautobiographical novel in Japanese dwelling on a return "home" to South Korea by a second-generation Zainichi (as narrated by a member of the family with whom she stays), theorizes how international *education* may be the only institutional means through which Zainichi and Korean Americans may interact. The first Zainichi woman to win the prestigious Akutagawa Literary Prize, Yi unspools the contradictions that a young Zainichi woman faces while studying abroad in Seoul. She yearns to discover a pristine Korean selfhood beyond the reach of Japanese discrimination but soon learns that "home" is in her imagination; the discrimination she encounters from Koreans, sends her running back to the comforts of Japanese culture. Most germane to this book is that both Yi and her protagonist compare her experiences studying in Seoul against those of relatives who studied abroad in America and accessed a Korean American subjectivity that released them from the limitations of being Zainichi. This "absent presence" operates as a gravitational force field that cannot help but dictate the terms of the narrator's relationship to Yuhi, and to herself.

The final chapter punctuates this book's thesis with readings of two texts that directly engage each other through the space of liminal minority *enterprise*: in one, a convenience store in a Black Los Angeles neighborhood, and in the other, the business of Korean-owned pachinko parlors. The first is Zainichi author Kim Masumi's *Moeru Sōka* (The burning Grass House, 1997), a novella set in the background of the 1992 Los Angeles riots, at the height of racial tensions between Korean Americans and African Americans. However, the novella is more concerned with the divide between the two protagonists, one Korean American and the other Zainichi. That Kim writes explicitly about the Korean American context aligns with what much of the rest of my book argues—Zainichi Korea engages in a transpacific interminority dialogue. Similarly, Korean American author Min Jin Lee's *Pachinko* (2017) is written entirely in English but is set in Japan with Zainichi protagonists—the first direct overture from Korean America to the Zainichi. The novel spans several generations of a Zainichi family, beginning in Korea and concluding in Japan with a slight detour in America. I argue that these texts are only half articulable in disciplinary silos of Asian or Asian American studies; a framework that I call a "diasporic minority transposition," triangulating the multitude of histories, racialization, and politics from all three national sites, is necessary to situate these works in a greater transpacific discourse.

CHAPTER I

The Japanese Empire, American Industrialism, and Korean Labor

Younghill Kang's East Goes West *as Colonial Critique*

I do not want to treat efficiency as mere technique or method. There is no other way for humankind beyond efficiency. I wish to emphasize that the way of man is in fact efficiency.

—Ueno Yōichi

In the past the man has been first; in the future the system must be first.

—Frederick Taylor

System, system, system!

—Reporter for the *Detroit Journal*, after visiting a Ford plant

NEW YORK, THE 1920S. Two friends on a desultory stroll across the Brooklyn Bridge pause to take in the city skyline. The Korean student, Chungpa Han, revels at the spectacle of New York's gleaming structures, while his mentor, Kim, stands grimacing beside him. Chungpa thinks,

What a picture! The arched City Hall against the afternoon sunset, these long columns and these high towers. What different rhythm from the Grand Canal of Venice or the Hankang of Hanyang! . . . [This city] links humanity to the world of mechanism, the world of mass production, this magnanimous gigantic structure. . . . All is the work of a short time, in a small space. It would have taken men in different ages hundreds of years to accomplish this. . . . The craftsman may have worked in deadening monotony, the engineer may have planned in routine formation. But the product emerges with individual creativeness, a monument to the American age. Precise, exact, swift, poignant, and powerful.[1]

What impresses Chungpa more than the sheer scale of New York is the fact that these monuments were made with such celerity and precision. It is *efficiency*—a "rhythm" so distinct from Europe and Asia—that enchants but also unsettles Chungpa; beneath the surface of his wonderment lies a quiet acknowledgment of the individual sacrifice needed for the New York building to rise—the worker and designer must labor in anonymous tedium. On the other hand, Kim has a decidedly more sardonic outlook:

> "This island," he muttered, "is rockbound. It can't grow any more. Yet the inhabitants in it increase more and more. Probably it is no longer than the span of a century since the New York of today emerged, from rural farmlands. . . . Now all the depraved creatures and exiled souls in humanity gather to help the big city's growth and add to the radical scare. . . . Well, science that tries to explain the how-and-where of truth, from simple to complex, from particular to general, is no help to me." (245–46)

Kim's despondency is perhaps reflective of the dark modernist vision of America ruled by an efficiency bereft of a humanistic core. He sees New York as a collection of alienated souls fueling the city's unmitigated expansion. Unable or unwilling to accept efficiency without purpose, Kim—as Chungpa's double—has been left hopelessly behind by the modern age.

With these two disparate views, Younghill Kang sets the crux of his argument enfolded within *East Goes West*, an admonition concerning all that can be achieved through efficiency, both beauteous and terrible. Crafted with strong autobiographical elements, the novel chronicles Chungpa Han's arrival and education in America, where he discovers the limits of his racialized potential through a series of humble jobs while pursuing his studies. Chungpa comes to realize that the art and literature so valued in Asia go unappreciated in America; instead, ruthless efficiency and market logic rule over all.

However, Chungpa and Kim's attitudes hold an additional layer of complexity, for the two men are former colonial subjects. The rise of the burnished metropole and the desperate mass of people from rural origins would have been familiar scenes first encountered in colonial Korea and imperial

Japan. Hidden behind Chungpa and Kim's views regarding the American way of efficiency lies an echo of the past—the Japanese way of efficiency. In America, Chungpa will learn that this efficiency has a name: Taylorism.

This chapter reconfigures Kang's critique of American capitalism as part of a more expansive argument about colonial labor and manufacturing techniques rooted in imperial Japan. While much of the scholarly discourse on *East Goes West* focuses on its critique of American cultural materialism, I concentrate on the efficiency mechanism driving it, "Taylorism," to link Japan with America. Chungpa's admired New York high-rises cast long shadows that stretch across the Pacific to Tokyo, for Taylorism found a home in not one but two modernist projects—modern industrialism in America and colonial modernity in the Japanese Empire.[2]

Furthermore, I show how within the projects mentioned above, manufacturing techniques contributed to the construction of race according to local environments. The strong connections between American and Japanese industrialism demonstrate how labor can be systematically racialized according to a Taylorist logic, which ethnic minority communities may replicate. Taylorism, within the context of extant racial tropes, may come to measure a labor force not necessarily by skill or education but by race. I also connect Kang's critique of race within a stratified economic system with his early experiences in Japan, which had originally imported systematized labor management from the United States.

Finally, I extend the transpacific conversation regarding the need for integrating Asia into discussions of Asian America. Despite the strong Japanese presence in *The Grass Roof* (Kang's first novel) and *East Goes West* (his second), where Kang's Japanese education and subsequent propaganda work against the Japanese as part of a US military operation, imperial Japan stands outside the ken of the prevailing scholarship on *East Goes West*.[3] I argue that a consideration of Japan is a necessary step in fully comprehending Kang's discursive meditation on America, for it was the colonial project that would first expose him to a similarly dehumanizing system. Mediating spaces such as Japan complicate the homeland-destination binary found in early Asian American literary criticism and theory, for, as Susan Koshy writes, "Ethnicity metamorphoses at multiple sites of transit, return, and arrival in the movement between and within nations."[4] Kang's novel, as well as his own personal backstory, evinces the need to reinscribe Japan as a powerful intermediary in the production of Korean American subjectivity.[5]

I divide scholarly discussions of *East Goes West* into four camps. First, early criticism retroactively introduced Kang to a new generation of readers. In 1977, Elaine Kim contested the popular reading of *East Goes West* as a feel-good memoir about overcoming racial discrimination and recast the novel as a pointed critique of American racism, thereby situating Kang as an early Asian Americanist.[6] Others such as Kyhan Lee credited Kang's book as the "true genesis of Korean-American literature."[7] The 1997 Kaya Press reprint of *East Goes West* picked up on the idea of Kang-as-vanguard, for on its back cover Chang-rae Lee, arguably today's most well-known Korean American author, claimed that *East Goes West* is "as vibrant and pointed in its vision today as it was 60 years ago, and may prove to be one of our most vital documents." A second faction of scholars has focused on Kang's critique of American materialism and racism. Joanne H. Kim argues that *East Goes West* "scans the panorama of American society to denounce the dehumanizing aspects of American capitalist machinery," and "the racism that pervades even liberal, leftist American institutions";[8] Walter Lew focuses on the loss that Chungpa experiences with his immigration to America as his ambitions deteriorate from acquiring scholarly knowledge to "a life of obsessive materialism and the loss of [his] psychic relationship with Korea";[9] David Palumbo-Liu examines the practice of ethno-cultural commodification with Chungpa's selling of encyclopedias whose value is signified by the Asian body;[10] and Patricia Chu and Karen Kuo funnel Kang's argument through gender and masculinity.[11] A third group interrogates Kang's complicated relationship to African American racial politics. Kun Jong Lee describes the intersectional maneuvers Kang makes in Chungpa's descriptions of his encounters with African Americans in Harlem; Stephen Knadler unpacks Kang's problematic reinforcement of racial stereotypes; and Julia H. Lee compares W. E. B. Du Bois's *Dark Princess* to *East Goes West*, seeing both as contestations of national projects.[12]

An emergent fourth camp, in which I include this discussion, frames Kang's bodily and literary migrations by a transnational framework. Leif Sorensen describes *East Goes West* as a novel that carves out an aesthetics of exile to create meaning: "The sheer power of aesthetics seems capable of un-doing the failings of modernity, as in the virtuosic moments of transnational intertextuality that produce a context in which Chungpa's and Kim's stories become intelligible, valuable, and desirable."[13] In other words, Chungpa and Kim are two sides of the same coin, representative of dueling approaches to colonial legacies in America that have yet to comprehend statelessness; Kang's aesthetic efforts are a means of bridging the gap between Asia and Asian America. And Joseph Jeon suggests framing Kang's work through a "historical temporality," which has "the virtue of putting Kang and his belated commentators in the same global historical frame, one in which Asian interests become increasingly intertwined—both in complicity and conflict—with American interests."[14] This has the advantage, he argues, of pegging scholarly discussion of Kang's work to ever-shifting global realign-ments, thereby contextualizing these conversations as snapshots in time.

Taylorism in America and Japan

Published in 1911, Frederick Taylor's *The Principles of Scientific Manage-ment* approached the twin problems of efficiency and waste by focusing on labor rather than on machinery, as Henry Ford did.[15] Taylor believed that repetitive laborers working in tandem naturally match the pace of the slow-est worker because of the inherent laziness of humans. This "soldiering," he observed, went unpunished on the assembly line, but the problem could be addressed by teaching a "one best method" for accomplishing certain duties. The key was to break tasks into smaller subunits to be addressed by scientifically selected workers according to their suitability for a given job.[16] For example, a repetitive, monotonous task was best accomplished by an equally obtuse worker, whereas brighter workers would be given more complicated ones to handle. While Fordism concentrated on the configura-tion of machines and how labor could augment them, Taylorism in its pur-est sense viewed workers *as* machines to be streamlined and economized.[17] Consequently, Taylor's management system in execution broke down not only tasks but time and motion into units to be measured under the watch-ful eye of the foreman and the *tick tock* of his stopwatch.

Both approaches faced considerable criticism. While Fordism and Tay-lorism enjoyed brief, intense attention as cultural phenomena (e.g., "Fordize or Fail," a Taylor-inspired "efficiency craze"), their detractors were equally vehement.[18] Taylorism in particular was met with immediate and explosive opposition from labor. David Montgomery details the sobering account of a machinist in the New England Bolt Company in Providence, Rhode Island: "'Cameras to the front of them. Cameras to the rear of them. Cameras to the right of them. Cameras to the left of them.' Pictures taken of every move so as to eliminate 'false moves' and drive the worker into a stride that would be as mechanical as the machine he tends."[19] The worker's sense of resignation belies the outpouring of panic felt by labor. Fear and anxiety of Taylorism spread throughout the workforce with surprising alacrity. Indeed, "The very appearance of stopwatches, time cards, or measurements of machine cutters, beds, or T-bolts that so much as hinted at standardization was enough to trigger anxious caucuses of craftsmen, strikes, or beatings of those who seemed to be collaborating with the systematizers."[20] In hindsight, it seems natural for labor to soundly reject Taylorism; management's and workers' economic interests were hardly in alignment, and scientific management's neglect of the individual led to the dehumanization of the worker. Fordism and Taylorism, as they were then constituted, would eventually fall out of favor for more flexible iterations.

Across the Pacific, Japanese manufacturers watched with keen interest, even if they held reservations.[21] After the violent sociopolitical upheaval of industrialization during the Meiji period, Japanese captains of industry studied and later integrated Fordism and Taylorism into their own manufacturing systems.[22] When the comparatively underdeveloped Japanese industry took notice and began integrating Taylorism into its own national efficiency movement, which would accompany it into World War II, the industry faced a labor shortage, at which point labor was outsourced to the colonies.

Taylorism spread rapidly, sparking—as it had already in America—a short-lived "efficiency movement" (*nōritsu undō*) that would infiltrate other realms besides industry. Journalist Ikeda Tōshirō returned from a visit to the United States and published a series of articles on Taylorism, writing that "a great revolution in work has recently swept through the United States, from the shop floor to the front office. This has come from the application of what is known as Scientific Management."[23] Ueno Yōichi, the "Taylor of Japan," tried applying the principles to every aspect of his life, including diet and transportation. Others followed, with serious studies "conducted on the most efficient arrangements for kitchens, the most efficient golf swing, and the 'one best way' in pearl diving."[24]

Yet as William Tsutsui cautions, it would be a mistake to claim that Taylorism was imported without undergoing a transformative process. Japan has long looked upon Western imports with suspicion, yet the Meiji period's policy of modernization required an unavoidable degree of Western exposure. Nationalist intellectuals compensated by compartmentalizing technology and ideology, formulating *wakon yosai*,[25] or "Japanese spirit, Western learning."[26] Kang himself notes that "[the Japanese] have a genius for adopting and imitating the skills of others."[27] Indeed, this trend continued with Taylorism, although it is arguable in which direction and to what degree.[28] Nevertheless, with the "Japanization" of Taylorism, Japan augmented rather than diminished its imperial ambitions. By dividing workers into subcastes along strictly racialized lines, Taylorism was the ideal manufacturing ideology for production efficiency without racial egalitarianism. It was in this context that a young Korean student named Younghill Kang sought access to the same Western knowledge that gave Japan and the US its scientific superiority. He would be left wanting.

"The Machine Age"

Kang entered the United States in 1921, when automotive industrialism was beginning its rapid ascent; he would have witnessed firsthand the secondary effects of the assembly line.[29] The novel demonstrates that he had serious qualms about the nature of industrialism and capitalism. New York City, in particular, seems to embody the machinery that Chungpa comes to revile.[30]

> New Yorkers all seem to have some aim in every movement they make. . . .
> Even the man who only goes to a show and is making arrangements about it
> has a business air. His every action decisive, orderly, purposeful . . . he must
> know exactly what he wants to do in his mind. Just to move in New York
> and not be ploughed under, man must prevision and plan out. Free, factual,
> man is reasoning from cause to effect here all the time—not so much think-
> ing. It is intelligence measuring, rather than intellect's solution. Prophets
> of hereafter, poets of vision . . . maybe the American is not so much these.
> But he is a good salesman, amidst scientific tools. His mind is like Grand

Central Station. It is definite, it is timed, it has mathematical precision on clearcut stone foundation. There may be monotonous dull repetition, but all is accurate and conscious. Stupid routine sometimes, but behind it, duty in the very look. Every angle and line has been measured. (152)

This striking passage, which seems to share affinities with the preceding description of oppressive time management, recasts the stereotypically frenetic New Yorker as subject to the logic of Taylorism, surrounded by "scientific tools"; Kang's reframing calls into question New York as a home of "the individual." Indeed, his caricature portrays the New Yorker as both a producer of widgets and a widget himself rather than an executer of self-will; he or she must step in line with the humming whir of the city, lest he or she be "ploughed under." The connection is made all the more salient by Chungpa's burgeoning opposition to the educational indoctrination—declaring a major field of study—needed for a life of "monotonous dull repetition." "Something in me all the while opposed such specialization. . . . like the man who helps to make machines, by working on a particular detail, say, driving a nail. So his life work means that he repeats that single routine work in one narrow channel. He is not a magnanimous creator of that gigantic machine, no, for he has lost the plan of it, he has been absorbed by it, he is the servant of it, not it of him. . . . Poor modern soul" (283).

Chungpa looks askance at the university education he receives because he fears becoming part of a larger system of economic efficiency. Declaring a major would be a capitulation of sorts, forever dooming the mind to "handle [its] specialty, never the infinite." Chungpa conflates intellectual myopia with assembly line drudgery; his attitude toward "specialization" appears an indictment of the Taylorist philosophy of task-oriented subdivision. He likens himself to an intellectual assembly line worker so involved with his specialized task that he cannot step back to view the finished product, factory walls, or all that stands outside its fences. By drawing connections between the electric energy of New York's streets with factory work, Kang effectively resituates his initial admiration from afar in a decidedly less flattering light. The "Machine Age" comes to be multivalent: New York is both a gleaming representative of modern technology and a machine itself. Thus American individuality is recharacterized as a fallacy. In actuality, it is a subspecialization—each person performs a compartmentalized role on the assembly line. The quickened pace of the New Yorker is a manifestation of an efficient machine-like worker in a Taylorist system.

From where did Kang's deep opposition to management science originate? I posit that his aversion to Taylorism may have been rooted in his understanding of colonial Korea and the Japanese imperial machine. Connecting the two locales with management science lends weight to the theory that Kang's critique of American capitalism's pernicious effects is not limited to industrial labor and ethnic minorities but points to its active participation in the formation of colonial modernity and colonized subjects across borders.

Kang's rejection of mechanization and scientific management may be understood in its wartime significance. Consider an early example of technology transfer, firearms. In 1543, a Japanese trader bought a set of rifles from a Portuguese ship and ordered local swordsmiths to make copies, but domestic craftsmen lacked the knowledge to replicate Portuguese technology, a deficiency indicative of the problems of nonstandardized manufacturing.[31] Even if rifles were still largely individually built, Portuguese gunsmiths could draw on standard tools, which the Japanese did not have access to.[32] Two hundred and fifty years later the underlying problem was revisited in antebellum America, with military arms once again. When the US government's demand for gun production skyrocketed in the early nineteenth century, Harpers Ferry Armory's craftsmen-based production system proved insufficient. In an early precursor to Taylorism, director John Hall designed a modular assembly system standardizing each component so that in addition to streamlining production and relying less on individual skill, the parts would be interchangeable, a feature useful in battlefield repair scenarios.[33] Military arms would again be the site of management innovation with Taylorism's introduction to Japan, another hundred years later. Returning from a two-year tour of wartime munitions factories in the US and England, engineer Godō Takuo began implementing what he had learned into the Kure Naval Arsenal's manufacturing system. His system "called for a revolution in the production process, with provision for accelerated division of labor, centralized planning, stopwatch time study, cost accounting, Gantt chart tracking, and instruction card procedures. Covering the full range of Scientific Management techniques, the 'limit gauge' even embraced controversial Taylorite prescriptions like 'functional foremanship,' a complex organizational program which divided shop-floor administrative duties among a number of specialized overseers."[34]

As the aforementioned examples have shown, scientific management tended to gravitate to the theater of war—it may have been that the urgency of war allowed for experimentation to meet demand and overrode labor disputes, allowing Taylorism to operate relatively unfettered. In a magazine article, Kang notes that Korea's disadvantage in arms technology contributed to its subjugation: "Owing to a lack of modern weapons, outward resistance to Japanese dominion in Korea was impossible."[35] That same sense of military urgency would introduce Korean laborers to the Japanese management system.

By the time *East Goes West* was published in 1937, colonial Korea had undergone significant economic transformation. Beginning in the 1920s, the largely rural population of Korea started to scatter and shift toward cities because of Japanese policies requiring industrialization and modernization. In the 1930s, industrial growth began to absorb a large agricultural labor surplus and siphon populations away from rural to urban areas, with about half heading to domestic industrial centers and the other half emigrating to Japan and Manchuria.[36] From 1930 to 1940, about 1.31 million voluntary workers emigrated in search for higher wages, with another one million Koreans involuntarily shipped out as industrial laborers or as so-called comfort women.[37] By 1940, 1.24 million Koreans lived in Japan, the vast majority of them working as day laborers or in other low-skill occupations.[38]

Soon-Won Park's study of a cement factory's labor structure provides an excellent model of scientific management at work in colonial Korea. Like Kang, Korean factory laborers came from largely agricultural backgrounds with their own cultural norms that had to be broken and re-formed to align with factory productivity. Park writes, "Factory work itself was a new experience. The year-round, eight-hour workday spent in one location with breaks only for meals caused much strain. Learning to observe exact starting and stopping times also required much effort. In addition, the workers had to overcome tensions and fears associated with working around frightening machines and complicated equipment."[39] Moreover, the Sŭnghori factory was a site of complex ethnic tension and racialized hierarchy interpolated with labor management. While labor and management have generally shared a history of conflict, this dialectic was more pronounced in colonial factories, with Korean low-level laborers overseen by Japanese managers. Upward mobility for more capable Korean workers was strictly limited, and Japanese management had to deal with a labor force that was at times only begrudgingly compliant, if not hostile: "Koreans, regardless of their experience or formal position, were always defined first and fore-most by their Koreanness. They could not have avoided serious reflection about the social rejection and contempt they had to endure as a colonized people. Their position in the ethnically segmented colonial labor market was driven home to them on a daily basis."[40] While Park does not directly address Taylorism by name in her study, it is apparent from her descrip-tions of Onoda Sŭnghori that scientific management had already made its mark in shaping production. Consider, for example, its rigid time manage-ment system: "The Sŭnghori factory used a time-card system to enforce punctuality for factory entry and exit. Sirens, one a half-hour before a shift began and another at the start of each shift, were used to alert workers, most of whom would not have had watches or clocks. Every worker had to carry a time card and stamp the card at the time clock in the security guard's box in front of the factory gate upon entering and leaving the fac-tory. The time card was used to calculate wages, paid every two weeks."[41] While American workers strongly opposed Taylorist mechanization poli-cies, Korean laborers, desperate for wages and conditioned by colonial oppression, had little recourse. Kang paints a strikingly similar picture of mechanized time management in an American department store. Chun-gpa, enduring one of his many temporary engagements, contemplates the rigidity of store regulation:

> It did not take me long to form an opinion that life in a department store was a horrible life for all people. What appalled me was the regimenta-tion. . . . Every employee had not a name but a number. His number was on his card on the wall, lined up with many other numbered cards. The first thing he did before taking off hat or coat was to punch the card by the automatic clock. . . . And four times a day you had to punch that clock, as a number coming in and going out. (289–90)

Kang's grim depiction of regulatory practices at a department store evinces the putative power of Taylorism, yet I think his larger critique lies with Taylorism's global reach; Chungpa must contend with the Foucauldian biopower of scientific management, a management ideology that recognizes neither border nor nation-state—a technique that not only follows the sub-ject but actively pushes him or her into the local liminality.[42] In this case, the *tick tock* of the foreman's stopwatch pursues the Korean subject in East Asia and America.

The Japanese Presence in East Goes West

It was in this setting that Younghill Kang and his fictional proxy arrived on American shores, where "the individualist was born, the individualist, demanding life and more life, fulfillment" (9). Having escaped the circumscribed conditions of his former life in Korea under Japanese rule, Chungpa intends to transcend nationhood in meritocratic and cosmopolitan New York to gain subjectivity. However, he quickly finds himself subsumed by the logic of "American efficiency" and similarly constrained as an "Oriental Yankee." Kang depicts the Taylorist logic through the specter of Japan in *East Goes West* in several ways. First, he reveals the false dichotomy of Japan and America as respective sites of individual oppression and liberation. Instead, he channels Japan through his observations of American life and culture to draw similarities and convergences. Second, he illustrates the differences between a Taylorist imperialist state and a Taylorist capitalist state, particularly with respect to ethnic minorities. I have shown how Taylorism in imperial Japan positions the Korean body under the category of racialized, low-skill labor. Kang demonstrates how the Taylorist capitalistic project actually exploits this difference as part of the commodification process. Last, he deconstructs Chungpa's pursuit of education as a futile endeavor reminiscent of the conditions of colonial Korea. His experience with the education system under Japanese rule punctures the illusion of American meritocracy.

Kang portrays Chungpa's initial experience in America as wonderfully sublime, a sheer pleasure—when he has the means of paying for it. When his funds dissipate, Chungpa quickly finds himself among the derelicts of New York in a homeless shelter, an ordeal that he associates with imperial Japan ("The only experience I have had to compare with this was in a prison of the Japanese"). Yet his enthusiasm for America never falters; the one distinction he can take comfort in is the fact that his fellow social outcasts stand apart as individuals. While Korean prisoners reek of homogeneity ("But the people—Korean revolutionists—had been put there for a single integrated feeling, a hard bright core of fire against oppression"), American dregs are "like pithless stalks, and the force that swept them here, the city's leavings, was for the most part the opposite one, a personal disintegration." In an astonishing display, Chungpa takes comfort in "clutch[ing] to a new world of time, where individual disintegration was possible, as well as integration, where all need not perish with the social organism, or, as in Japan, all rise in savage blood, a single fighting man" (22). In other words, so attached to the idea of subjectivity is Chungpa that he prefers individualized poverty in America to political solidarity in Korea.

As a site of national opposition, Japan functions as a homogenizing force transforming Korean individuals into a singularity, "a single fighting man," a condition that persists in America. Consider the case of Chinwan, a unique character who appears early in the novel. Korean by birth but educated in Japan, Chinwan transgresses nationhood and has the ability to penetrate the membrane of ethnicity: "Long before Japan took Korea, Chinwan had emigrated to Japan and he remained there. As a child, he had passed through the Japanese schools, and he had taken degrees from the Imperial University of Kyoto, and in all things he was pretty well Japanized. Many of his Japanese friends did not even know he was a Korean. But he spoke Korean and knew Korea well. And at present, he wanted to associate with Koreans, perhaps because he had just married one" (65). Chinwan's biographical heterogeneity is a reflection of Kang (and presumably Chungpa), who was also educated in Japan before coming to the United States. More than simply linguistic, Chinwan's difference lies in his choice to straddle both worlds—perhaps naively so—oblivious to the political impact that his transgressivity implies.[43] Chungpa's description intimates the nebulous space Chinwan occupies; he is "Japanized" but speaks "Korean and [knows] Korea well." Lacking an epistemological framework, Chungpa cannot effectively articulate Chinwan's multiply located identity—instead he is both/neither Korean and Japanese. Characterized as apolitical but affable, Chinwan ends up literally impaled by Korean nationalist Mr. Lin for his slippery politics. Yet Lin privately confesses to Chungpa that he actually likes Chinwan, and that his attack "was nothing personal" (68). He and the Korean expatriate community read Chinwan's hybridity as a rejection or betrayal of Korea, despite Lin's personal affection for Chinwan. National politics embody a galvanizing force that dehumanizes even as it unifies, a condition Chungpa explicitly rejects.

Chungpa's subsequent disassociation with the Korean Institute, where the attack on Chinwan occurred, ostensibly extricates him from the totalizing politics of Japan. He turns instead toward the rest of America, which he hopes will afford him subjectivity. Yet by the novel's ambiguous end it is not clear whether Chungpa has found his much-sought-after selfhood. Instead, Kang depicts America as equally dehumanizing and nonindividualistic, albeit in slightly modified form.

Beyond the Korean Institute of New York, Chungpa discovers a similarly totalizing force that constructs race according to Taylorist modes of labor.[44] Consider the slave plantation; it is, as described by Thomas Holt, a model of "the modern virtues of rationality and rationalization. Many plantation ledgers display calculations of work routines and nurture as meticulously as those of Frederick Taylor. . . . In some cases such calculations led to the decision that it was cheaper to work a slave to death and buy new replacements from Africa than to provide the nutrition and care that would promote biological reproduction of the labor force."[45]

With manumission, the construct of Blackness did not simply dissipate but remained tied to old modes of economy. The Black body, historically tied to menial labor, is itself considered a capital commodity; the body cannot occupy any other space other than that relegated to pure labor. Here lies the delimited difference; a Taylorist logic within a capitalist system uses the easiest signifier of difference, skin color, to signify both menial labor and capital commodity. In Japan, the Korean body is similarly associated with menial labor, but with a decidedly different purpose.[46] Taylorism, as a mechanizing force, integrates the Korean body into the imperial machine. For example, Japanese policy made an effort, however disingenuous, of incorporating the Korean body into itself. Colonial Korea was subject to a propaganda campaign, *naisen ittai* (Japan and Korea as One), designed to transform Koreans into Japanese subjects.[47] American slave owners had no such intentions; the slave body was always already considered an Othered object. The mechanization of the worker in conjunction with the larger colonial or capitalist project determines the space a racialized body may occupy.

Consider Chungpa's encounters with several African American characters, all of whom occupy the same space defined by Blackness. During the week Laurenzo works as a live-in cook for the Schmitts; on the weekends, Chungpa witnesses him drunkenly raging against his stagnant social position: "I'se been to Williams College, and to Washington, and then I come up here to go to Harvard. . . . But a niggerman's only good to cook and wait, that's all" (262). Here Kang highlights the dual role Laurenzo must perform to make his meager living under the Schmitts' roof: during the day, Laurenzo acts as an obsequious "house slave," and during his dark, private

moments, he briefly, explosively casts off the facade, revealing ambition beyond the scope of Whiteness.

In contradistinction, the similarly educated Wagstaff is able to more con-
structively articulate his anger. He has worked as a porter and as an elevator
man and has played cornet in a minstrel show, typical of most acceptable
positions for African Americans. His frustration lies, like Laurenzo's, with
the knowledge that even if he continues to educate himself it means little
socially and economically. He asks bitterly, "What room is there in America
for an educated Negro?" (273). Even if he wants to engage the capitalist system wholeheartedly, he understands that there is little opportunity for him
to gain any economic returns as a laborer.

At a party of young progressives in the village, Chungpa meets Alfred, a
stoic young Black intellectual who displays a nuanced knowledge of modernist art. Kun Jong Lee notes that this disturbs Sally, a "drunken bohemian"
who is "deeply troubled at Alfred's uncommon behavior" (336). For her,
Alfred is "definitely over-educated, cramped by moral and cultural norms
and . . . not a 'Negro,' since he is unfaithful to his race and 'outwhites' the
bohemian Villagers" (337). Chungpa notes that he, Kim, and Alfred share
a solidarity as the quietest group at the party, but he refrains from drawing
any explicit connections between African American and Asian American
receptions in White America. The three characters—Laurenzo, Wagstaff,
and Alfred—are all struggling against constructed racial roles but from different vantage points. Laurenzo's duality tears him apart, Wagstaff's education enables him to contemplate "the Negro question" but he suffers from
self-enclosure, and Alfred's full engagement of the system on its own terms
proves haplessly ineffective.[48] All three characters' denied subjectivity is signified by positions in labor or the inaccessibility of occupations beyond
strictly circumscribed boundaries.

The Korean body in America occupies a slightly different space. As I
have recounted, the Black body signifies pure labor, but the cultural logic
of capitalism engrafts the Korean body onto a larger discourse regarding
Asia. While slaves were commodified both in body and in labor, Asian
immigrants voluntarily arrived as plantation hands in Hawaii, and on the
mainland as unskilled labor.[49] And while both Black and Asian labors were
sold as goods, Asian bodies did not have exchange-value mapped onto

them within the American labor trade context.[50] Furthermore, the Japanese victory over Russia in the Russo-Japanese War underscored Japan's rapid modernization, which problematized capitalism's manufacturing of race. A consciousness of the fact that Eastern powers had the ability to challenge the West engendered a brief period of cultural fetishism; Asian goods, particularly Japanese, became associated with a degree of cultural capital.[51] Here is where the portability of Asian Otherness within the larger capitalist project takes a decidedly Taylorist bent.

Take, for instance, Chungpa's venture into Rev. Bonheure's religious commune. Bonheure's commune serves as a critique of ethnic enclaves that claim to support their denizens while internalizing Taylorist patterns. On the surface, the Saints' world appears appealing, a self-contained system ("But my, what a marvelous and effective organization!" [335]) in which there is no racial predetermination conflating Blackness with menial labor. Just as Taylor's *Principles* states that the workman should be scientifically selected, Bonheure makes certain that each occupation is given to someone with the proper disposition; Chungpa notes that Bonheure "devoted a good deal of talent to picking the right person for the right job. He was really a genius at this, and all the saints seemed happy and industrious"; Bonheure "saw that there was a job for every man. And no new jobs were taken without consulting him" (335–36). However, with the exception of Bonheure, everyone remains a common worker, with no room for individual growth and agency; theirs is a meretricious world, for it "killed all initiative and was just like slavery" (336). Lee argues that Kang portrays Bonheure as a trickster figure using religious rhetoric to convince his followers to labor under his rule: "The Elder is basically a con man, 'a pious fraud,' who is interested in money-making rather than the glorification of God or the uplifting of African Americans."[52] Stephen Knadler argues that Kang fashions Bonheure after encyclopedia salesman D. J. Lively, suggesting "that Bonheure, and his way of speaking, may be no less illegitimate—and authentic—than any other 'American' way."[53]

Bonheure may be all of these things, but his behavior is a symptom of his indoctrination into the church of capital. Bonheure has taken up the role of master in another incarnation of the master-slave dialectic, differing only in using the threat of spiritual and religious, as opposed to physical, punishment. He has "quite simply," in the words of Frantz Fanon, taken "those unfair advantages which are a legacy of the colonial period" into his own hands and exploited them for his own gain.[54] Chungpa's racial difference is used by Bonheure as a testament to the miraculous power of religion, which he uses for his personal profit; Chungpa's integration into the Saints' circle is predicated on his status as a "Chinee." At the conclusion of a speech given by Chungpa at a spiritual revival, the audience remains impressed more by the mere fact that Chungpa speaks English than by the substance of his talk: "The people . . . only see the 'miracle' of an articulate Korean who does not confirm their stereotypes of the Chinaman."[55] The audience credits his speech to the infallibility of the system they serve, a "miracle" from on high. Under this logic, no matter how ratiocinative Chungpa may seem, or how convincingly he flaunts his erudition, his efforts amount to a tautological exercise. Using scientific management, Bonheure has selected Chungpa for his racial difference to function within existing racial tropes to support his organization. In American Taylorism Chungpa's labor does not matter; all that matters is its signification of Asia. Only when Chungpa realizes that his intellectual efforts go unappreciated does he commit apostasy. Bonheure's obvious desire for a "new Pierce Arrow car" leads to Chungpa's awareness that knowledge-seeking has no place in the Temple of the Saints; it can serve him only as one more contributor to the drive for material commodities. Education, labor, and race are appropriated into a Taylorist system serving capitalism, leaving no opportunity for subjectivity.

Bonheure's system suggests a degree of interethnic mimesis, for it obviously parallels a preceding scheme trading upon race, Chungpa's employment as a traveling salesman. Chungpa first arrives at D. J. Lively's office with the intention of selling him pens of dubious worth but soon finds himself sold on Lively's own pitch of working as a salesman hocking worthless encyclopedias titled *Universal Education*. During Chungpa's initial sales pitch, Lively disingenuously buys the pens, but not out of any charitable intent. Faced with an incredulous Chungpa, who mistakenly credits the sale to his skilled rhetoric, Lively explains, "You have sold yourself to me already" (134). In purchasing the pens, he purchases Chungpa's body, which is of more value than what he has initially invested. After the "purchase," Lively explicitly constructs a narrative, which he maps onto Chungpa's body: "An Oriental salesman for books. . . . A fine clean Christian young Oriental earning his way through college" (134). Clearly, Lively sees that Chungpa is a terrible salesman but believes that capitalizing on his Asian difference will win him an untapped market share. Chungpa's ability as a salesman is irrelevant; his body's signification of the sales pitch already imbued in the public's consciousness is what sells books. As David Palumbo-Liu notes, "The body becomes both a sign of difference and a token of exchange within a particular economy."[56] Indeed, in the rare event when he actually sells a copy of *Universal Education*, Chungpa apparently succeeds because of his race.

Chungpa's encounters with Lively and Bonheure are typical of his employment pattern; hired more for his racial capital than his competence, Chungpa serves simply to transfer the legitimacy of the commodity product—a synergetic relationship between race, capitalism, and Taylorism. In Chungpa's first disastrous venture, a White woman in suburbia hires him as a manservant for his value as an Oriental rather than for his ability, or as she later learns, his lack thereof. Her remarks make clear Chungpa's purpose: "My former cook was a very tall Negro. He was able to do the work of two. But I hired you to be presentable" (59). Palumbo-Liu observes that "the 'presentability' of the 'oriental' is thus of higher value than the productivity of the 'Negro.'"[57] What occurs is an exercise in economy: with the "Negro," the woman receives only labor and not much else. The Black body signifies little cultural value other than labor; it *is* labor. With Chungpa, she receives not only labor but the added value of domesticated Orientalism. Later, working as a salesman in a department store's Oriental goods section, Chungpa resigns himself to legitimating products of dubious worth; Chungpa is located in the "Chinaware" department, ostensibly because his body signifies the authenticity of the wares, even if he is cognizant of their poor quality and illegitimacy. Race, rather than Chungpa's intelligence or skill, becomes the measure of specialization within the Taylorist logic.

"'Japan has conquered Korea by Western science,' [my uncle] told me again and again. 'We, too, if we are to live again, must master the Western learning. Go, my boy. Travel. Ignore poverty and hardship—but master the Western knowledge.'"[58] Following the entreaty of his poet uncle, Kang has pursued the education needed for personal and national liberation. Likewise, it is the "Western learning," in Christian missionary and Japanese schools, Chungpa believes, that creates "the individualist, demanding life and more life" (9). In America, Chungpa encounters walls reminiscent of the barriers confronted in provincial Korea, and he attempts to scale them the only way he has found success—through education. But through the course of the novel, he realizes that education in America has become subsumed by the very system that he fled from in Japan; attempting to transcend race with education when they are both elements of the same overall structure is ineffectual. Writing in 1946, Kang reflects on the futility of education within a system saddled with institutional safeguards restricting mobility: "Everybody knows Korea needs science and industrial development. What more promising than the field of engineering? But here again there were difficulties. No Korean engineer could get any important contract under the Japanese. If he got a job at all, his salary would be one tenth of that given a Japanese with the same training."[59] Chungpa's world-weary friend and mentor, Kim, knows the truth of the matter long before Chungpa does. Upon hearing of Chungpa's intention to pursue a university degree, Kim admonishes him: "You will study a little of everything and not much of anything, and you will have no time to think until you come out. The education method is that of acquiring superficial factual knowledge. Ranging and shallow, rather than searching and deep. It is just like going into a New York subway. They try to educate too many. You can see the same in the Dearborn assembling plants: It is the business method. It works to turn out Fords . . . but not to turn out scholars. A dry, mechanical, tedious atmosphere!" (160).

Kim's critique of American education suggests that Chungpa will literally become a product of Fordist practices. Chungpa, unable or unwilling to heed his warning, replies, "Well, it seems I can do nothing until I go to college and learn something . . . Not even cooking or waiting or dishwashing. When I get out of college, then I may begin to master American civilization, American culture" (160). Chungpa continues to have faith in education's romantic qualities; he believes education to be a means to an end. Already well aware of capitalism's success in appropriating education, Kim shifts tactics with his intransigent protégé by giving more pragmatic advice: "In making a living, Oriental scholarship may help you more than your American education, though this seems strange to contemplate now. But in such a field, you would have the advantage. There would be less competition. . . . As a transplanted scholar, this is the only road I could point to, for your happy surviving" (257). Kim recognizes the function of race within a mechanized system, so he directs Chungpa to trade upon it. Chungpa would remain subject to the vicissitudes of racial construction, but he would have some semblance of agency, within confines.

In many respects, Chungpa has made little progress as a former colonial subject. Kang recalls the case of a friend who made a similar attempt: "A good many years ago, I knew a Korean who studied agricultural science in America, and went back with high hopes for improved farming. After struggling for fifteen years to realize his dreams in Korea, he gave up in hopeless discouragement."[60] Japan acts as a mediating space for Chungpa's initial exposure to Western learning, but a transnational mode of labor efficiency haunts him through economic models, race, and education.

Chungpa's journey ends with an ambiguous dream sequence in which he returns to an underground shelter surrounded by subalterns, hinting, as Walter Lew has noted, at his capitulation and destruction.[61] The novel's somber conclusion contrasts with the ebullient, near-quixotic optimism of its beginning; Chungpa realizes that he cannot obtain subjectivity within this system and finds himself, much as he feared he would, living under "the futility of the martyr," the individualist gone.

Taylorism's flexibility as a system of mechanization and role construction makes possible its adaptation to the larger goals of a nation, an economic mode, or a cultural logic. Through the utilization of the racialized subject, America and Japan engage in a socioeconomic dialogue resulting in the subjugation of the Korean body. Chungpa discovers too late that although he has escaped from the Japanese Empire to the United States his condition differs only in the local modernist project (from colonial to capitalistic): the system used to achieve it remains the same. Japan dehumanizes the colonial subject; but in America, Korean nationals encounter the same homogenizing tendency. Chungpa flees to America to search for subjectivity, only to find in America a more pernicious iteration—a more efficient means of producing uniformity that acknowledges and even encourages circumscribed heterogeneity as a selling point.

Always Already Transpacific

Younghill Kang always had imperial Japan on his mind. In addition to introducing Korean culture and history to the American public, Kang's writerly projects included a propaganda campaign against Japan. In a fortuitous turn, the United States viewed Japan with increasing suspicion, and Kang, as a former colonial subject of the Japanese and as an admirer of American democracy, was the ideal agent to report on the Japanese threat. To that end, he wrote a series of articles in popular journals vilifying the Japanese state and warning American readers of its insidious designs on the United States. The collaborative nature of Kang's writing is evident in "When the Japs March In" (1942), in which two established voices legitimate his screed, including Pearl S. Buck, author of *The Good Earth*, who writes in a blurb, "Out of the heart of a Korean today, Younghill Kang speaks. I think this article is the best thing that Dr. Kang has ever written, and I congratulate *The American Magazine* on publishing it."[62] Kang enumerates an array of injustices committed by Japan against Korea, including the stripping away of civil liberties, and admonishes, "What Japan has done in Korea she will do in the Philippines, in Burma, in the East Indies, in China, and in India, if she wins this war. She will do it in the United States if she makes good the boast of Jap admirals who say they will 'dictate the peace terms in the White House in Washington.'"[63] But in a curious turn that illustrates his ambivalence, Kang's "The Japanese Mind Is Sick" (1945) accuses the Japanese government of exploiting an immanent pathology in the Japanese psyche by conscripting the unwitting culture industry "to feed the fever of the Japanese mind" for the purpose of total war.[64] That is, through a selective reading of Japanese literary figures and the prevalence of suicide in Japan, Kang argues that intrinsic neuroses and angst in the Japanese have been directed against the West in the name of nationalism; therefore, the Japanese citizenry will not hesitate to sacrifice their lives in the name of nationhood. The article is fraught with contradictions and reveals conflicting lines of tension, as Kang openly admires Japanese literature and culture, having translated works into English.

What of a postcolonial Kang? By 1946, with liberation from Japan accomplished, Kang would turn to convincing the American reading public that their intervention in the Pacific was entirely justified but, in the gentlest terms, would suggest that their military presence had overstayed its welcome. Borrowing heavily from *The Grass Roof*, Kang catalogs the many injustices suffered by himself and the Korean people at the hands of the Japanese, giving credit to the United States for their successful resistance: "[Korean resistance] was inspired by President Wilson's words at the Versailles Conference."[65] But his writing bristles at the continued occupation of Korea by Russian and American forces, which he modulates by ventriloquizing his voice through others: "The six Koreans told me that the people in Korea are determined to win complete independence, and they are waiting patiently, hoping America and Russia agree to withdraw their forces as soon as possible. The arbitrary division of Korea, along the thirty-eighth parallel, by the United States and Russia was originally made to facilitate military operations in crushing the Japanese. The continuation of this artificial wall long after the defeat of the enemy of the United Nations is very unfortunate."[66] The disappearance of a lifelong objective—Korea's liberation—seemed to take the wind out of Kang's sails. He found himself at odds with the United States' geopolitical objectives—instead of a shared goal of defeating Japan, Kang found himself urging US departure from the peninsula and respect for Korean sovereignty. It is, perhaps, a partial explanation for his career's decline after liberation.

All this is to say that early Korean American literature such as *East Goes West* must take Japan into consideration, aligned with the idea that transnational Asian American literary studies must account for the presence of tertiary national actors; otherwise, Asian American criticism will forge ahead with critical blinders. Indeed, as Koshy has articulated, we "have entered a transnational era where ethnicity is increasingly produced at multiple local and global sites rather than, as before, within the parameters of the nation-state."[67] Kandice Chuh points out that "critically acknowledging the material effectivity of multiply located histories and chronologies . . . means recognizing the limitations of knowledge produced by distancing 'America' from 'Asia' as limitations that do ideological work."[68] In other words, critics must recognize the importance of Asia in Asian American literature to circumvent scholarly provincialism. Korean American literature in particular is a rich site for the study of an incorporated imperial Japan—whether conscious or not—in framing Asian American subjectivity. In the following chapter, I wonder if the same could be said of *Zainichi* fiction: that is, how does America and/or Korean America figure into Zainichi literary meditations on race in Japan?

CHAPTER 2

American Racial Discourse
in Zainichi Fiction

*Transpacific Cultural Mediation in
Kaneshiro Kazuki's* GO

In addition to specific instances of intervention by the American occupation
prompting the Japanese government, for instance, to quash an emergent
Resident Korean organization as part of the "red scare," American global policy
as manifested in the Korean War promoted a Japanese economic recovery, with
dubious consequences, however, for the democratic emancipation of Korea.

—Norma Field, "Beyond Envy, Boredom, and Suffering"

IN 2004, famed Japanese actor "Beat" Takeshi wryly mused on the sudden
and unexpected "Korean wave" in Japan. Attempting to make sense of the rapid
influx of Korean cultural goods—culminating in the opening of a Korean "host
club" in Shinjuku's red light district—he wondered, "Why are Korean men so
good?"[1] Thanks to a thaw in import-export policy between South Korea and
Japan, Korean serial television dramas were beginning to make their way to
Japan, and one series in particular, *Winter Sonata*, found an eager audience
in Japanese housewives. The male lead of the show, Bae Yong-joon, soon discovered that he was the object of adoration by a large constituency of Japanese middle-aged women, much to his bewilderment. "Yon-sama," as he was
dubbed by Japanese media, became an industry unto himself, the projection of
innumerable romantic fantasies, which ushered forth a pop cultural fad for all
things Korean. It was a turn that caught many by surprise, since Korean men
in Japan had long been considered to be undesirable. The intervention by the
Korean culture industry, aided by governmental changes in trade policy, altered
Japanese perceptions of reality.[2] It was of course a gauzy construct, but it would,
for better or worse, influence the racialization of Koreans in Japan.

Economic policy, popular culture, and history—three components, none
of them isolated to a single national site, working in concert to radically
shift public perceptions of race. Dwelling on the malleability of those perceptions, this chapter considers how interrelated elements across multiple
national sites affect self-racialization in Kaneshiro Kazuki's 1996 novel
GO. While Asian American studies scholars traditionally focus on domestic Asian diasporic literatures, I look abroad to uncover connections that
expose the collaborative—and knotty—formulation of these communities
through politics and culture in both the United States and Japan.

Part of a long tradition of *zainichi bungaku* (Zainichi literature), *GO* is an
accessible rendering of the alienation and subjectivity of Zainichi (Resident
Koreans in Japan) in a familiar Japanese genre—the chronicle of a schoolboy
brawler.[3] The plot of *GO* is as follows: Sugihara, a Zainichi Korean high
schooler struggles to find his place in a Japan that discriminates against the
Zainichi, who are considered alien residents despite being born and raised
in Japan. Sugihara falls in love with a Japanese girl named Sakurai, who is
oblivious to his Korean heritage. During their courtship, Sugihara, who passes
for Japanese, struggles with the decision to reveal his ethnicity to Sakurai.
Meanwhile, Sugihara's father chooses to switch nationalities from North Korean
to South Korean, ostensibly for the purpose of vacationing in Hawaii—a move
that sends Sugihara spiraling down an existential hole. Sugihara then decides
to transfer from his North Korean state-affiliated school to attend a Japanese
high school, where he has to contend with incessant bullying. It is only before
they consummate their relationship that Sugihara admits to Sakurai that
he is Zainichi; she initially rejects him, but the novel concludes with their
reconciliation when she finally accepts him, absent labels.

Complicating the standard high school romance between our protagonist and love interest are subtextual plotlines centered on racial anxiety, national politics, intergenerational conflict, and discrimination. Beneath the
surface of *GO* are several sites of discourse wrestling with the ethno-national
politics of Japan, Korea, and the United States in formulating a Zainichi
minority subjectivity. This chapter argues that the novel strives to formulate
an epistemology for *racial* rather than national or ethnic subjectivity beyond
the ken of Korea and Japan by importing racial discourse through American
popular culture.[4]

I engage with both Asian and Asian American studies as part of a longer conversation on transnational, multidisciplinary, and multilingual studies. Disciplinary boundaries in area studies have traditionally precluded meaningful dialogue, but there have been attempts at rectification, with scholars moving across Japanese, Korean, and Chinese studies.[5] Studies of Zainichi history and literature for instance, require an alignment between Korean and Japanese studies. Asian American studies has made concurrent shifts; however, that dialogue has been largely unidirectional. Elaine Kim and Lisa Lowe write, "There will need to be a variety of connections between Asian studies and Asian American studies, though these encounters will surely have to take account of the long history of dissymmetry between the two fields."[6] They call for such a dialogue in hopes of creating a more comprehensive critical framework to account for an influx of new immigrants from Asia to America, which has had the secondary effect of altering the makeup and character of Asian America. However, this approach still relies on a "homeland-destination binary" centered on the United States as the final resting place of inquiry.[7] This chapter takes the opposite tack by calling for dialogue between Asian studies and Asian American studies to account for immigrants in Asia who have been indelibly affected by American political interventions, cultural imports, and racial discourse. I hope to rectify the lack of consideration for mediating tertiary spaces in order to critically account for the presence of American cultural and racial discourse in the literary constructions of race in Asia.

Transpacific Cultural Mediation

A comparative transnational approach is essential to create a comprehensive understanding not only of minor literatures in Asia but of Asian American literature as well. An Asian Americanist should go beyond domestic minority fiction to account for the specter of empire, both American and Japanese, as Shu-mei Shih and Francois Lionnet argue in *Minor Transnationalism*: "When non-U.S. forms of transnationalism and transcolonialism are brought into play, the 'minority discourse' model is helpful only to a limited extent. Not all minorities are minoritized by the same mechanisms in different places. . . . By looking at the way minority issues have been formulated in other national and regional contexts, it is possible to show that all expressive discourses . . . are inflected by transnational and trans-colonial processes."[8] That is, to understand Asian American fiction—and Korean American fiction in particular—a transnational approach to comparative minor literary studies not only is justified because it "refutes any notions of a natural and wholly bounded national identity while simultaneously iterating the historic and material power of the nation-state" but also is necessary as "a critical methodology that mediates interpretation, counseling deliberate disruption of normative understandings of nationhood and social subjectivity, and that insists on recognizing the ideologies conditioning national identity formation."[9] In other words, threading the needle between two traditions of minor literature across the Pacific enriches our comprehension of both, while resisting totalizing forces such as ethno-nationalism and increasing the opacity and interplay of political, social, and cultural discourses.

Asian studies scholars generally approach Zainichi subjectivity as a matter unique to the area's particular history and circumstances. Sonia Ryang argues that the prevailing approach by Western scholars is to treat Zainichi as Japan's foreign minority, thereby tacitly internalizing the logic of Japanese monoethnicity.[10] Instead, Ryang argues for the reframing of Zainichi in discourses of diaspora. In her formulation, there are two models of diaspora, the *classical* and the *cultural*. The classical model, best exemplified by the Jewish diaspora, is premised on several traits: an ethnic persecution causing the dispersal and loss of the homeland; a sense of collective connection to the homeland; a nostalgic sentimentality and desire to return; and an emphasis on the phylogeny (collective genesis) of the diaspora. The cultural model, on the other hand, is less bound by physical space. Instead, it is more concerned with a general state of instability and crisis of identity related to loss of the homeland (real or imagined), and a self-labeling as displaced and dislocated.[11] The most decisive criterion for identifying a diaspora is "an irreducible diasporic consciousness or state of mind," with an emphasis on ontogeny (individual genesis) of the diaspora.[12] Ryang argues that while first-generation Zainichi may be best described by the classical model, subsequent generations are more accurately described by the cultural model. Thus, even within the same ethnic group, generational differences may affect members' racialized subjectivity. Furthermore, the complicated politics and history of citizenship constitutes a web fraught with tension, creating multiple modes of statelessness in one ethnic group.

Yet according to Lisa Lowe's *Immigrant Acts*, those legal constructions of the Asian Other can be contested and refined by subsequent cultural forms: "If the state suppresses dissent by governing subjects through rights, citizenship, and political representation, it is only through culture that we conceive and enact new subjects and practices in antagonism to the regulatory *locus* of the citizen-subject."[13] Lowe posits that the state produces one definition of race through *legislation*, but Asian American communities can seek to challenge and question those definitions through culture, a move that parallels Ryang's articulation of Zainichi diasporic discourse.[14] "Culture is the medium of the *present*—the imagined equivalences and identifications through which the individual invents lived relationship with the national collective—but it is simultaneously the site that mediates the *past*. . . . It is through culture that the subject becomes, acts, and speaks itself as 'American.'"[15] I would add that first-generation Asian American immigrants may be disproportionately defined by juridical machinations, which Lowe characterizes as a mechanism for reproducing capital labor structures; however, if culture is the central means by which Asian Americans can contest legal definitions, then culture would be largely the arena of subsequent generations.

While Ryang and Lowe speak to different inflections of culture with respect to diaspora and minoritization, both are intimately related with the "memory work" explored in Lisa Yoneyama's comparative *Hiroshima Traces*. Speculating that "the Korean resident aliens' reality in Japan appears perhaps as fragmented as that of the 'Asian American,'" she discusses how a memorial to the Korean victims of the atomic bomb in Hiroshima crystallizes several lines of negotiation in forming ethnic subjectivity against the backdrop of a competing national project.[16] Most compellingly, Yoneyama's broader argument acknowledges the plasticity of ethnic subjecthood in the national imaginary through her examination of dialectic memory work. Similarly malleable, Sugihara grapples with his cultural diaspora, inherited from the first-generation Zainichi, by sifting through imported cultural objects through which he can redefine Zainichi in Japan.

For these reasons I propose reading *GO* through what I call *transpacific cultural mediation*, extending Ryang and Lowe's theoretical emphasis on culture as a means of self-definition, in the sense that Sugihara's relationship to the homeland is largely imaginative and negotiated through tertiary national spaces. The early history of Zainichi racialization is predicated on colonial-era labor practices and myriad legal definitions—and that relationship dictated the terms of initial debates and produced an ideology of return. But second-generation Sugihara contests his father's more classical model of diasporic subjectivity (though it is not without its own plasticity) and appears to operate under the cultural model; he rejects legislative and political mobilization, instead opting for a cultural means of self-determination. Situated at the nexus of Japanese, North/South Korean, and American politics, the second-generation Zainichi subject's pathway to a self-constructed racialized subjectivity is quite narrow.[17] The emphasis on culture as means of contesting and defining the citizen-subject is central to my thesis with regard to the younger Zainichi; it is a strikingly postmodern approach to racialization that is afforded to a *specific* dimension of a *specific* minority group in Japan at a *specific* time.[18] Transpacific cultural mediation makes it possible to navigate these specificities precisely because it addresses the particularities of the Zainichi. First, it makes visible the intimate histories and discourses of the United States, Japan, and Korea by forging connections that transcend boundaries. Second, it disrupts the notion of a "wholly bounded national identity" by demanding consideration of secondary and tertiary national sites as essential components. That is, it recasts the transnational and transcolonial minority as *the* radical element that upends ethno-national ontologies and is especially devastating to Japan's ideology of monoethnicity.

Kaneshiro's novel and Sugihara's search for selfhood are culturally mediated not only through Japanese and Korean ethno-national politics but through American racial discourse and popular culture. That is, in the process of negotiating a Zainichi identity for himself outside an either/or dichotomy, Sugihara must detour through another cultural space—in this case, American cultural and racial discourse—to find the latitude to break free from reified cultural identities that have been thrust upon him. John Lie argues that the meaning of Korea for Zainichi cannot be considered without Japan, and vice versa;[19] in fact, Zainichi ideology's totalizing politics precludes even considering the formation of an ethnic minority subjectivity.[20] I posit that to fully comprehend Sugihara's rejection of alien resident status and heretofore absent ontological construction of Zainichi as minority subject, a triangulation of Japan, Korea, and the United States as political, cultural, and racial intermediary must be considered.

The Myth of Monoethnicity and American Intervention

Beyond racial formation theory, there are tangible historical connections between the United States, Japan, and the Zainichi population. In a sense, the US occupation and Allied Powers had a hand in the reemergence of "Korean" as an ethnic and national category. Koreans were legally considered Japanese citizens until Japan's surrender, after which they suddenly found themselves in a stateless legal limbo.[21] That is not to say their citizenship status was clearly delineated; as Erin Aeran Chung shows, the question of the Korean population's "contingent citizenship" was quite complicated. Initially, the Supreme Commander of the Allied Powers (SCAP) decided to repatriate all Koreans; consequently, it did not concern itself with clarifying the legal status of Zainichi Koreans (figure 5).[22] This would prove to be problematic for the six hundred thousand who remained behind, finding themselves somewhere between second-class Japanese and foreign nationals with murky legal statuses.[23] It was a position that was embraced at the time, since to be "foreign" in the moment meant to be a member of the Allied forces during the occupation; and as newly minted foreigners, Koreans openly rejected the legitimacy of Japanese law.[24] In fact, an early Zainichi Korean organization called Joryeon, perhaps sensing the power disparity of "foreignness," would try to take an active hand in reshaping Japanese politics (but it was eventually dissolved by SCAP for its work with the Japanese Communist Party).[25]

If the Japanese Empire considered their colonized subjects lesser beings, why grant citizenship to the colonies? A closer look at the particulars of their imperial project shows how a myth of monoethnicity—necessitating citizenship—was integral to its success. Japan sought to create Japanese subjects of its colonized peoples, not out of any benevolent intent, but as a consequence of its peculiar position with regard to very material conditions. Having recently modernized in relatively short order, it had to somehow reconcile its lack of resources with its ambitions of becoming a global power; its shortage of capital created unique conditions for its imperialist project.[26] Japan had to accrue land, labor, and capital quickly, so unlike most European projects that reached into distant lands, its empire was initially limited to neighboring regions—essentially, the northeastern Asian continent. That brought about a particular dynamic, because, according to Western classifications, Japanese imperial subjects shared a common

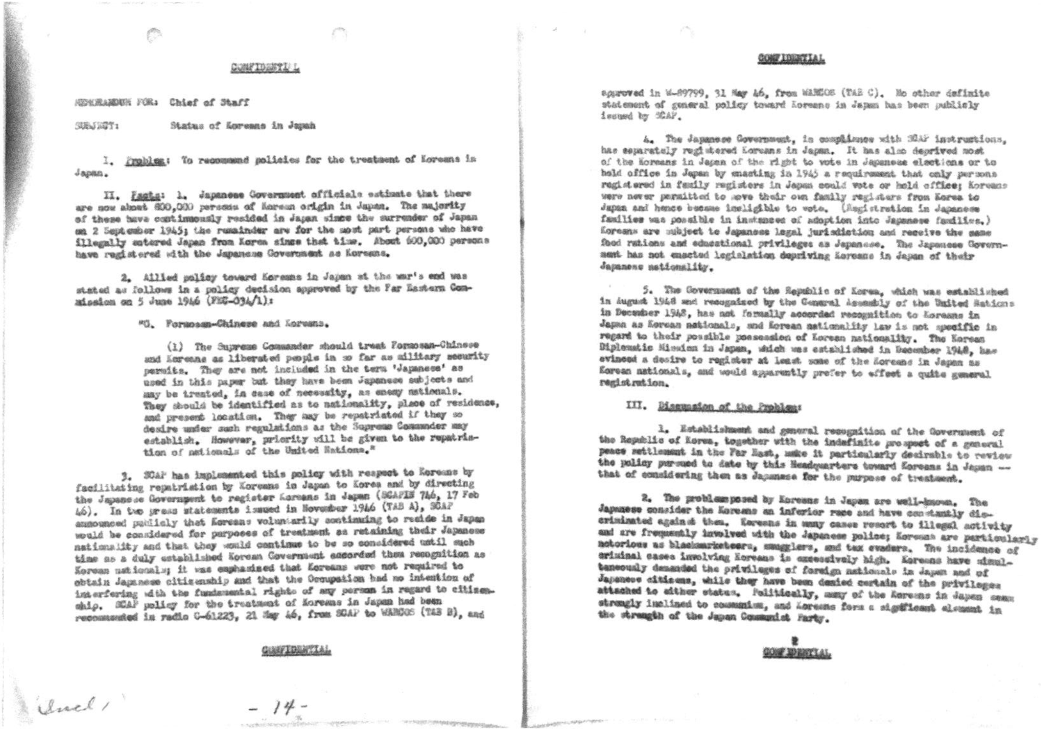

CONFIDENTIAL

MEMORANDUM FOR: Chief of Staff

SUBJECT: Status of Koreans in Japan

I. Problem: To recommend policies for the treatment of Koreans in Japan.

II. Facts: 1. Japanese Government officials estimate that there are now about 800,000 persons of Korean origin in Japan. The majority of these have continuously resided in Japan since the surrender of Japan on 2 September 1945; the remainder are for the most part persons who have illegally entered Japan from Korea since that time. About 600,000 persons have registered with the Japanese Government as Koreans.

2. Allied policy toward Koreans in Japan at the war's end was stated as follows in a policy decision approved by the Far Eastern Commission on 5 June 1946 (FEC-034/1):

"G. Formosan-Chinese and Koreans.

(1) The Supreme Commander should treat Formosan-Chinese and Koreans as liberated people in so far as military security permits. They are not included in the term 'Japanese' as used in this paper but they have been Japanese subjects and may be treated, in case of necessity, as enemy nationals. They should be identified as to nationality, place of residence, and present location. They may be repatriated if they so desire under such regulations as the Supreme Commander may establish. However, priority will be given to the repatriation of nationals of the United Nations."

3. SCAP has implemented this policy with respect to Koreans by facilitating repatriation by Koreans in Japan to Korea and by directing the Japanese Government to register Koreans in Japan (SCAPIN 746, 17 Feb 46). In two press statements issued in November 1946 (TAB A), SCAP announced publicly that Koreans voluntarily continuing to reside in Japan would be considered for purposes of treatment as retaining their Japanese nationality and that they would continue to be so considered until such time as a duly established Korean Government accorded them recognition as Korean nationals; it was emphasized that Koreans were not required to obtain Japanese citizenship and that the Occupation had no intention of interfering with the fundamental rights of any person in regard to citizenship. SCAP policy for the treatment of Koreans in Japan had been recommended in radio C-61223, 21 May 46, from SCAP to WARCOS (TAB B), and

CONFIDENTIAL

Incl 1

- 14 -

CONFIDENTIAL

approved in W-89799, 31 May 46, from WARCOS (TAB C). No other definite statement of general policy toward Koreans in Japan has been publicly issued by SCAP.

4. The Japanese Government, in compliance with SCAP instructions, has separately registered Koreans in Japan. It has also deprived most of the Koreans in Japan of the right to vote in Japanese elections or to hold office in Japan by enacting in 1945 a requirement that only persons registered in family registers in Japan could vote or hold office; Koreans were never permitted to move their own family registers from Korea to Japan and hence became ineligible to vote. (Registration in Japanese families was possible in instances of adoption into Japanese families.) Koreans are subject to Japanese legal jurisdiction and receive the same food rations and educational privileges as Japanese. The Japanese Government has not enacted legislation depriving Koreans in Japan of their Japanese nationality.

5. The Government of the Republic of Korea, which was established in August 1948 and recognized by the General Assembly of the United Nations in December 1948, has not formally accorded recognition to Koreans in Japan as Korean nationals, and Korean nationality law is not specific in regard to their possible possession of Korean nationality. The Korean Diplomatic Mission in Japan, which was established in December 1948, has evinced a desire to register at least some of the Koreans in Japan as Korean nationals, and would apparently prefer to effect a quite general registration.

III. Discussion of the Problem:

1. Establishment and general recognition of the Government of the Republic of Korea, together with the indefinite prospect of a general peace settlement in the Far East, make it particularly desirable to review the policy pursued to date by this Headquarters toward Koreans in Japan — that of considering them as Japanese for the purpose of treatment.

2. The problems posed by Koreans in Japan are well-known. The Japanese consider the Koreans an inferior race and have constantly discriminated against them. Koreans in many cases resort to illegal activity and are frequently involved with the Japanese police; Koreans are particularly notorious as blackmarketeers, smugglers, and tax evaders. The incidence of criminal cases involving Koreans is excessively high. Koreans have simultaneously demanded the privileges of foreign nationals in Japan and of Japanese citizens, while they have been denied certain of the privileges attached to either status. Politically, many of the Koreans in Japan seem strongly inclined to communism, and Koreans form a significant element in the strength of the Japan Communist Party.

2

CONFIDENTIAL

FIGURE 5 Supreme Commander for Allied Powers, "Status of Koreans in Japan," Confidential Memorandum. Note how the racialization and inherent criminality of Zainichi are asserted: "Koreans are particularly notorious as blackmarketers, smugglers, and tax evaders. The incidence of criminal cases involving Koreans is excessively high." Source: National Archives and Records Administration.

cultural heritage and were ethnically similar in appearance.[27] That allowed Japan to exercise a rhetoric of inclusiveness even as it subjugated its colonies and made it possible for Japanese nationalists to describe their colonial practices as more "humane."[28] The push toward incorporating the colonial subject, then, stemmed from Japan's material and practical goals: to integrate the colonized into the imperial project quickly but at arm's length, and to distinguish the Japanese Empire from Western nations as morally superior, with an eye toward defending against or expanding into the West.

Interestingly, in formulating its colonial policies, Japan studied European and American models of empire and assimilation, which intimates that their respective minoritized communities share a prehistory.[29] Mark Caprio sketches three broad categories of colonial administration: external, internal, and peripheral. External colonial administration concerned the handling of distant territories with racial and geographic differences from the homeland—which would apply to many European colonizing projects. Internal administration best describes the US model: it was mostly a nation-building project whose primary concern was securing the political allegiance of the people by installing a hegemonic culture and dismantling local, social, and cultural barriers. Japan, however, would adopt the peripheral model for colonial administration—a policy that promised the colonized assimilation into the interior but, in reality, continued to marginalize them at the exterior. Japan's project required its colonies to buy into the monoethnic argument as an incentive for participating in empire. Ultimately, its goal was to use their suzerain states to protect the colonial center from the West.

Thus the relationship between the United States and Japan, with the Zainichi population caught between, informed the Zainichi's definition as colonized subjects, their ephemerality as citizens, and finally, their formulation as resident aliens. My point is that the particularities of Zainichi colonial status may explain the move toward cultural mediation. First, citizenship for Zainichi Koreans is a sensitive matter, for in the postwar period they vehemently opposed their categorization as Japanese citizens—a label that functioned not to include but to exclude. Second, for first- and even second-generation Zainichi, citizenship was not to be sought after but categorically rejected for a favored state of "foreignness," since that would include a recognition of their existence as liberated people. Still, living in Japan as an ethnic minority and as permanent resident aliens enabled the perpetuation of discrimination and disenfranchisement. Third, in conjunction with a gradual

shift in attitude toward Japanese citizenship, it has been necessary for the
Zainichi Korean imaginary to construct a strong racial subjectivity that goes
beyond nationality and ethnicity, and the most effective theater for that exercise is cultural. Still, culture cannot be created in a vacuum, so Sugihara must
negotiate a position between Japan and Korea, as he feels he cannot do so
unless he travels through another cultural space—America.

Hypermasculinity and Ambivalence

GO has been critiqued for its hypermasculine bent and emphasis on individuality; as others note, the novel could even be read as a rejection of
Zainichi identity politics. For example, Sugihara's proclamation at the novel's
dénouement rejects labels, names, and categories, taking to task the very term
Zainichi. In a reading of both the text and the film adaptation, Ichiro Kuraishi points out that "Sugihara's claim, repeated in the movies, that he dares to
erase the national borders . . . in this sense embodies the zainichi generation
gap, with the younger generation's eye on the possibility of going beyond
the homeland orientation, as if to forget about the lost homeland, colonial
history and diasporic reality. But this desertion of the past obviously carries a
conservative, almost reactionary message of antidiaspora and antiethnicity."[30]
In other words, Sugihara's denial of national circumscriptions might appear
to transcend the limits of a state-inflected Zainichi identity, but by failing to
embrace and redefine Zainichi he reverts to a default Japanese identity. Indeed, his reformation is in the mold of the student archetype—studying for
exams so that he may eventually become a professional salaried worker and
follow the conventional path toward economic stability and success.

Furthermore, Sugihara's coming to terms with himself is predicated on
the romantic acceptance of him by a "native" female character. Sugihara and
Sakurai's initial attempt at sexual congress takes place at the Imperial Hotel
(Teikoku Hoteru), where Sugihara reverses the naming dynamic by giving
Sakurai a pseudonym on the hotel registry.[31] Within the confines of the
room, Sakurai finally reveals her first name (Tsubaki), whose conventional
Japaneseness embarrasses her. Sugihara decides to reciprocate by revealing
his ethnicity, which results in Sakurai rejecting him. It is only at the end of
the novel when they reconcile that he comes to terms with his racial identity.
Thus Sugihara's resolution depends on the conquest of the feminized Japanese figure—a simplistic reversal of the colonial dynamic. Melissa Wender

characterizes the resolution as disappointingly heteronormative—Sakurai confesses that she loves him for his fierce passion, his skill as a fighter, and his leaping ability.[32] Thus it is through Sugihara's "male heterosexuality . . . that this book proposes [he] define his relationship to his identity."[33]

Yet Kuraishi and Wender's readings of *GO*'s heteronormative underpinnings and exaltation of typical Japaneseness are still predicated on the finality of Sugihara and Sakurai's reconciliation despite his revelation, which appears contradictory. To resolve that contradiction, I read the text as having an ironic position on Sugihara and Sakurai's relationship. Similarly, Christopher Scott's queer reading of *GO* attempts to recover the novel's ambivalence and vacillations on racism and homophobia as a reflection of the peculiar positionality of Zainichi Koreans in Japan.[34] Moreover, I do not think that Sugihara's polemic betrays an "antiethnic" message, for Sugihara never considers passing for Japanese; instead, it is important to him that Sakurai acknowledge his Korean background before they further their relationship.

Rather, I would argue that something much more complicated and ambivalent is at play here—that Sugihara's inelegant diatribe is a stumbling first step toward bridging the gap between Zainichi as racial minority and Japanese subject. In truth, I am more interested in the means and process of Sugihara's journey. He does not have the sophistication or knowledge to formulate, from the ground up, his own racial ontology. Instead, his is a generation of Zainichi that, while acutely aware of the history and trauma of Japanese colonialism, is acculturated to and speaks the postmodern language of popular culture; thus he references music, television programs, literary works, and a sundry list of cultural imports to process and negotiate space for himself. In short, he occupies each space, taking anything that might be of use, to formulate his own racialized alterity.

Nationality, Ethnicity, Race, the "Third Way" and Beyond

Sugihara's haphazard search for an ontology beyond the Korean-Japanese binary reflects a complicated institutional and historical legacy. First-generation Zainichi considered themselves temporary guests in Japan and had every intention of returning to Korea. Second- and third-generation Zainichi, however, were more interested in permanent status in Japan. With first-generation Zainichi intellectuals largely dictating the terms of a Zainichi subjecthood in Japan, a conflict between generations was inevitable if any move toward settlement in Japan was considered assimilation (and implicitly collaboration). As a possible answer, Zainichi intellectual Kim Tong Myung introduced a "third way" (*daisan no michi*): "The third way was a way to live in Japan as home, without being totally Korean or Japanese but by being 'zainichi' (resident in Japan). In other words the third way was the creation of a space for multivocal negotiation away from dominant notions of identity located in hegemonic definitions of nationhood to a space where new identities could be imagined."[35] However, there are drawbacks to the third way that is predicated on racialization above all else. For example, there is little room for discourse in addressing patriarchy within the Zainichi community, and the third way accepts a colonizer/colonized binary, which, as Lionnet and Shih argue, can be restrictive.[36] Consequently, a "fourth way" (*datsu zainichi-ron*, the discourse of abandoning Zainichi), according to Jeffry Hester, addresses these drawbacks by acknowledging the slippery nature of defining a Zainichi subjectivity dependent on so many moving parts, caught between the trauma and history of empire, racialization, and popular culture.[37]

Within these generational tensions the novel contests identity according to three dimensions familiar to ethnic studies scholars with respect to the particular history and placement of Zainichi: nationality, ethnicity, and race. The novel first dismantles nationality as absurdly fluid, particularly in the case of Zainichi, with its "contingent citizenship" legacy, which produces "residents" rather than subjects of Japan who can apparently switch nationalities at will. Next, Sugihara attempts to challenge ethnicity with a discourse on genetics, which he ultimately abandons. Finally, Sugihara redirects intellectual and emotional labor to constructing a racialized self through culture. He understands that despite his shared ethnic heritage, he has little in common with either North or South Koreans—as underscored by his rejection of North Korean ideology and of South Korea.[38] He must dwell in a tertiary cultural space to process and formulate a cultural identity outside the bounds of nationality and ethnicity.

Opening with the Sugihara family's desire to vacation abroad, the novel quickly explicates the tensions surrounding the subject of Zainichi nationality. The Sugihara family want to go to Hawaii but are confronted with a problem—the matter of their North Korean citizenship.

> It was New Year's and I was fourteen when my old man started muttering about "Hawaii." . . . Up until then, Hawaii had been a symbol of capitalist decadence in our house. At the time, my old man was fifty-four, had North

Korean citizenship (in other words, a *zainichi chōsenjin*) and was a Marxist communist. . . . I think an explanation is in order. Why is it that my old man, who was born in Jeju-do, Korea, has North Korean citizenship? And why is it that to go to Hawaii, he has to change his citizenship to South Korean? This might be a bit dry, but I'll try to explain as simply as I can.

When the old man was a kid—that is, during the war—he was *Japanese*. The reason's simple. It's because back then, *chōsen* (Korea) was a colony of Japan. Supposing he grows up, the old man—who's had Japanese citizenship, a Japanese name, and the Japanese language forced on him—was to become a soldier for the [Japanese] Emperor. . . . Being in Japan was good, but as the decision to decide on citizenship got closer, my old man picked *chōsen* [North Korean] citizenship. The reason is, North Korea subscribed to Marxism, which was supposed to be better for the poor, and cared more for the Zainichi Koreans than the South Korean government did. (9–10)[39]

Unlike US citizenship, Japanese citizenship is not determined by place of birth; so although Sugihara was born in Japan and has never set foot in North Korea, he has North Korean citizenship because his parents selected North Korean citizenship upon their liberation.[40] In the eyes of the Japanese government, he is *zainichi chōsenjin* (a Resident North Korean in Japan), an alien resident. Therefore, he has no right to vote, is discriminated against by businesses and universities, and has limited mobility.[41] So Sugihara Senior decides to switch from North Korean to South Korean. Nationality, then, in the initial framing of the novel, is quickly dismissed as a farce. It is a means to an end; to change one's nationality is seen less as a betrayal than as a pragmatic maneuver. In the end, Sugihara's father bribes officials from Min-dan—a South Korean Zainichi group—to change the family nationality to South Korean, at which point he turns to Sugihara and quips: "You can buy nationality. Which one do you want?" (12). Their insouciant attitude toward nationality is reinforced when Sugihara, after revealing his ethnic heritage to Sakurai, jokes: "I was *chōsen* [North Korean] until the eighth grade. Maybe I'll become Japanese in three months. Maybe I'll become American in a year. Maybe Norwegian by the time I die" (186). The move Kaneshiro makes here is not insignificant. For earlier generations of Zainichi, national citizenship was integral to subjectivity. Koreans had their national and ethnic identities systematically dismantled by the Japanese and fought, bled, and died for the sake of nationhood. This discourse would leave a lasting impression on Zainichi politics, as many early efforts of organizing tended to focus on

South Korean and North Korean politics rather than domestic Zainichi af-
fairs. But Kaneshiro dismisses nationality as a consequence more of practical
calculations and politics than of destiny or essentialism.

If nationality or citizenship is no longer a deciding factor in Zainichi
subjectivity, Sugihara must next address ethnic determinism, which he believes he has refuted. At one point, Sugihara attempts to reconcile ethnic
differences by citing a television program on human genetic history. He
explains to Sakurai that tracing of mitochondrial DNA shows all permuta-
tions of human genes to have arisen from a single genetic line originating in
Africa (174–75). He finds comfort in a scientific narrative that accounts for
the shared genetic ancestry of Koreans and Japanese but fails to recognize
that racial discrimination is not about genes. Tracing mitochondrial DNA
shows how everyone is related—a merging of "pollution" and "purity" ideologies (176). At the end of his explanation, Sakurai, missing the point, asks
him what he's really trying to say. Still anxious about revealing his ethnic
heritage, Sugihara simply states that he admires the bravery of the early
travelers who spread out through the various continents. When he finally
does confess his Korean ethnicity to Sakurai at the hotel, he returns to this
line of thinking in a lengthy cross-examination:

> "How do you tell the difference between a Japanese, Korean, or Chinese
> person?"
> "How do I tell the difference . . . ?"
> "Nationality? Like I said before, citizenship can change."
> "Birthplace then, or language . . ."
> "Okay, then, what about returnees with foreign citizenship who were
> born and educated abroad because of their parents' work? They're not
> Japanese?"
> "If their parents are Japanese, then I think they're Japanese." (188–89)

Having pointed out that nationality is no determinant of Japaneseness,
Sugihara proceeds to dissect Sakurai's ethnicity rationale—that Japaneseness is determined by parental lineage. He points out that genetic forensics
traces Japanese DNA to China and that Koreans and Japanese share the
same ethnic heritage if you go back far enough. Intellectually, Sakurai
understands the logic of Sugihara's argument, but an inarticulable barrier
remains: "Sakurai sighed deeply: 'You really know a lot. But that's not really
the issue. I understand the reasoning behind everything you say, but that's
not good enough. It's scary . . . the thought of you inside me is scary . . .'"

(190). Thus, regardless of the logic and reasoning behind Sugihara's DNA explication, Sakurai finds his blood *kitanai* (dirty); his mistake is in believing that rationality and reason are enough to overcome racialization.

Both nationality and ethnicity take a figurative beating when Sugihara's long-festering resentment toward his father bursts out. Oyaji (Old Man) has been on a bender, distraught over the news that his brother has passed away in North Korea. In his despair, he wallows in guilt over the fact that he had not fulfilled his familial obligations in sending enough money back to his brother and that because he has switched nationalities, he is unable to visit North Korea to bury him. Sugihara, however, has little sympathy for Oyaji or his late uncle. Much to Oyaji's astonishment, Sugihara responds, "If North Koreans want to eat [well], then they should bring the revolution. What are those bastards doing?" (221). Sugihara expressly rejects the idea of having any obligation to North Korea; in his view, its people are responsible for their own fates. This does not go over well with Oyaji, and they spill out into a small park, where they have a brutal boxing match, which Oyaji wins by spitting blood into Sugihara's eyes. Sugihara thinks, "This blood, my old man's blood, won't get out of my eyes," perhaps reflective of Sugihara's futile efforts of washing away ethnicity (226). Later, Oyaji confesses that he realizes that he is of an older generation and that Sugihara will have a very different relationship with nationality and the idea of the homeland; he switched nationalities to liberate Sugihara, but he cannot help conflating kinship with the nation. The same blood that is key to Sugihara's universalizing DNA argument is the cause of his downfall. Oyaji's blood cannot be scrubbed away or made benign through scientific rationales—it has been racialized.

Racial Formation and American Cultural Imports

Racial formation, which Sugihara belatedly stumbles upon, is the arena in which his subjectivity is both based and contested. In some ways, part of Sugihara already knows that his DNA thesis will fail to reconcile ethnic differences; and he has always known how little nationality matters in terms of his acceptance by Japanese society. It is the third and final element that Sugihara uses to formulate a cohesive Zainichi subjectivity, but this cannot happen without several US-based intermediary steps from nation- and DNA-based racial formation toward culture and discourse—the putative transpacific cultural mediation. Stuck between the binary of Korean and

Japanese, Sugihara must try to formulate an ontological space between, but that cannot occur in a vacuum. Instead, he temporarily enters a tertiary cultural space as a means of negotiation—a mode of being outside the domestic realms of power to rehabilitate, reshape, and revise.

The first move toward mediating spaces comes in the aforementioned vacation to Hawaii. While Sugihara does not accompany his parents to Hawaii, his father's change in nationality, he later realizes, was more for Sugihara than for himself: "I understood why this asshole-of-an-old man suddenly changed nationalities to South Korea. It wasn't for Hawaii. It was for me" (227). Going to Hawaii, then, is more than an ideological break; it is the beginning of Sugihara's entrance into Japanese institutionalism, for he uses the money that would have been used to fund his Hawaii trip to take the entrance exam to enter a Japanese school. And it is significant that his family does not take the much easier option of going to Okinawa, a similarly tropical vacation spot with a large US military presence—it must be Hawaii. His father returns from Hawaii and places their vacation photo in the *genkan* (hallway entrance) as a declaration of the family's break from totalizing North Korean politics and ideology; and Sugihara embarks on his journey toward racial formation. It is also significant that Hawaii is not a permanent space for Sugihara's parents; it is a fantasy projection, a construct of American empire. In a pattern that will be repeated, tertiary national spaces (both geographic and cultural) are means, rather than ends—places to occupy temporarily in order to renegotiate the domestic self.

American cultural references are not particularly unusual in Japanese fiction, and indeed, allusions to other cultural sites, such as *Romeo and Juliet*, pepper the novel. But Sugihara's intertextual travels often return to a narrative theme—the transformation and construction of the racialized American. For example, he is fascinated by the *Godfather* films; he describes his favorite scene as the one in which Vito Corleone arrives at Ellis Island and gazes upon the Statue of Liberty, indicative of how appealing he finds the American immigrant narrative (131). However, he also betrays an acute cognizance of the dark side of American racial discourse. At one point, he expounds upon phrenology—how it was used to persecute Native and African Americans, and how the same logic could be used against Koreans (80).

It is through popular culture—with the attendant political and racial underpinnings—that Sugihara negotiates a pathway for Zainichi subjectivity. Christopher Scott notes that *GO* appears to be unusually "infatuated with American culture, particularly that produced by African Americans."[42] For example, Sugihara ponders how African American culture has produced a rich array of musical genres such as jazz and hip-hop, when nothing analogous has been produced by Zainichi culture (134). Scott reads these cultural references as evidence of Kaneshiro's own anxieties and perhaps a circuitous way of layering a queer framework onto Sugihara's relationship with his best friend, Jong-il. American popular culture is indeed conspicuous in the novel, but I would suggest that the intertextuality goes beyond an expression of Zainichi anxiety; Sugihara actively adapts American cultural discourse for his own ends. For instance, the first chapter closes with Sugihara reworking lyrics from Bruce Springsteen's "Born in the U.S.A.":

> Born in a rich home and country
> I did bad and got kicked by my old man
> You lose sight and end up like a dog that's been beat too much
> Even though you spend most of your life in style
> I was born in Japan
> I was born in Japan
> (19–20)

Here Sugihara rewrites the subtext of Springsteen's lyrics—a lamentation over the plight of the working class in the richest nation in the world, a nation with imperialist ambitions in Vietnam—by inserting himself as the subject in a Japanese context.[43] His intertextual framing begins with a universalist undercurrent—that of the struggling worker in an exploitative system—but he also positions Oyaji as part of a larger system of oppression, perhaps representative of the totalizing politics of his Zainichi heritage. Later in the text, Sugihara ruminates on the life and times of Jimi Hendrix.

> After wrapping up an hour and a half of practice, I listened to a CD of "The Star Spangled Banner" by Jimi Hendrix at Woodstock—a half-Cherokee, half-Black rock star. Hendrix played in protest of how minorities were being sent to the front lines of the Vietnam War. . . . No matter how many times I hear it, it still kills me. There's no way for minority voices to get through to the establishment, so they've got no choice but to be as loud as they can by any means necessary. There might come a day when I want to play the Japanese national anthem in protest. I'm practicing my guitar for when that day comes. (97–98)

This time, Sugihara explicitly identifies with the positionality of the mixed-race Hendrix and his attempt to give a voice to the voiceless through his instrument. Betraying a sharp awareness of the injustices suffered by African and Native Americans, Sugihara envisions a time when he will be able to follow in their footsteps. Both musical performances in their original contexts are attempts to negotiate and redefine the meaning of the United States according to working-class and racial struggles, to take ownership through extralegal means. In each case, Sugihara internalizes their historical and political contexts and negotiates a language and space for himself; his cultural travels are a form of "practice" for the day when he will have to assert his subjecthood as Zainichi.

Using culture to mediate relationships is not limited to ethno-national politics. Even *Oyaji* is not immune; he croons "Silent Night" in the style of Bing Crosby. Perhaps unamused by his father's ironic appropriation of the All-American singer's image, beset by violent impulses, Sugihara thinks to himself, "Aren't you supposed to be a Marxist?" (243). Another evening, Sugihara watches *Star Wars* with Oyaji, who nods approvingly at the training sequence between Yoda and Luke Skywalker. Afterwards, Oyaji jokes that Sugihara should refer to him as Yoda—to which Sugihara mutters that he's more Darth Vader than Yoda (66). The text layers and complicates their relationship through ironic intertextuality as a means of negotiating an understanding that cannot be captured in father and son's "native" (or adopted) language of Japanese, let alone Korean. In a moment of vulnerability, Oyaji empathizes with Sugihara when he sarcastically mentions his plans for moving to Norway to become Norwegian; Oyaji reveals that he once harbored a similar dream of moving to Spain to become Spanish (101).

It is significant that the majority of cultural imports mentioned in the book are American in origin. I would suggest that the US's postwar function as Supreme Commander for the Allied Powers (SCAP) gave these imports a special significance among Zainichi Koreans, who initially greeted SCAP as the harbinger of their release as liberated people. That relationship would deteriorate rapidly, as SCAP's priority was the rebuilding of Japan's government and people: For example, when the Zainichi population began to organize with communist labor forces, SCAP quickly turned on them, as they considered them to be ideological enemies who undermined the rebuilding of Japan.[44] But SCAP would also at times intervene on the behalf of Zainichi Koreans, who were subject to discrimination and intimidation by Japanese authorities (154). Thus, in the Zainichi consciousness, US occupational forces, despite their at times oppositional stances, would be considered an external tertiary force that might be used to the Zainichi population's advantage when dealing with an adversarial Japanese government. Extending this dynamic to American culture, I would argue that a similar dynamic is at work in *GO*—the use of US interventions in cultural form to liberate the Zainichi from the shackles of ethno-nationalist discrimination. Thus negotiation of a Zainichi subjectivity in Japan has always been mediated by external tertiary forces, for it was the arrival of SCAP that enabled Zainichi Koreans to escape Japanese citizenship, and it was SCAP's status—or at least its perceived status—as an arbiter of universal human rights that afforded Zainichi some leverage, however minimal. For better or worse, Sugihara occupies American culture as a neutral zone while he grapples with his Zainichi subjectivity in a *racial*, rather than an ethno-national, sense.

I recognize that this is a problematic formulation, for it buys into the global hegemony of the United States as a military power and cultural force. By undermining Japan's situating of itself as the gleaming metropole of modernity, the novel necessarily accepts the United States as the political and cultural arbiter of modernity, which manifests in a distinctively hypermasculine bent in the novel—collectively critiqued by Wender, Kuraishi, and Scott. However, Sugihara tempers that by tapping American racial discourse, particularly regarding African Americans, to contextualize his occupation of a tertiary national space that has a long history of racial discrimination; and he takes pains to highlight comparable prejudices in Japan while simultaneously taking advantage of the US's privileges. The conflation between culture and politico-militaristic power is made most apparent when Sugihara faces several metonymic discriminatory forces.

For example, when Sugihara confronts bullies at his Japanese high school, he quotes a recent cinematic rendition of Billy the Kid: "I'll make you famous" (22). Invoking rugged individualist imagery from the American West seems to align with the archetype that Sugihara enjoys emulating—the cowboy making his way in a lawless land. His prowess as a fighter notwithstanding, Sugihara attempts to transcend his school reputation as racialized pariah by fighting his way to the top. By mimicking Billy the Kid, he imagines himself rising above his status from outlaw to legend. When he is faced with a domestic juridical disciplinary force, the novel's solution is to offer the same radical individualism that repairs Sugihara's relationship with Sakurai, mediated once again by American cultural forms. Zainichi subjects, as alien residents, are always required to carry their Alien Registration ID card with them;

failure to produce identification upon request by the authorities can result in heavy fines or jail time. After Sugihara leaves the hotel, he spies a policeman approaching on a bicycle, upon which he begins to ventriloquize Raymond Chandler's hard-boiled private eye, Philip Marlowe: "No way has yet been invented to say goodbye to the cops" (194). The officer stops Sugihara, who, upon being questioned, channels detective noir: "I was irritated, angry, and annoyed. If I were Philip Marlowe, I'd make some crack and somehow get myself out of this, but instead I went with The Continental Op and decided to hit and run" (196). Sugihara pushes the officer, who hits his head on his bicycle and is knocked out. In a curious scene, after returning to consciousness and realizing that a remorseful Sugihara poses no threat, the young officer laments that he is not very good at his job. Sugihara responds, "There's no way you could've avoided that. . . . Nobody's ever dodged it. It's a technique taught in hand-to-hand combat by the U.S. military" (199). Sugihara thus not only expresses his discontent internally by channeling American detective noir but physically lashes out using US military tactics, presumably learned from training sessions with Oyaji. A fearful symmetry between the cultural and the tactical results in self-destructive acts of anger.

While prone to violence, Sugihara still evinces an understanding that there should be a purpose driving it. Lest he be judged as an impulsive reactionary, Sugihara proves more thoughtful at times in his choice of cultural and political avatars, at one point tapping into the legacy of another American icon and trailblazer, Malcolm X:

> The black civil rights leader Malcolm X said, "I don't even call it violence when it's in self-defense; I call it intelligence."
>
> I despise violence too, just like Malcolm X. But there are times when there's no choice. If my left cheek gets hit, should I turn the other cheek? No way. There are guys out there who don't go for the cheek, they go for more vital regions. (24–25)

Here Sugihara aligns himself with the civil rights movement, in apparent parallel with his burgeoning consciousness as Zainichi. He is not an outlaw but a champion of racial equality, even if his methods call for violence. He considers himself the subject of discrimination, fighting to be recognized and acknowledged as a human being; thus his acts of aggression are justified. This is not the first or last time that he repurposes American racial discourse to self-define Zainichi racialization.

Pathways to Self-Formation

Yet there are limits to how far transpacific cultural mediation can travel; it is more a means of negotiation than a permanent solution. Sugihara's abilities as a brawler give him little satisfaction, and even then, he understands that fighting his way to the top of the heap will result in a Pyrrhic victory. For instance, Sugihara goes to his friend Kato's birthday party, where Kato invites Sugihara to go into business with him, and is confronted by a racist bully named Kobayashi. Upon being called *chonko* (a racial slur for Korean) by Kobayashi, Sugihara wearily proceeds to pummel him, but not before pointing out that there will always be a difference between himself and Kato, despite their both being social outcasts (143–45). Similarly, Sugihara immediately regrets knocking out the young officer, intimating that his violent outbursts come at a cost to himself and are counter to his character; his anger dissipates as soon as he hears the officer's bike crash to the ground, and he returns to check the officer's injuries. Even his admiration of Malcolm X's defense of violence speaks mainly to his fascination with African American culture, which has carved out a strong identity for itself in its battle for equality.

The impracticality of Sugihara's strategy is made all the more clear when juxtaposed with other exceptional Zainichi characters' methods of subject formation. Tawake is perhaps the most tragic figure, a superb physical specimen and natural-born leader who should have excelled but is nevertheless constrained by systematic discrimination. Tawake shares much of Sugihara's anger and recounts an episode to Sugihara in which that anger went unexpressed. At the age of fourteen, Zainichi Koreans must have their fingerprints registered at the ward office (a requirement much protested by Zainichi organizations in the 1980s and 1990s); when Tawake's day finally arrived, he found that his anger was disarmed by the human faces of the city employees, a middle-aged man who apologized profusely and a nervous young woman (73–74). Tawake confesses to Sugihara that he fully intended to confront the injustice of the exercise and disrupt the bureaucrats' office, but that, when caught up in the ritual exchange of apologies, he could not help responding to the official's stream of *gokurōsama* (my apologies) with *sumimasen* (pardon me) more times than he had ever uttered in his life. Juridical dehumanization is achieved through a low-intensity, diffused, and nebulous bureaucracy immune to individual action. Frustrated, Tawake recedes from view to live out his days as a subaltern, resigned to the fact that he alone cannot defeat systematic racial discrimination.[45]

Jong-il, Sugihara's former classmate and best friend, is a soft-spoken intellectual who is deeply invested in the Zainichi community and has the acumen to improve the Zainichi condition. In an incident that perhaps foreshadows the specter of doom haunting Sugihara and Sakurai's relationship, Jong-il intervenes in a mirror-image courtship on a train station platform. A young Japanese student, spurred on by his classmates, approaches a female Zainichi student who is marked by wearing a *ch'ima chŏgori* (traditional Korean dress) instead of a Japanese school uniform—there is no "passing" here. The Japanese student approaches the Korean student with a butterfly knife for "courage" hidden in his pocket. Conditioned by the political and social context, the girl mistakes the boy's approach as an act of aggression, and Jong-il intervenes, only to find himself stabbed by the boy's knife, which has been reflexively thrust into him. Faced with the naked politics of Zainichi and Japanese conflict, these bodies are shoved into a combative space with their roles predestined, regardless of their individual desires. The Korean girl mistakes the boy for an aggressor, the Japanese boy moves his arm without thinking, and Jong-il, the intellectual, ends up getting killed.

The third exceptional Zainichi Korean character to reach beyond the Japanese-Korean dialectic is Naomi, a manager-owner at a *yakiniku-ya* (Korean BBQ restaurant) where Sugihara's mother works. Naomi stands apart for several reasons. Her distinctly Japanese name made her a target for bullying at the North Korean school she attended with Sugihara's mother. Then, as a former fashion model, she naturalized to Japan because her North Korean status precluded international modeling jobs. Despite her beauty, she retires from modeling before the age of thirty, explaining in vague terms that "there were some things" (J: *iro iro atta no yo*「色々あったのよ」) (87). She returns to take over her father's restaurant and eventually departs when she marries an American businessman who works in international trade. Sugihara, at the conclusion of his journey, runs into Naomi again:

> "Missing your front teeth—it's very *cute*," Naomi said, brushing my cheek. "If you become *cute*-er, then you can *get* a good girlfriend. And, more than anyone else, you'll be *happy*."
>
> I nodded, and said: "You know, English pops up when you talk."
>
> Naomi's cheeks turned red, and then she smiled coyly. (235–36)

Again, it is a problematic formulation that Naomi's means of extrication depend on an agent of American capital—that she has to "marry out" as a means of legitimating her hybridity. Stuck between Japanese and Korean identities, she has no real means of reaching beyond until she meets and marries a US citizen, whose access to capital—both financial and social—allows her to revel in heterogeneity.

Tawake and Jong-il both purport to fight discrimination by ensconcing themselves in their identities as Zainichi Koreans, yet they fail to recognize the degree to which they are Korean *and* Japanese. That misrecognition causes Tawake to freeze when confronting the ward office bureaucrats and causes Jong-il's death when he assumes the mantle of racial defender in a terrible misunderstanding. Naomi's marriage latches onto social and cultural capital of American-ness that fails to negotiate space for Zainichi subjectivity. The lives of all three present a critique of the myth of individual exceptionalism in the absence of hybridity.

For these reasons I contest the prevailing criticism of the much-maligned conclusion of *GO*, which ends with Sugihara and Sakurai's reconciliation after they both denounce ethnic and racial difference and reconnect on the basis of a nearly primal attraction contingent on their individuality. According to that reading, after all his introspection, Sugihara finally renounces his efforts to find a rationale for equalizing the national, ethnic, and racial differences between Japanese and Korean, only to find that his physicality and raw animal magnetism transcends those categories. It is a troubling and weak resolution, if indeed that is what occurs.

However, I argue that their reconciliation is one idealistic track of several that the text seems to offer with regard to formulating Zainichi selfhood. Sakurai confesses that she was attracted to Sugihara's primal anger—but where was the anger directed, and where did it come from? It seems odd and facetious that Sakurai would decouple that anger from Sugihara's racial angst. It is a bizarre courtship, as if they have agreed to efface all that has occurred between them and regress to another point in time. In the end, it is precisely because of Sugihara's rage against discrimination and racial anxiety that Sakurai is drawn to him. To read their reconciliation as the disavowal of race would have to include ignoring the entirety of the text and the journey they take to get to that point.

Indeed, another Zainichi character on a similar path presents another means of achieving something akin to a "third way."[46] Politically conscious and socially active, Miyamoto "outs" himself as Zainichi to Sugihara (212), articulating a similar awareness of American racial discourse, particularly Korean American subjectivity.[47] He tries to recruit Sugihara to form a unified Zainichi group beyond the nationalist politics of Mindan or Soren—his interest is in creating a Zainichi identity endemic to their lives in Japan. Sugihara declines Miyamoto's invitation, not because of any ideological opposition, but because he has another project in mind—he struggles for a Zainichi subjectivity so that he can find love.[48] Miyamoto understands, but his project is larger in scope and scale—they come to a sympathetic understanding that they seek similar ends, if by different means. However, they hold in common a third national referent—in the form of American racial and cultural discourse—as a means of negotiating their space between Korea and Japan. Transpacific cultural mediation is the means by which both Zainichi characters, Sugihara and Miyamoto, encounter lines of tension running in multiple directions as they seek a way beyond a Korean-Japanese dialectic. They are two subjects working toward a distinctive Zainichi subjectivity by sympathetic means; to uphold one method as superior to or independent from the other would show an incomplete understanding of a multifaceted effort.

For similar reasons I frame my reading of *GO* through an Asian American critical lens; while the novel's cultural and political context falls within the purview of Asian studies, neglecting American racial discourse results in an incomplete and two-dimensional picture. *GO* engages in an interminority and transnational cultural dialogue as a means of rehabilitating a fragmented history, generational alienation, and political absence. Transpacific cultural mediation, then, resolves how East Asian minor literatures speak to diasporic subjectivities in the US and elsewhere. Asian American scholars looking beyond domestic literature might see how American racial and cultural discourse is integrated in diasporic communities abroad; and conversely, Asian studies scholars might perceive connections to minority fiction in the United States as well as the attendant scholarly body of work. It may be that in the future, as bodies and capital flow through porous national borders, a truly comprehensive picture cannot be drawn without an engaged, sustained conversation between the two disciplines.

CHAPTER 3

Korean American Literature Has Always Been Postcolonial

Clay Walls, A Gesture Life, *and Colonial Trauma*

Clay Walls and *A Gesture Life* . . . point to Korean nationalism, Japanese colonialism, and U.S. racism as distinguishable but inseparably linked historical narratives that simultaneously underwrite the production of Korean and Korean American subjectivities.

—Kandice Chuh, *Imagine Otherwise*

Trauma . . . is a story of a wound that cries out, that address us in the attempt to tell us of a reality or truth that is not otherwise available. This truth, in its delayed appearance and its belated address, cannot be linked only to what is known, but also to what remains unknown in our very actions and our language.

—Cathy Caruth, *Trauma: Explorations in Memory*

IN 1943, Second Lieutenant Young-Oak Kim arrived at Camp Shelby in Mississippi to join the 100th Infantry Battalion, part of the famed World War II 442nd Japanese American regiment. His commander, the story goes, immediately offered Kim a transfer, for it was well known that Koreans and Japanese despised each other. Furthermore, Kim was not only Korean American but also an officer, which would further complicate efforts to bond with the Japanese American enlisted men. Kim declined the offer. "Sir," he said, "they're Americans, and I'm an American. We're going to fight for America."[1]

It is a pleasant, patriotic story. It has clean lines. The Japanese American narrative was already well under way—internees leapt at the chance to prove their loyalty to the Stars and Stripes, and the 442nd would become the most decorated unit in American history. Kim's story furthers a subnarrative—even

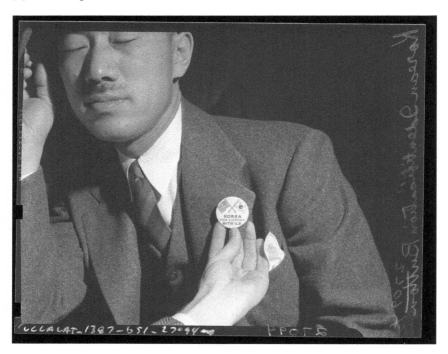

FIGURE 6 Korean American man wearing button stating, "Korea for victory with U.S." in 1941, Los Angeles, California, Los Angeles Daily News Negatives (Collection 1387). Source: Library Special Collections, Charles E. Young Research Library, University of California, Los Angeles (UCLA) / CC by 4.0.

the Koreans could not help but join the Japanese in pan-ethnic Asian American solidarity in the war effort. In one fell swoop, colonial tensions were left behind in the old country; as Americans, Kim and his regiment put aside their differences to make room for apple pie on the window sill of history.

But material and cultural history is rarely this neat. Even as Lieutenant Kim bonded with his battalion, back home in Los Angeles other members of the Korean American community had different sentiments. In the introduction to this book, I refer to Hisaye Yamamoto's "Wilshire Bus," in which the Japanese American narrator registers her shock at seeing an elderly Asian man wearing a pin that identifies him as Korean as opposed to Japanese. That story, it turns out, was based on the proliferation of lapel pins produced by the United Korean Committee in America, in addition to automobile decals and identification cards (figures 6 and 7).

Furthermore, Japanese American soldiers from Hawaii might have had good reason to be suspicious of Lieutenant Kim's motives. Koreans in Hawaii bristled at being placed under wartime restrictions and curfews along with the Japanese and campaigned the state for distinction from them.[2]

Ultimately, it was the story of racial solidarity and pan-ethnicity that took root—it is the one that mobilized Asian America. But the second story never went away, really; it has always been present but has become unseen. The question I raise in this chapter is, How can we create room for both narratives? How can a critical Asian American studies account for multitudes that complicate rather than resolve?

This chapter exhumes literary bodies to underscore the primacy of the Japanese Empire in Korean and Asian American formation and to articulate a corresponding framework. It is, I recognize, a sensitive and politically fraught subject. But the historical and generational trauma of colonialism must be absorbed, rewritten, and integrated into Korean American literary

FIGURE 7 Button, detail. Used under CC by 4.0.

history as part of a comprehensive formulation of Asian American literature. First, inasmuch as Korean American fiction belongs to Asian American literature, it also belongs to Japanese postcolonial fiction. In contradistinction to, say, anglophone postcolonial literature, which tends to emerge from decolonized sites, Korean American fiction is doubly displaced by an anxiety wrought by an inability to return to a precolonial state, and the additional complication of undergoing a transformative process in the United States, with its own imperial inflection. There is a tension between Korean American fiction and the prevalence of Japanese colonialism that receives little attention. Second, literary constructions of "comfort women" are an instantiation of the Japanese imperial legacy in Korean American fiction, part of which is the result of a confluence of intersecting elements, including an idealized American global justice, Asian American social justice, and colonial trauma. A number of novelists have tackled the subject of comfort women in English-language fiction, including Nora Okja Keller and Chang-rae Lee, but an even larger number of Asian American writers have touched upon Japanese colonialism and its repercussions. The literary subject of comfort women is in equal parts visceral tragedy and injustice but also provides an opportunity for Korean American fiction to grapple with empire and colonialism writ large. Third, reconceptualizing Korean American literature as contact zone between transpacific minority discourses complicates the broader justice-oriented narratives and a flattened Asian American political homogeneity—a means of articulating an anti-Japanese sentiment that became politically fraught after the 1960s. In chapter 1, I examined an early example in Younghill Kang's *East Goes West* (1937), but contemporary Korean American fiction ranging from the 1970s to the 2000s persists in portraying the Japanese imperial presence. To that end, I offer a reading of *Clay Walls* and *A Gesture Life* through theories of colonial racialization.

Decolonizing Asian American Studies

Even a cursory survey of Korean American fiction reveals a preoccupation with Japanese imperialism, particularly early instantiations such as Younghill Kang's *The Grass Roof* and *East Goes West*, and Richard Kim's *Lost Names: Scenes from a Korean Boyhood*. A wide spectrum of more contemporary Korean American fiction, to a lesser degree, acknowledges colonial history in some capacity, including Theresa Hak Kyung Cha's *Dictee* and Susan Choi's *The Foreign Student*. The problem is that Korean American fiction's tendency to dwell upon the Japanese imperial presence is inconvenient for the larger Asian American political project. Of course, Japanese Americans, who were cast as traitorous outsiders and forcibly interred during World War II, should not be conflated with the Japanese Empire, but that has led to an overcorrection by Asian American criticism that has produced a critical blind spot regarding Japanese imperialism in Korean American literature. It is particularly egregious given that Japanese imperialism is constantly and consistently present through the entire corpus in one form or another, yet little commentary exists in Asian American studies.

A parallel neglect in Asian studies and Korean studies is instructive. For many years, colonial-era Korean authors who wrote in Japanese were ignored by Asian studies—Korean studies scholars in particular. The politics were simply too radioactive; a strident anticolonial nationalism in Korean studies precluded serious study of authors suspected of collaboration. Such a starkly defined colonizer-colonized binary led to a critical disregarding of an important and large body of work that was more ambivalent and complicated than nationalist politics would allow.[3] Only recently did Korean scholars begin to explore the literature of colonial-era Zainichi (Resident Korean in Japan), and this has led to an interest in minority discourse in America and elsewhere. Writing about author Yi Kwang-su, Nayoung Aimee Kwon notes that he was largely ignored for many years after liberation: "Such confluences of cultures between Korea and Japan (especially but not limited to their literatures) have long been evaded in both *postcolonial* nation-states: Although Yi would subsequently grow up to become one of the most prominent figures (not only in colonial Korea, but in the Japanese empire at large), this work—like other Japanese-language writings by former colonized subjects—was long forgotten after the abrupt collapse of the empire in 1945 in both Japan and Korea. Only in 1981 would it become available in Korean translation."[4] It would take a generation to begin the task of recovering these authors and mining their ambivalences and paradoxes in the shadow of empire, eventually leading to the work of other Zainichi authors such as Kim Sa-ryang and Kim Tal-su.

While Asian American studies does not ignore Korean American fiction by any measure, until the 1990s there was inadequate discussion regard-

ing the relationship between Korea and Japan, particularly during the colonial era. As I discussed in chapter 1, much of the prevailing scholarship
on Younghill Kang largely disregards *The Grass Roof* or focuses instead on
his immigration narrative in *East Goes West*, and even then his strongly anti-
Japanese rhetoric goes unmentioned. However, in the 1990s, Asian American studies began to produce criticism regarding Japanese imperialism in
relation to Asian America. What had changed? Two things: first, Asian
American studies turned toward a transpacific analytic; and second, in 1994
and 1995 two Asian American writers—Nora Okja Keller and Chang-rae
Lee—published novels about the comfort women.

Comfort Women: Intersecting Asian and Asian American Studies

Why have comfort women captured the attention of Asian American
scholar and writers? After all, the subject would appear to belong to the
purview of Asian studies rather than Asian American studies, which has
traditionally focused on domestic issues of race and social inequality. There
is no evidence of mass migration of comfort women to the United States,
nor did formative Asian American activism directly target Japanese war
crimes and sexual slavery. The subject did receive attention—it made international news and penetrated the American consciousness—but it appears
incongruous with an Asian American studies' emphasis on social justice.
There is an argument to be made that comfort women overlap with matters
of human trafficking in the United States, but the question stands: What
draws Asian American studies (and Asian American writers) to comfort
women as a subject of study? Were Lee and Keller's respective publications
enough to overcome decades of reluctance on the part of Asian Americanists to tackle the ramifications of Japanese imperialism? A possible answer
comes in the critical assessment that the comfort women issue happens
to neatly align with multiple political projects. In "Discomfiting Knowledge," Kandice Chuh observes that "what follows from this articulation of
'comfort woman' as a term of analysis and history rather than personhood,
is the understanding that the claiming of 'comfort woman' as an Asian
American issue might productively shape Asian Americanist inquiry inso-
far as it translates into the advancement of a critique of the racialized and
sexualized practices of the intersecting modernities of Japan, Korea, and

the United States."[5] That is, what disturbs Chuh is that comfort women are once again objectified in service to larger critiques of global hierarchy. The problem, she explains, is that in exploring the subject, Asian Americanists rightfully interrogate Japan's war crimes but also justify the United States' intervention in the Eastern theater. In other words, Asian American studies, in embracing comfort women as a subject of study, may find itself inadvertently affirming US hegemony. Lisa Yoneyama, in her study of the transnational context of juridical order, is even more explicit in her dissecting of postwar redress involving the United States, Japan, Korea, and Asian America: "American discourse on Japanese war crimes is profoundly shaped by U.S. nationalism and assumptions about modernity, liberalism, colonialism, and postcoloniality that are embedded in Cold War epistemologies. Asian/America, as a discursively constituted terrain, is deeply implicated in this knowledge production. . . . Asian/Americans, as the agent-subjects of U.S. state apparatuses, tend to secure their nationalized status by underwriting America's Cold War myth of liberation and rehabilitation vis-à-vis Asia."[6] In her reading, mobilizing around comfort women fits into a larger project driven by a hypernationalism that has strategically recruited Asian/Americans to reify the United States' global supremacy. But the process is messy and often syllepsistic—Asian/American antiracism and American hegemony may unintentionally intersect. Finally, even as there is recognition of the importance of comfort women, Chuh admonishes that it may lead down an undesirable path:

> Discourses like Asian American studies that are engaged in and indeed motivated by social justice, by the desire to correct inequities in the distribution of power and resources, cannot but unfold in the context of the unavoidable problematics that inhere in epistemological objectification. A certain watchfulness is necessary to avoid the pitfalls of what Rey Chow has called "self-subalternization," a process by which the critic identifies with a position of powerlessness in order, paradoxically, to claim a certain kind of academic power. Like minoritized discourses generally, Asian American studies' genealogy includes the language of powerlessness and victimization, a rhetoric that has participated in the institutional growth of Asian American studies and the establishment of its practitioners.[7]

This critique has teeth. It offers a possible answer to the questions of why and how Asian American studies has been drawn to comfort women as a subject of study—that comfort women provide a means of self-abjection ("self-subalternization") to define Asian America.[8] Read in that light, Lee's and Keller's novels and the comfort women operate as a kind of traumatic backdrop against which Asian Americanists can integrate the colonizer-colonized binary into their criticism of racial exclusion and discrimination in the United States—but at a cost.

Korean America as Postcolonial Site

I offer an alternate reading, one that is not necessarily antithetical to Yoneyama's and Chuh's. While they hypothesize that the phenomenon of comfort women penetrating Asian American discourse is a consequence of geopolitical tectonic shifts, with Asian America as a junior partner, I posit that this may be part of a long tradition that until recently has been relegated to the background by a different kind of institutional pressure—an Asian American pan-ethnic solidarity. If we contextualize Lee's and Keller's interest in comfort women as part of a long-standing practice of integrating Japanese colonialism into Korean American fiction, the subject becomes more legible. Both Keller's and Lee's renderings of comfort women are part of a multigenerational narrative that crosses the Pacific from Korea and Japan to Honolulu and New Jersey. Initially, indirect or direct allusions to Japanese colonialism had a distinctly political purpose: to galvanize the American public against Japan to intervene during World War II and thereby recruit them to the cause of Korea's liberation from colonial rule. But why has that tendency persisted well after liberation? I argue that it is evidence of a Korean America that has been indelibly altered by colonialism, a gesture toward the postcolonial condition that an Asian American pan-ethnicity cannot allow: in short, Korean America is inextricable from Japanese imperialism.

I acknowledge the perilousness of the preceding statement, for it contravenes nearly a century of anticolonial rhetoric. Or does it? Postcolonial studies, after all, argues that a decolonized site does not simply revert back to a pristine precolonial state. Instead, much of postcolonial literature is marked by a national anxiety over questions of language, discourse, race, education, and infrastructure that has been forever altered.[9] Likewise, after World War II, South Korea did not miraculously return to the halcyon days preceding colonialism. To be fair, it did its best to cast off all traces of Japanese influence, to varying degrees of success, but its remnants are undeniable and persist despite decades of counterprogramming. Yet the story of Korean America fails to acknowledge Japan as anything other than an unhappy nuisance that was overcome thanks to American intervention. According to Chuh, that is nonsensical: "The history of Japanese colonization . . . decisively transformed the meaning of Koreanness, ineradicably complicating what it means to be 'one hundred percent Korean'—a condition already made impossible by the complex histories underwriting the emergence of Korea as a modern nation-state."[10] If the prevailing sentiment in postcolonial studies is that a clean break between a recently departed colonizing nation and the colonized is illusory, then why is the diasporic community not included in that conversation? It is as if once a postcolonial population arrives on the shores of the United States, they transform into ideal immigrants who have left their histories and attendant complications behind—a statement that borders on the absurd.

Asian American studies, as a result of disciplinary contours, tends to categorize racial demographics according to national origins, which simply reinforces ontological divisions. Furthermore, its social justice– and racial inequality–oriented projects create a disincentive for acknowledging and studying interethnic histories—it behooves Japanese Americans and Korean Americans to stand in solidarity in the face of the greater threat of racial discrimination in the United States. A similar dynamic has limited our understanding of literary constructions of comfort women in Asian American literature. Instead of a nationalist anticolonial politics occluding a wider critical perspective, Asian American pan-ethnic solidarity has had the unintended consequence of circumscribing discourse. It is, as Yen Le Espiritu explains, a by-product of the history of Asian American studies as a discipline and "Asian American" as a racial categorization:

> Ethnic groups are formed and changed in encounters among groups. To interact meaningfully with those in the larger society, individuals have to identify themselves in terms intelligible to outsiders. Thus, at times, they have to set aside their national or tribal identities and accept the ascribed panethnic label. . . . Ethnic resurgences are strongest when political systems structure political access along ethnic lines and adopt policies that emphasize ethnic differences. When the state uses the ethnic label as a unit in economic allocations and political representations, ethnic groups find it both

convenient and necessary to act collectively. In other words, the organization of political participation on the basis of ethnicity provides a rationale for, and indeed demands, the mobilization of political participation along ethnic lines.[11]

Asian Americans had the racial categorization projected and mapped onto them; consequently, it was advantageous for them to embrace and co-opt the label as a means of gaining legitimacy and political capital within the system. There was nothing natural or innate about the inclusion of East, South Asians, and Pacific Islanders in the same category, but once that schema was in place, for the sake of expediency and efficacy, the label stuck. However, that meant that the field might have had a disincentive to study or analyze interethnic tensions and histories. More recently, calls for critical reevaluations of Asian American pan-ethnicity have emerged particularly from Pacific Islander studies, for which the strategic advantages are less clear or even harmful, because of neglect. For example, in "Asian American Studies and the 'Pacific Question,'" J. Kēhaulani Kauanui launches an incisive broadside against an uncritical bent in Asian American studies:

> It should also be noted that "Pacific Islander and Hawaiians" are included as "sub-components" of Asian American studies, as stated in the AAAS's statement of purpose. Why are Chinese, Japanese, Korean, and Filipino ethnicities named while the categories "Southeast Asian" and "South Asian" are left disaggregated? This is comparable to having a statement list: Hmong, Vietnamese, Cambodians, Laotians, Indians, Pakistanis, Bangladeshis, Sri Lankans, and East Asian Americans. Also, problematically, Hawaiians are included as a sub-component of Asian America named separately from the category Pacific Islanders. Moreover, the category of Pacific Islanders is hanging in this line-up, as though it is an ethnic group, rather than a disaggregated panethnic group. This amounts to deracination and de-racialization.[12]

Kauanui raises an important point—the structural divisions within Asian American studies, absent critical self-reflection, inadvertently engage in a form of erasure, which may do a disservice to Pacific Islander studies. That is, aggregating Samoans, Tongans, Maori, Hawaiians, and Tahitians into a pan-ethnic term elides important differences in a way that blunts critical approaches.

Similarly, I argue that there are unforeseen consequences of pan-ethnic approaches within Asian American studies. Now, it may be problematic to equate the politics of the homeland and any spillover to first-generation immigrants with the body politic of Asian America, but there are clear indications that those historical tensions exist in Asian American fiction. Consider, for example, that 340,000 South Korean soldiers served in Vietnam as a junior partner to the United States, yet that until recently there has hardly been any meaningful study of those tensions and any effect they may have had in the formulation of an Asian American pan-ethnicity.[13] Furthermore, I think the delicacy of the matter is underscored by the false equivalency of Japanese and Japanese Americans that led to internment—a watershed moment in Asian American history demonstrating the weaponization of ethnic heritage against American-born minorities. But if the field is to continue its transpacific turn, it cannot have it both ways: either it must accept that preimmigration histories are meaningful touchstones in Asian America, or it must claim Asian America to be sui generis and somehow ignore those moments of contact—but it cannot do both. The consequence of the latter approach is clear to me: an Asian American studies that cannot integrate pre-pan-ethnic histories can position the subject of comfort women only within a broader discourse on human rights, human trafficking, sexual exploitation, and anti-imperialism, and not within the context of Korean American and Japanese/Japanese American relations. All of this is to say that these kinds of conversations are sacrificed to greater forces for the purposes of establishing social and political legitimacy, but perhaps the time has come for them to occur more openly, so that the interethnic tensions and histories make for a richer and more nuanced discipline.

The Longue Durée of Korean American Fiction

Postcolonial Korean American fiction is not veiled or even particularly subtle. It does not speak in code or drape itself in oblique allegory.[14] Early Korean American fiction is the most obvious; Younghill Kang was unequivocal in his intent, if not execution, to highlight Japanese imperialism (chapter 1). But even some fifty years later, Japanese imperialism persists, most notably in Ronyoung Kim's *Clay Walls* (1987), which paints a more complicated picture. Her novel chronicles two generations of Korean immigrants as they make their way from Korea to Los Angeles. Chun and Haesu have to escape from Korea because Chun has been accused of subversive activities by the

Japanese colonial police, and ultimately they land in the United States. Although Haesu detests and resents the Japanese for forcing her to flee Korea with Chun, she and her daughter have several encounters that problematize her view of Japan. During a return trip to Korea by way of Hawaii, Haesu has a dispute with the head of their ship, Captain Yamamoto, who bristles at her accusation that he discriminates against her because she is Korean. To her shock, Captain Yamamoto reveals that he is actually Korean, not Japanese. By confessing he risks discovery, yet he does so not out of a shared sense of nationalism but out of a desire to be free of national labels: "I hate being on land. Entanglements, unresolvable commitments, a web of illogical complications. Because of what happens on land I am forced to be an impersonator at sea.'"[15] The sea offers him refuge from national politics—on a channel that flows through the Pacific. He believes that he can escape national politics: "The sea swallows everything. It is impossible to plant a flag on water. Not so on land. Men plant their flags in the ground and begin the battle. We are born to our nationality by fate. Why should one be considered better than another?" (77). Yamamoto pines to be free and is tormented by his conflicting commitments and allegiances; his only wish is to remain at sea, stateless, untouched by politics. Yet although Yamamoto may eschew national politics, national politics does not ignore him. A ship employee by the name of Kudara, as the captain's foil, secretly works for the Korean state, and his mission, it is revealed, is to arrest Koreans passing as Japanese.

During Haesu's travels between the United States and Korea, Kim begins to question if the nation can account for the multitudes of humanity and the complexities of national and class identities. Haesu finds, unexpectedly, that her sympathies lie with Yamamoto rather than Kudara, even though Kudara works on behalf of Korean Independence. Things are not as simplistic as she has envisioned them; how can she sympathize with a Korean passing as Japanese and find the spy repulsive when he works for the Korean state? While it is hinted that Yamamoto seeks to straddle both nations as a consequence of his collaborative activities, he undergoes considerable risk when he sympathizes with her aggrieved sense of justice. The either/or binary of Korea-Japan exhausts him—perhaps he betrays himself because he wishes to be discovered. Indeed, Kudara reports him to the authorities, and the captain, it is hinted, is swept away by the secret police.

Kim's characters are not shy about expressing anti-Japanese rhetoric in private, but there is little evidence of that combativeness when they are actually faced with Japanese characters. In the second half of *Clay Walls*, the narrative mostly follows Haesu's American-born daughter, Faye, who struggles with her Asian American selfhood in 1960s Los Angeles. Faye has a similarly conflicted relationship with Japan, having inherited colonial trauma from her parents through their anti-Japanese rhetoric. When Jane Nagano, a Japanese American friend from school, invites Faye over to her home, she is initially met with stiff resistance from Haesu, who eventually relents. Still, Faye cannot escape an ethno-nationalist guilt the night before she visits Jane's home: "I thought of torture chambers and Koreans shouting 'Mansei!' My head began to ache. I ran the conversation with Jane through my mind again and tried to forget that she was Japanese" (212).

Faye's friendship with the Nagano family begins to splinter and fray her understanding of the Japanese. Her visit to Jane Nagano's home shows that they are comparatively comfortable and enjoy a strong family bond; meanwhile, Faye's family is fragmented and drifting apart. During her visit, it dawns on Faye that the Naganos enjoy a class of comfort, wealth, and American hybridity that is alien to her and her family. Jane's father, who wears a suit at home while reading the newspaper, stands in stark contrast to her own taciturn, absentee father. In a brief exchange between the two, Mr. Nagano and Faye exchange pleasantries belying a colonial language game between them:

> Mrs. Nagano waited while Mr. Nagano folded his newspaper. He took the cup from her hands. "Aah, the tea smells good," he said as he ran his nose over the cup. "There's nothing like green tea from Japan. Don't you agree, Faye?"
>
> "Uh, well, uh," I stammered. "My mother usually makes coffee."
>
> "Jane tells me your parents are from Korea," he said, as if they should know about Japanese green tea.
>
> "I think the tea we drink is Chinese," I said.
>
> As he nodded, he brought up his cup to his lips and blew gently. "Do you speak Korean?" he asked before taking a sip.
>
> "Yes. We speak it at home. My mother's English isn't very good." To keep him from thinking Momma was stupid, I quickly added, "But she speaks Japanese and can read Chinese."
>
> He raised his eyebrows. "Is that so?" He put down his cup. "Where did she learn?"

> "In Korea. She had to."
>
> He was quiet for a moment then said, "I see. Did she teach you Japanese?"
>
> I shook my head. That was the last thing in the world she would do. Momma always sounded angry when she spoke Japanese, as if she were punishing each word as it came out of her mouth. (214–15)

At first blush, this may appear to be an innocent exchange, but the subtext speaks volumes. Jane's father begins by remarking on the superiority of Japanese green tea, inviting Faye to agree with the sentiment. Faye demurs, not wanting to offend Mr. Nagano, but also refusing to acquiesce to his declaration—she instead takes refuge in American coffee and Chinese tea as third national spaces that are neither Korea nor Japan. When he asks her if she speaks Korean, the conversation turns to a tacit discussion regarding the colonial linguistic legacy imparted to her mother, Haesu. Nothing is ever stated directly; it is a conversation of subtle turns and intimations, but the context is clear, as are the respective messages by Mr. Nagano and Faye. It does not occur to Mr. Nagano that Haesu would speak Korean thanks to educational policies outlawing the Korean language; and he either does not care or misses the fact that Haesu would be reluctant to pass on Japanese to her daughter, even when Faye hints at the compulsory nature of Japanese language learning in Korea ("She had to"). It may be that Mr. Nagano has bought into the *naisen ittai* (Japan and Korea are One) campaign, which claimed that Korea was Japan's blood relation and that the Koreans welcomed the Japanese with open arms. It may be beyond his comprehension why the racially inferior Korean would not aspire to pass on the supremacy of the Japanese language to her children.

While Faye retreats to a third national space as a means of avoiding offending Mr. Nagano, the Nagano family occupies American culture as a means of demonstrating superiority. The Naganos perform a synergetic blend of both American and Japanese cultures; at one point in the evening, Jane Nagano's sister recites a poem for the family:

> "Oh, Margaret. That was nice," I said. "Did you write it?"
>
> She laughed. "I wish I had. It's from *The Grass*, by Walt Whitman."
>
> Mrs. Nagano said something to Mr. Nagano. I recognized the word "*Chosen-jin*" and knew it was about me. I felt ill at ease. Was it about my ignorance of Walt Whitman? I wondered, or about the way I laughed, or

the way I don't drink Japanese green tea? Was it about my being Korean? We had our opinions about the Japanese; perhaps they had formed some about us. Did Jane have to beg her parents' permission to invite me to her house?

Mr. Nagano smiled at Dale and Margaret with approval. "You have improved a great deal. You have developed duplicity into a fine art. It is difficult to tell if you two are acting as one or one acting as two."

The word "duplicity" opened a crack in my memory. I had tried desperately to forget a secret, tried so hard that I could never forget. I remembered Captain Yamamoto of the Taiyo Maru. (216)

Several points stand out in this key passage. First, Margaret and Dale recite "What Is the Grass?," not "The Grass," Whitman's childlike meditation on death and rebirth, a questioning of the mortality of humanity and democracy. It appears to be no accident that Margaret selects Whitman—that most American of poets—as her artifact to make her claim to America. Second, Faye's ignorance of American poetry apparently triggers a remark in Japanese by Mrs. Nagano—we can only speculate about what—but Faye can make out enough to know that the comment marks her racial difference as Korean. It is not difficult to assume that Faye's innocent question affirms the Japanese stereotype of colonial-era Koreans as intellectually inferior—in this case, by her lack of knowledge of American culture and therefore modernity. Finally, Mr. Nagano remarks that the two children work in tandem, perfecting the art of "duplicity," a word that floods Faye's mind with images of Captain Yamamoto. Yamamoto's ghostly presence is evocative of the inescapability of colonial politics, despite the intermediary space that Faye and her family occupy in the United States and its poetry.

Structurally, the entire immigrant narrative of *Clay Walls* depends on the conflict between Korea and Japan, with the United States serving as an intermediary between, yet for most Asian American critics the importance of that relationship appears to be secondary. Chun and Haesu escape to America because the Japanese colonial police mistake their identities; Haesu's return trip to Korea is framed by her encounter with Captain Yamamoto; and Faye's venture into Asian American subjecthood is situated against her evening with the Nagano family, complete with colonial tensions. In other words, life in the US does not mean a complete withdrawal from colonial politics—indeed, that politics is inescapable—yet with few exceptions critical scholarship on *Clay Walls* tends to gloss over it.[16] *Clay Walls* would be better served with a comprehensive theorization of Korean American literature that does not push imperial Japan into the background—it should be recognized as an equally important site in the Korean American immigration narrative. Should the matter remain inconclusive, I now turn to another novel that dwells on the ternary relationship among Korea, Japan, and America in an even more tangible—and traumatic—manner.

Turning Japanese in America

In the early 1990s, comfort women began to go public with their stories after decades of private shame, and heated public discussion followed. Chang-rae Lee traveled to Korea to interview comfort women in hopes of gathering material to tell their story; he began to weave a draft of their tale but found the results unsatisfactory. Throwing out much of the material, he began again but retained a minor character, Doc Hata, and rewrote his second novel from Hata's point of view. Resisting the conventional trajectory in Asian American literature, half of the narrative takes place at a remote military outpost in Singapore during the Pacific War, with mostly Japanese and Korean characters. Told in a series of interspersed flashbacks, Lieutenant Kurohata, an ethnic Korean educated and raised as a Japanese citizen, serves as a medical assistant and officer. He begins to question his ethnic duality when a group of Korean comfort women arrive at base camp, and he is further torn when he falls in love with one of the women, "K." In the second half, he is Doc Hata, fragmented in both name and identity, living quietly in a small suburb of New Jersey and passing as a Japanese immigrant. As such, Doc Hata has little interest in Asian American identity; indeed, anytime he faces such questions, he tends to politely deflect and demur. The novel follows Doc Hata as he tries to navigate his strained relationship with his adopted biracial daughter from Korea, Sunny, who has rejected him only to return to town years later with a young son in tow. On the surface, Hata provides everything that Sunny would need, including piano lessons and a warm, meticulously kept home. However, she grows weary of her unfairly assigned role as his spiritual salve and eventually rejects him to run off with a young man, leaving Hata with only the haunted memories of K to keep him company. Doc Hata, and by extension Sunny, strive to fashion some kind of cohesive identity fragmented by war, trauma, and racial politics in both the past and the present, East and West.

The prevailing scholarship on *A Gesture Life* speaks only tangentially about Franklin Hata as a Japanese citizen and about his work as a medic in the Imperial Army; indeed, critics tend to mirror Hata's narrative reluctance to engage completely with his ethnic heritage.[17] It is an understandable reaction, since the work does not easily fit within the contours of the conventional Asian American novel.[18] In contrast, I write against the grain by foregrounding Hata's knotty racial identity as a Japan-born ethnic Korean—a Zainichi.[19] I do so to circumvent the deterministic inclination to categorize the novel as Asian American. That decision liberates—and requires—us to take into consideration Zainichi history. The conventional approach is to read for moments of hybridity and American racial formation in *A Gesture Life*; however, by framing the novel according to the various theories of Zainichi racial formation, we can gain a more comprehensive understanding of the novel. Otherwise, we cannot fully appreciate the levels of displacement Hata experiences as he processes, revisits, and replicates national and individual trauma. First, I frame Hata as a Japanese collaborator, a term reserved for Koreans who facilitated or cooperated with colonialists in undermining sovereignty. Second, Hata's assimilationist practices, which I contend were cultivated by colonial Japan, are frustrated in the United States by a racial logic that is arguably more pervasive and successful in remolding its minoritized subjects. Third, Hata continues to live and practice a colonial logic even after he has immigrated to the United States, until his fragile and untenable existence falls apart. The bitter irony is that it is the racism of the United States, not Japan, that reveals the futility of Hata's methods, which he finally rejects.

The standard reading of *A Gesture Life* argues that the novel reflects a slippery transnationalism at the nexus of trauma, colonialism, and American racism. Some critics read K as a gendered and violated victim of colonial Korea, and Doc Hata as a colonial success story—a native Korean used to subjugate his own nation. Hamilton Carroll argues that the novel's "traumatic narrative orchestrates the production of a historiography that exposes the workings of gender and race that cut between and across the novel's doubled national locations."[20] For example, the name Kurohata—"Black Flag"—reflects Doc Hata's stateless condition, a symbol of his inability to decide whether he is Korean or Japanese by taking action when K pleads for his help. In a more generous reading of Doc Hata's journey, Young-Oak Lee notes that "Hata's diasporicity, initiated by his adoptive stance as a child and intensified by his traumatic experience with K, pushes him to face, and to decolonize his mind from, false ideologies—nationalism, racism and sexism—and, finally, to launch out once again for an unknown destination. He has now learned that national ideals can be misleading and threaten to destroy both individuals and other peoples."[21] Most English-language scholarship on Lee's novel gravitates toward Hata's life in the United States and his estranged relationship with Sunny. Mark Jerng, for example, takes up the transnational adoptee as a representative of the novel's conflicting, paradoxical, and open narratives: "Adoption thus constitutes something of a problematic mediation between these two narrative movements: its place as a pivot between past and present exemplifies the non-synchronous nature of the adoptive relationship."[22] Although both Hata and Sunny are adoptees, Jerng tends to focus largely on Sunny and her relationship with Hata, rather than Hata and his adoptive family.

Kandice Chuh provides a formative reading of both *Clay Walls* and *A Gesture Life* that underscores their colonial politics but falls short of a comprehensive study despite its transpacific bent. For instance, while Chuh argues that both novels address colonialism, her study is decidedly limited by the disciplinary isolation that she has critiqued in the past.[23] She positions *Clay Walls* and *A Gesture Life* according to a chronology defined by Korea's liberation and thereby falls into the trap of conceptualizing Korean American subject formation by a precolonial and postcolonial binary: "In contrast to *Clay Walls*, whose preindependence chronological frame arguably compels the identification of anticolonial nationalism as a primary factor in the subjectification of Koreans and Korean Americans, *A Gesture Life*'s critical interests articulate the shifting historical conditions—from formal coloniality to postcoloniality—that its broader temporal frame encompasses."[24] It is a categorization of convenience that is seductive in its readability, but as I have written above, even Kim's rendering in *Clay Walls* is much more nuanced and ambivalent than Chuh's analysis gives it credit for. To be fair, Chuh's study better articulates the complexity of Doc Hata's multiply formed subjectivity in its discussion of *A Gesture Life*, acknowledging that, "like *Clay Walls*, *A Gesture Life* thematizes Japanese colonialism, but does so from an entirely different perspective, one that might be seen as 'postcolonial.' Dramatized through three distinctive spatiotemporal frames that ultimately converge though they never resolve, Franklin Hata's story makes almost impossible the use of such terms as 'Korean,' 'Japanese,' and 'American' as signifiers of identity, for in many ways, for him, they are but empty gestures."[25] Indeed, Chuh goes as far as recognizing a kind of hybridity that Doc Hata enjoys: "Doc Hata, the representative colonial subject, is neither and both 'us' and 'them,' a rendering that does not negate the wages of Japanese colonialism but allows for recognition of its ensuing and troubled hybridities."[26] But Chuh does not articulate what that hybridity means, because she appears to be unaware that a large body of work on the subject already exists in Asian studies. Furthermore, despite Chuh's gesture toward the narrative triptych, there is little effort to decipher its assemblage. It is instead declared to be "impossible" to resolve: that is, her dismissal of the long history of Korean Japanese immigration and subsequent minority formation leads her to declare that Hata is unknowable. It is a neglect that is representative of the central problem in Asian American criticism of *A Gesture Life*—Hata's minoritization as read solely through the lens of an Asian American frame that places other forms of minoritization in a penumbra.[27] When faced with moments in the text that do not fit neatly within the boundaries of Asian American studies, Chuh tends to rely on Hata's elusiveness as a crutch: "While the details of Doc Hata's life are fleshed out as the narrative progresses, evoking the complicated histories of the Japanese-Korean colonial relationship as it does so, never do we arrive at a sense of the ultimate truth 'about' Doc Hata. Never is there a moment at which the novel turns to reveal his name at birth, nor does it offer much information about his family prior to adoption."[28] There is a blind spot in Chuh's reading that is attributed to Hata's narrative ellipses—he is unknowable by the nature of the tale he weaves for the reader.[29] While it is true that Hata's references to his shrouded past are light on detail, and that his bifarious nature compounds the narrative's unreliability, I am struck by the inclusion of the "complicated histories of the Japanese-Korean colonial relationship" as part of the same unknowability. On the contrary, interrogating that relationship is more illuminating and reliable than any of Hata's interior monologues.

To adequately consider a Korean American diaspora that triangulates Japanese colonial practices, American racial politics, and Asian American identity, Asian American literary studies should consider a minor transnationalism.[30] Japanese racial colonial practices follow Hata across the Pacific and make their way into the United States. Two parallel projects, embodied by dual narratives, account for *A Gesture Life*'s central narrative tension—a delicate balancing act that Hata attempts (and fails to achieve) between Japanese imperialism and American nationalism. The first centers on bodily mobilization—K's, Hata's, Sunny's, and, menacingly, her son's—in service to another incarnation of the imperial project. Understanding Hata's American project requires reaching back to his time in Japan as an imperial soldier—we cannot understand one without the other—and how it came to be that he, as an ethnic Korean, fought for the emperor, and ended up turning Japanese in the US. His identity as a Japanese soldier was produced by colonial modernity; but becoming Japanese was not a simple, linear affair. Indeed, the colonial center jealously guarded the rights and privileges of Japanese citizenship, but it still needed to mobilize the bodies of the colonized to die for the emperor, and considered it ideal for the colonized to do so voluntarily. The second project consists of the means by which these bodies are mobilized—*dōka* (assimilation) and *kōminka* (imperialization). As Leo Ching writes in *Turning Japanese*, colonial Japan sought to convince its colonies that they, too, could become Japanese through these processes, which would enfold their bodies into the colonial center. That is, convincing the colonized to mobilize for the colonizers required the promise of citizenship and its privileges, but the truth was that Japan had no intention of realizing that vision in full. The reality of *dōka* created a bit of a conundrum for the racial logic of Japanese colonialism, predicated as it was on the essentialist superiority of *yamato damashii* (the Japanese spirit). Would not the inclusion of the Other threaten the preciousness of Japaneseness?

To address the aforementioned contradiction, an ambivalence took hold, which sheds light on Hata's (at times) bizarre relationship to his biological and adopted parents. *Dōka*, prior to 1937, was a colonial project that projected a "vague contour" of what a colonial society should be, but it also included a contradiction: to assimilate the Other, the basis of the Japanese self had to be first defined and confirmed.[31] Thus colonial assimilation raises questions—What is the Japanese national essence, and what constitutes the basis for a Japanese national identity? In other words, even as *dōka* functions as an instrument of assimilation, it always already differentiates, creating the basis of discrimination against the Other. To overcome this contradictory discriminatory assimilation, *dōka* constructs an "ambivalent relationship" between the colonial subject and colonized object.[32] There was not to be a wholesale assimilation, but a blurred adoption of the Other into the Japanese center that was both contingent and separate. Oguma Eiji argues that the Japanese "adopted child" (*yōshi*) system is crucial for the conceptualization of this relationship.[33] Unlike patrilineal systems like Korea or China, the Japanese system of a family name is attached to the household and is not exclusive to the paternal blood line. Adoption, then, can often be about preserving the institution of the family name rather than strictly about raising a child;[34] indeed, this system can be oppressive in that the child has to adapt to the family ways.[35]

Hata's own relationship to his Japaneseness is similarly marked by contradiction and ambivalence. The son of ethnic Koreans in Japan, Hata is adopted by the Kurohata family under somewhat vague circumstances. What is clear, however, is that Hata recognizes that he is better off materially and socially with the Kurohatas than with his birth family, who "were ethnic Koreans, though we spoke and lived as Japanese, if ones in twilight."[36] It is also revealed that they live in a Korean ghetto of "hide tanners and renderers," which would make them doubly ostracized, part of the *burakumin* caste of untouchables, in addition to being Korean. It may appear that the Kurohata family were exceptionally generous and liberal-minded to adopt Hata, who may have been particularly attractive as an adoptee because he has scored "exceptionally high on several achievement tests" (72). However, Hata hints at a measure of distance between himself and his parents: "I think of them warmly, as I do my natural parents, but to neither would I ascribe the business of having reared me, for it seems clear that it was the purposeful society that did so, and really nothing and no one else" (72). It appears that he has internalized the logic of the *yōshi* adoption system—that he is adopted not as an individual child to embark on a lifelong relationship of love and affection with a host family, but more out of necessity in service to the larger body of the family name and household. Moreover, Hata notes that discrimination against his ethnic heritage does not abate, but continues: "I had certainly despised others before, particularly the boys in the school I attended after being adopted by the Kurohatas, boys who treated me with disdain most of the time and at worst like a stray dog" (262–63). Though he is adopted by the Kurohatas and leaves his Korean identity behind, his assimilation into Japan is always incomplete—this, despite Hata's sincere efforts to give everything colonial Japan asks of him, the fallacy of which only reveals itself to him later in life: "For isn't this what I've attempted for most of all of my life, from entering the regular school with my Japanese parents when I was a boy, to enlisting myself in what should have been a glorious war, and then settling in this country and in a most respectable town, isn't this my long folly, my continuous failure?" (205). In short, Hata has been integrated into the colonial center but kept at a distance, and the racialization of his self continues—there is no subjecthood within the *yōshi* adoption system. In fact, the *yōshi* system is designed to subjugate the individual and absorb him or her into the larger institution of the family register; Hata carries on the family name and household, but his own personhood continues to be ill-defined and ambivalent. Both adoption and its colonial counterpart, *dōka*, prove to be inadequate.

If *dōka*'s nebulousness and incoherence frustrate Hata, *kōminka* (imperialization) perhaps offers a clearer pathway.[37] After 1937, *kōminka* came into use in a military context—Japan's expansion into China and Southeast Asia—as the "complete regimentation and Japanization of its colonized peoples intended to ensure their loyalty to the Emperor and their sacrifice for the Japanese war effort."[38] In other words, *kōminka* was the systematization of *dōka* that was projected onto the colonized.[39] That is, "Japanization" through an external force such as *dōka* failed; in contrast, *kōminka* internalized "Japanization" within the colonized, who were always incomplete as imperial subjects. Only then did the struggle over colonial identity emerge in Taiwan, where becoming Japanese was desired. When Hata enters the army, he takes part in a long process of *kōminka*—imperialization through institutions, including education (Hata enters a Japanese school) and renaming (Kurohata). The military, he hopes, will offer him the solution to his inner struggle. In his exhaustive *Race for Empire*, Takashi Fujitani shows *kōminka* in action with his study of the history and logic of integrating Koreans in the Japanese armed forces: "The military provided a particularly compelling site from which to witness this passage, since the more the Japanese empire came to depend on the Korean population for soldiers and sailors, the more difficult it became to exclude them from the nation—in both the conventional meaning of a political community and in Foucault's bio-political sense of a population."[40] In the final two years of the Pacific War, there were 190,000 Koreans in the Japanese army and navy combined. The military is, in a way, an extension of the "purposeful society" that Hata gives credit to raising him, rather than his biological or adoptive parents. It grants him a logic, order, and coherence that have eluded him in the past, yet he finds it to be lacking in the end: even the military does not offer him the respite he seeks, and discrimination continues unabated.[41] Moreover, even as the scale of total war calls for the mobilization of colonized bodies, necessitating inclusion, racism remains, though in muted form—what Fujitani calls "polite racism," which "insisted upon the illegitimacy of formal racial discrimination, even as it reproduced a racist logic through a discourse of differential histories, lagging development, and culture."[42] The logic of *kōminka*, therefore, operates on the mobilization of colonized bodies to defend the metropole, using a regimen of Japanization to inculcate the colonized. *Kōminka*, however appealing and coherent it may have seemed to Hata, would have been similarly disappointing as a means of acceptance.

With the liberation of Korea and the demise of Japan's imperial ambitions, the impetus for *dōka* and *kōminka* dissipated, but I argue that that logic never dies in Hata. The majority of Koreans in Japan, after a period of statelessness, eagerly embraced a return to Korean citizenship, but even that involved considerable conflict. As I discuss in the Introduction, only in the ensuing decades would the Korean minority in Japan come to think of Japan as a home and begin to articulate a hybridity rather than an either/or binary. Hata, however, being adopted, would have not had to face the same uncertainty. In contrast to Germany, Japan never had to consciously grapple with its multiethnic colonial history, and what took its place was an ideology of monoethnicity.[43] As an early Zainichi with Japanese citizenship, Hata could avoid struggling between Korean citizenship and an eventual Zainichi hybridity. In fact, Hata leaves Japan long before the Zainichi come to a collective consciousness, which would emerge only after he arrived in the United States. But precisely because of his experience with a colonial policy of assimilation, he takes a similar tack when he immigrates to the United States. Rather than embrace a return to "Koreanness," he furthers the colonial project by passing as Japanese in the US. In moments during his encounters with K and the comfort women he vacillates between his Korean and Japanese halves, but even then his Koreanness is often projected onto him by K or others. Indeed, the fallout from his encounter with K leads him to bury his Koreanness deep within the recesses of his consciousness. It would not have been possible in Japan, where his ethnicity would be a matter of official record as part of his *koseki* (family registry), where facts of heritage, paternity, adoptions, and so on are meticulously tracked. Instead, he flees to the United States, where the social infrastructure lacks similarly detailed recordkeeping, and his ruse can continue.

In some ways, Hata is more successful in the United States in executing colonial Japan's mission than he ever was in his previous life. He executes a doubled assimilationist performance, where he can fully inhabit a Japanese identity, something he could never do completely in Japan. Here, his Japanese assimilation is complete, but he comes to realize that despite his attempts he cannot fully integrate into the fabric of the US. His conversation with Renny Batterjee, an Indian American, suggests as much; Renny notes, "It seems everyone has completely forgotten who I am" (133), echoing Hata's own concerns that he, too, is quickly going "from good Doc Hata to the nice old fellow to whoever that ancient Oriental is" (200–201). Despite that realization, he insists that it is his responsibility to fit into Bedley Run, rather than expecting to be accommodated by everyone else. That belief leads him to a life of superficial acts, performance, and gesture, for which he is roundly critiqued by Sunny, and by Mary Burns, a widower with whom he has a brief romance. Just as he internalized colonialist logic in Japan, he has likewise internalized the racist logic of America, where he finds no respite.

The problem facing Hata in the United States is that he imports a colonial logic that is specific to a very different political and ethnic condition—and it runs headlong into another national project that is particular to American history and context. The US operates by an "internal" mode of colonial administration, as opposed to, say, British colonialism, which was largely "external." That is, an external colonial administration is primarily occupied with exploiting, for economic benefit, distant territories that are racially and geographically different, with a secondary interest in securing the protection of the colonial center. Japanese colonialism was "peripheral"—rhetorically dangling the promise of assimilation but refusing access to the colonial center as a means of control. The primary goal of the American system's internal mode of colonization is to secure a variegated people's political allegiance, even among vast cultural and ethnic differences. That required the wide dissemination of a hegemonic culture among its constituents and was contingent on the newly formed state's ability to dismantle local, social, cultural barriers that political bodies traditionally maintained.[44]

Thus, in the United States, Hata has to adapt his method of transformation, building a hybrid program of *kōminka* and model minoritization to become the paragon Asian American. He continues to replicate and reinforce the racist practices of Japanese colonialism through adoption, recruiting Sunny to take part of his shared pan-Asian America prosperity campaign with an army of two: "My Sunny, I thought, would do much the same. Not be so thankful or beholden to me, necessarily, but at least she'd be somewhat appreciative of the providence of *institutions* that brought her from the squalor of the orphanage—the best of which can be only so happy—to an orderly, welcoming suburban home in America, with a hopeful father of like-enough race and sufficient means" (73; emphasis added). Here, Hata reveals the rationalization he uses to adopt Sunny; he displaces his own importance (and culpability) in likening himself to an extension of the "institutions" (at other times, "purposeful society") uplifting Sunny from humble origins to be integrated into the broader fabric of model minority suburbia. But his project hits several obstacles. Others have already noted Hata's problematic racial politics and notions of purity with regard to Sunny. Indeed, Hata's adoption is largely transactional, with him bribing an adoption agent to secure the success of his application, under the pretext of Japanese custom (73). In a sense, Hata purchases Sunny to take part in his American assimilationist project, as she is to be his legacy and representative in the US. His first disappointment is in realizing that Sunny is biracial, possibly African American and Korean, which already dilutes his dream of redemption and the ideal model minority daughter (204). Indeed, his project splinters and falls apart when Sunny refuses to play the role, rejecting her piano lessons and, much to his horror, claiming her body and sexuality (29, 114). His racial colonialism is so overbearing that it leads Hata to force Sunny to have an abortion when she becomes pregnant by someone of whom he does not approve—it is hinted that he is of an "undesirable" race—which leaves their relationship in tatters. Suk Koo Rhee argues that Hata's project is to prevent further racial miscegenation: "Hata's anxiety is understandable if Sunny's sexual involvement with a black male is seen to deal the deadliest of blows to the protagonist's lifetime project of demarcating himself off from the colored race. Hata's de-racializing efforts include not only separating himself from other colored people but also purging himself even of his own ethnic history."[45] I argue slightly differently; I view Hata's opposition, while certainly based on racism, as a product of his American *kōminka* project of model minoritization.

Sunny's mixed-race body is already tainted, but her child will be unrecoverable if fathered by a Black man. Hata must mobilize Sunny's body—and her son's—correctly, for they exist to serve a greater purpose. It is a practice he imports from his military experience: Hata recounts how enchanted he was when his commanding officer, Captain Ono, experimented on a Burmese peasant who had been condemned to death for petty theft. Captain Ono kills the patient on the operating table, only to bring him back to life by massaging his heart, repeating the procedure several times (76–77). Hata is transfixed by Captain Ono's skill and the process, and cares not at all about the patient, who is a dehumanized object for medical study.[46] He takes the same attitude in examining "the recruits" for their duties in the clinic, framing them in the same ways as soldiers in the field. They are not vulnerable humans but part of the empire, in service to the Pan-Asian Prosperity Project. His attempts to reject Captain Ono fail, and he never expressly rejects the ideology of the empire—despite his supposed love for K, he fails to act other than by subjecting her to his desire and will. He continues to do so with Sunny, violating her will and body through subtler means, but operating on a similar logic nonetheless for the greater good of his newly adopted American empire—modern, model, and minor.

Doc Hata's chameleonic nature is nearly too effective. Asian American critics, in their preoccupation with his Asian Americanness, miss the camouflage with which he has adorned himself. His is a mode of living defined by transformation: he and his parents begin as Zainichi; then he turns "Japanese" while in the Imperial Army but is widely known to be ethnically Korean; next, in the United States, Hata assumes and passes as "a noble Japanese" without the Korean qualifier; and then—in that final transformation to which I object—with the help of scholarly criticism, he and his narrative are rendered as wholly and utterly Asian American.

Eventually, Hata realizes that the premise of his colonial project is fatally flawed. Throughout the novel, he is haunted by his ephemerality, his conditional acceptance, and the ambiguity of his home space. His initial attraction to Bedleyville is predicated on its resemblance to his hometown in Japan, yet he never truly feels at ease (2–3). Moreover, he grows aware of the fragility of his legacy, acknowledging to himself that once a certain number of years have passed, he may fade from the town's collective memory. "It becomes even more troubling a notion to consider how quickly the memory of the store will fade away . . . and how swiftly, too, the appellation of 'Doc Hata' will dwindle and pass from the talk of the town, if it's not completely gone already" (192). The irony is that only in America has he succeeded in transforming himself from Korean to Japanese; but instead of becoming whole, he discovers that his methods for assimilation prove disastrous for his relationships. The tragedy is that he has hollowed himself to accommodate to the racial logic of Japan and the United States, and in doing so has harmed many others, particularly those to whom he is closest.

Colonial trauma is an obstinate creature. The literary history of Korean American fiction is inextricably tied to Japanese imperialism; it is rife with colonial imagery and tensions, yet Asian American studies, as Chuh and Yoneyama argue, tends to read them along the well-worn grooves of domestic social justice and global human rights. Moreover, the American project of constructing Asian America according to political alliances precludes or obscures interethnic tensions and histories. My aim in bringing forth preimmigration historical antipathies and integrating them into a broader Asian American discourse is not to introduce divisions in long-standing political alliances but to complicate and enrich discussion that has been simplified for the sake of expediency. A transnational approach that integrates critical postcolonial studies provides another dimension of reading *Clay Walls* and *A Gesture Life* that actively includes rather than excludes minoritizations across bodies of water, continents, and time.

CHAPTER 4

International Study and Sojournship

Absence and Presence in Seoul Searching *and* Yuhi

> In the summer of my first year of high school, when I took the AFS
> exam—a recruiting test for studying abroad in America—I looked in
> my family register and learned, definitively, that I was Korean.
>
> —Yi Yang-ji, "Watashi wa chōsenjin"

THE 2016 INDEPENDENT FILM *Seoul Searching*, set in the 1980s, opens
with a montage of Korean American high schoolers parading through a
crowd of people upon their arrival to Gimpo International Airport in South
Korea. A kaleidoscopic array of characters make their entrance, each fitting
into an American high school archetype with an Asian American inflection—
the punk rocker, the junior ROTC, the pop diva, the B-Boy crew. Added to
the mix are members of the extended Korean diasporic universe, including
an oversexed Mexican, a cosmopolitan German, and a mixed-race adoptee.
Adapted from John Hughes's American Midwest and transported to Seoul,
our social misfits alight in their ancestral homeland, cultural and racial bag-
gage in tow, only to collide with staid Korean faculty members of the host
school (figure 8).[1] Hijinks ensue.

The film encapsulates a specific experience of a summer session abroad in
South Korea by *gyopo* (Korean Americans), who are depicted as brash, hor-
monal, insecure, and burdened by the effects of alienation in White America.[2] The film follows an array of outsiders as they grapple with their shared
ethnic histories and lineage and come to terms with the fact that they are
not Korean but some kind of hybrid middle ground that has yet to be fully
articulated. Complicating the narrative is a challenge to American hegemony in the form of characters from Europe, Latin America, and Japan. It
is a rite of passage that is assumed to be funded by misguided parents, who
hope that summer abroad will reconnect their children with their roots;
the film subverts that intent by displaying myriad encounters that lead to

their discovery of a global kinship rather than one rooted singularly in the homeland. Despite their differences, they come to a collective understanding of themselves and carve out a third means of Korean diasporic subject formation. Yet it is through one particular mechanism that these characters, who are not likely ever to otherwise come across each other, are forced to interact, face their shared cultural heritage, and encounter parallel zones of contact—the study abroad system.

I begin this chapter with an examination of *Seoul Searching* because it is a belated narrative exploration of a distinctly Asian American subgenre that has few examples in the cultural canon. To be sure, there are many examples of Asian American novels portraying time abroad—that is, not novels consisting of flashbacks or parallel narratives that feature a distant point of origin, but literature in which time abroad is integral to the present tense of the narrative.[3] Rarer still are the few texts whose story is entirely located abroad.[4] Instead, in Asian American literature, international study is usually portrayed as a pathway to citizenship.[5] In general, these narratives follow the transformation of immigrant to citizen, or some semblance of citizenship, neatly concluding in the United States. But this is not an examination of return, nor does it focus on the phenomenon of the "boomerang" population—migrants coming home after a period in the West. Instead, this chapter explores study abroad as a mechanism for diasporic minority encounters in third national sites—one of the few institutional structures through which Korean Americans and Zainichi (Resident Korean

FIGURE 8 Korean American students arrive at Gimpo International Airport in *Seoul Searching* (Mondo Paradiso, 2016).

in Japan) may come into direct contact, however incidentally. Put another way, study abroad offers a means of resisting a stolid immigration narrative and rearticulating of Korean diasporic subjectivity—what I am calling minority *sojournship*.

International Study as Diasporic Mechanism

This chapter examines one of the more established means by which Korean America and Zainichi Korea might stumble upon each other. Whereas preceding chapters discuss how minor literatures informally encounter one another through colonial labor (chapter 1), cultural and racial discourse (chapter 2), and trauma (chapter 3), this chapter focuses on an institutional conduit. Study abroad, usually through the university system, is the institution by which Korean Americans and Zainichi Koreans can return to the homeland. Beyond that, I cannot think of another structured means by which Korean America and Zainichi Korea could possibly come into contact, other than pure serendipity or immigration to the United States by a relatively small number of Zainichi or Korean Argentinians. However, in Zainichi fiction such as Yi Yang-ji's *Yuhi*—which I discuss at length— the time-abroad narrative, often in South Korea, is quite common.[6] Often Zainichi authors have spent extensive periods in Korea studying the language and culture, particularly since it is relatively close and inexpensive in comparison to Japan. However, it is not conventional, bidirectional travel I am interested in exploring; instead, I want to unpack and interrogate the liminal moments of contact that emerge between and among minority subjects in third national spaces.

In the Western cultural tradition, study abroad in fiction is the stuff of American insecurities and anxieties. At the turn of the nineteenth century, traveling abroad functioned as an expression of genteel sophistication and class display—a return to European locales to escape the bustle of American industrialism and an opportunity to exercise conspicuous consumption.[7] As study abroad has evolved from its elitist origins and become accessible to middle-class students in American life, so too has its cultural representation.[8] In the contemporary context, study abroad is more likely to be experienced through the robust international educational system in the United States.[9] Despite these gains, the number of minority students studying abroad lags—the overwhelming majority of American students abroad are White.[10] In its modern instantiation, the study-abroad narrative usually entails the adventures of younger characters—university students or recent graduates—as they attempt to discover a budding sense of self through unfamiliar yet safely first-world experiences in Madrid or London.[11] A particularly well-worn trope entails a young American embarking on an existential crisis while traipsing through European backdrops or meditating upon historical artifacts—a combination of heteronormative American fears regarding the home country's relative lack of historicity as feminized vulnerability. One school of thought is that study abroad, particularly for White American students, can awaken in them a national and cultural awareness of American-ness.[12]

Yet this dynamic does not apply directly to minority students, particularly Asian American students. Beyond a myriad of factors influencing minority students in their decision-making process beyond finances, Asian American students' study-abroad experiences tend to look different.[13] First, Asian American students do not study abroad at the same rates as their White counterparts, because of a combination of factors including cost, concerns over racism, lack of administrative support, and familial obligations. Second, Asian American students who do choose to study abroad, unlike the majority of their White peers, who choose anglophone countries, tend to study abroad in Asia.[14] The prevailing reason for their preference for Asia is a desire to learn about their cultural heritage. Thus we can extrapolate on the basis of their preferences and reasons for or against deciding to study abroad, that their priorities and experiences may take on a different flavor than those of their White American classmates.

International education inflects differently in the South Korean context and, accounting for local contexts, in Asia writ large. In a hypercompetitive environment, South Koreans looking to gain an edge in the global marketplace see studying abroad as a means of "alternative human development." Because they see international study as a means of gaining fluency in English and learning to break through stereotypical tendencies to shy away from active discourse and outspokenness, Koreans send their children abroad through a patchwork system.[15] The practice has become so ubiquitous in contemporary South Korea that a national conversation has emerged questioning the phenomenon of young mothers moving with their children to the United States or other English-speaking countries while their fathers remain behind to earn capital to finance their time abroad—called "wild goose" (K: *gireogi*). It is somewhat of a continuation of study abroad to the United States in the early twentieth century, when access to the American education system was a means of accessing modernity for the still-developing and primarily rural Korea.[16]

Study abroad for Zainichi Koreans, who have steadily increased in number since the 1988 Seoul Olympics, runs the gamut. Overall, it appears that Zainichi Koreans study abroad in South Korea to connect with their ethnic heritage, learn the language, and arm themselves with a sense of Koreanness against a Japan that actively erases their presence. In their qualitative study, Terasima Takayosi and Koike Miyako interviewed several Zainichi subjects who had studied in South Korea, who gave an array of reasons. In some cases, interviewees wanted another perspective of a history that had eluded them in their Japanese education; for others, it had been a lifelong dream to study in Korea; and for still others, the impulse grew out of a natural inclination from having attended North Korean–sponsored schools in Japan.[17]

What is interesting to note is that both Asian American and Zainichi students appear to be motivated mainly by a mutual interest in cultural heritage, whereas South Korean students seem to be motivated by gaining a competitive edge in the global marketplace. That hints at another aim driving heritage international students to visit South Korea, the consequences of which may transform Asian America and Zainichi Korea.

Sojournship

Asian American studies has a complicated relationship to study abroad and to Asian international students. Chih-ming Wang, in *Transpacific Articulations*, provides a comprehensive literary reexamination of international students writing Asian America. Wang points out that, like so much of Asian American studies, the reluctance to engage or include international students in Asian American discourse stems from the field's early political mobilization and focus on a domestic identity rejecting Asia and foreignness.[18] Instead, he proposes positioning Asian international students' contributions to Asian America as an important component of the field's transnational turn, while carefully acknowledging its specific historical and economic context. Placing foreign students in the context of transnational intellectualism, he argues that they are uniquely situated in the bilateral relationship between the projections of Asia and those of Asian/America, dependent on larger structural dimensions—cultural, economic, political. That is,

> In tipping Asia toward America, Asia/America represents the transpacific passage as an asymmetrical relation of knowledge, movement, and power within which the foreign student emerges contradictorily as at once the vanguard of national consciousness, the victim of transcultural forces and racializing policies, and a transnational identity that signals elitism and mobility. . . . Foreign students have partaken in Asian America with a deliberate Asian orientation; however, at the same time they also rely on America as a transnational platform on which to operate their political activities and perform a sense of alterity to their homeland culture.[19]

Wang's recuperation of the Asian foreign student is specific to his study of early intellectuals and their respective national histories. It is, as he acknowledges, an extension of Aiwha Ong's notion of "flexible citizenship," in which "these logics and practices are produced within particular structures of meaning about family, gender, nationality, class mobility, and social power."[20] He frames his exploration of the intellectual and cultural contributions of Asian foreign students to early Asian America formation as part of a broader discussion on transnational discourse between American studies and Asian American studies; by stressing that early Asian American movements were not solely about identity formation and civil rights but were anti-imperialist, antiracist, and necessarily engaged in geopolitics, particularly in the eastern and southeastern theaters, Wang is able to effectively argue that the international student is "a transnational figure of diasporic difference that is both embedded in and constitutive of Asian American cultural politics as articulated in Third World struggles."[21] In other words, the international student is a flash point or a tangible conduit for transnational discourse between Asian and Asian American studies.

Framed thus, a longitudinal study of international students can detect how discourse by Asian and Asian Americanists evolves, as international students mature and contribute not just culturally but as intellectuals. It should be obvious by this point that the purpose and context of study abroad read differently depending on the local and national environment. Even within the United States, the context for Asian American study abroad reads differently than the context for White Americans. Namely, Asian Americans who study abroad, while fewer overall than their White counterparts, gravitate toward Asian countries because of ethnic, linguistic, and cultural familiarity and/or familial ties. Accordingly there is already a decentering of Europe and the West in the structure of Asian American study abroad. Moreover, Asian foreign students offer a means of access to modernity beyond a Eurocentric or Western center of gravity.[22] Of particular interest to the subject of this study is the push and pull between Asian scholars interested in Asian American studies and Asian American scholars.

I contend that study abroad for the Korean diaspora is not merely a "return" sojourn; it is another valuable means of domestic racial subject formation that can include exposure to third national sites. I want to build upon the aforementioned work on international students by uncovering study abroad narratives by second-generation Asian American and Zainichi Koreans whose purpose is quite different from that of their forebears—not immigration or modernity, but the *decentering* of the West in connecting with their cultural heritage. First, study abroad formulates a contact zone for diasporic minority students to encounter one another, be it directly or indirectly; and it creates a unique opportunity for members of the Korean diaspora to encounter each other in a structured, systematized fashion that has no parallel. Some second-generation Korean Americans or Korean Europeans may visit the homeland on occasion, but beyond an educational setting there is no organized means by which they might encounter one another.[23] Second, I seek to theorize how to account for international study as a structural conduit for Asian American cultural integration in a bilateral manner. That is, I hypothesize that as much as it is valuable for Korean Americans to learn about themselves in a Korean context, it is equally if not more important for them to process encounters with other members of the Korean diaspora in their respective racializations.[24]

Efforts to theorize international study thus far, reflective of the field, follow the homeland-destination binary—that is, from Asia to America. Instead, I propose focusing on the postimmigration period, to explore study abroad as a mechanism for interminority encounters in third national spaces. Study abroad is no mere educational experience hermetically sealed from national politics and migratory flows; it is, as the literature shows, a highly national, cultural exercise, and makes for a different experience for students depending on local contexts as well as global economics and their attendant hierarchies. For minority students in particular, that experience is fraught with complications, as they not only juggle their national, ethnic, and racial histories but may also be unsettled by the diasporic interminority encounter.

Theorizing sojournship in Zainichi and Asian American literature offers a method for integrating the interminority encounter—a means of grappling with a comparative diasporic subjectivity for Korean Americans and the Zainichi. By decentering both the homeland and the point of origin, sojournship avoids the ideology of return and a transformative experience defined wholly by a "native" ethnicity. While sojourners might travel to South Korea to reconnect with their ethnic heritage, in encountering another minority context they widen the perspective of a global identity or diasporic identity beyond the confines of dualist relationships (US-Korea or Japan-Korea). Finally, those encounters are generative and productive in that students are brought back to their respective points of origin to be integrated into a trilateral, transpacific ethnic identity. To that end, I examine two cultural productions that depict the interminority encounter, both implicit and explicit.

Yuhi, Movement, and Transitions

Yi Yang-ji's life was remarkably transitory. In 1988, she became the first female Zainichi author to win the prestigious Akutagawa Prize, for her novella *Yuhi*, which critics consider a harbinger of a number of Zainichi writers following her footsteps, with the most common comparison being Zainichi novelist Yu Miri.[25] What sets Yi apart from her predecessors is that she enjoyed a degree of acceptance by literary culture that had eluded others—her work was perceived as *literature* rather than minority literature.[26] Yi's work is also unique in that the catalyst for her writing came from her time abroad in South Korea, where she earned her bachelor's from Seoul National University and her master's in dance at Ewha Women's University. She did so belatedly, having been raised in a household of divorce and neglect. It was not until she explored the possibility of studying abroad in America that she discovered much to her surprise that she was not Japanese—her parents had decided to assimilate and pass as Japanese, and her childhood was completely bereft of Korean culture and language.[27] After a suicide attempt, she fled home as a teenager and settled in a rural area near Kyoto, where she worked at a Japanese-style inn before completing high school. Several desultory years later, Yi eventually gained admission to Waseda University, where she attempted to connect with other Zainichi students but found the experience inadequate and decided to continue her education in South Korea. There she began to write fictionalized renderings of her time abroad—the short story "Koku" and *Yuhi* being the most notable examples.[28] Her life was tragically cut short at thirty-six when she passed away from a heart condition.

Several threads in Yi's biography and *Yuhi* are worth dwelling upon. First, critics have noted the strong autobiographical bent of *Yuhi*, as Yi took a similar path to Seoul National University;[29] and it is noteworthy that study abroad was the catalyst that sent Yi on her lifelong search for her Korean ethnic heritage—in this case, exploring the possibility of studying in the United States. Second, Yi traveled to South Korea through the mechanism of international study to continue her search for a Zainichi selfhood, but it was not an isolated, domestic Zainichi subjectivity that she sought. Third, Yuhi's failure—and the narrator's own failings—are always set in juxtaposition against the narrator's cousin's successful transplantation to the United States.

Yuhi is told through the perspective of an unnamed female narrator—referred to as Onni (big sister)—and chronicles the perceived failure of the titular Yuhi to complete her studies at S. University (read as Seoul National University, the most prestigious university in South Korea). By the opening of the novel, Yuhi has already left Korea and returned to Japan; the bulk of the text involves the narrator coming to terms with Yuhi's absence and impenetrable silence. Yuhi, a Zainichi Korean enters our narrator's life as a boarder in her aunt's home, but just as she mysteriously arrives, she departs not long after, having been unable to grasp the contours of South Korean culture and language. Onni, in a series of flashbacks, recalls her affection for and frustration with Yuhi, describing her as childlike and her mastery of Korean as exasperatingly incomplete. As Yuhi's failures mount, she retreats into her room, nearly mute, reading Japanese literature and expressing herself only through a flute and a diary written entirely in Japanese. Thus the novel places the reader and narrator in a double act of linguistic displacement, as the text is written in Japanese but is told through a narrator who is supposedly digging through her memories, in Korean, about her onetime friend, who cannot grasp Korean.

Language Games

It is little wonder, then, that most of the scholarly discussion on *Yuhi* tends to gravitate to the play on languages in the novel. After all, in an interview with Kawamura Minato, Yi herself admits her frustration with Korean culture and language; and critics widely read her autobiographical fiction as a reflection of her own experience while studying abroad at Seoul National University. "The novel just poured out from inside me. And that led to a bit of a crisis. After entering Seoul National, I started wanting to write in Japanese and protect myself from Korean. Shield myself from it, no matter what. The first words I really heard from my mother, my mother tongue, were a kind of violence."[30]

Several linguistic tensions emerge from a basic structural reading of the novel. Yuhi fails to master Korean and retreats into Japanese. Our unnamed narrator, who is likewise frustrated by Yuhi's grammatical mistakes and mispronunciations nearly to the point of misophonia, still yearns to penetrate the facade of Yuhi's inscrutability, but when she discovers Yuhi's diary—a window into her mind—she cannot understand or read it because it is entirely in Japanese. The narrator's aunt—Yuhi's landlady—speaks some Japanese, thanks to colonization, but resists doing so. The novella itself is written in Japanese, yet it takes place in the interior monologue of a Korean character who is thinking and speaking in Korean. Additionally, Korean words are sometimes written phonetically in Japanese katakana—the equivalent of italicized foreign words in English—and at other times written in Hangul (Korean), underscoring a dual linguistic displacement and dissonance.

Clearly, language is an important object of inquiry, but the question is, to what end? Conventional readings of *Yuhi* explore and deconstruct these linguistic tensions, but there is some disagreement about the target of Yi's meditation on the disjuncture between Korean and Japanese languages. For example, Catherine Ryu posits that Onni's frustration with Yuhi's language should be seen as a moment of Lacanian Othering that eventually leads to her understanding Yuhi on her own terms.[31] Onni, despite her frustration and sense of betrayal by Yuhi's abrupt departure, identifies with Yuhi in her alienation from her ancestral homeland and mother tongue, and comes to realize a decoupling between language and ethnicity. Atsuko Ueda reads language in *Yuhi* as a means of building ambiguity between the two national sites, forcing readers to perform a kind of "translation" that forces a linguistic dissonance upon the reader, constantly blurring the line between Korean and Japanese.[32] In his analysis, Takayuki Yokota-Murakami frames the linguistic duality as a kind of "implicit bilingualism" in service to his building a theory of polylingualism in Japanese literature.[33] In particular, he is interested in Zainichi literature, for Zainichi authors had a transitional period in which they anguished over writing in Japanese rather than Korean, but with generational turnover they have come to embrace Japanese without much consternation.[34]

Another strain of readings looks beyond the linguistic play to uncover alternate ontologies. In her early survey of Zainichi history and its peculiar positionality, Norma Field looks past national politics in *Yuhi* to highlight the book's homosocial subtext:

> Now, there are too many hints of a charged relationship between the mature woman narrator and the young Yuhi to be ignored. . . . The narrative is un-reflexive on this aspect, and Japanese critics have also failed to comment, as if the national issues overwhelmed the possibilities for this sort of investigation. Beyond the complex, troubling semantics of the structure—the subdued but still emotional Korean acknowledgment of the impossibility of return for a Korean born and raised in Japan on the one hand, and the alienation approaching autism induced in the same by a Korea experienced as primitive by comparison to a technologically sanitized Japan on the other—the ethno-erotic attachment between the two women, perhaps precisely for being un-marked, suggests the beginning of yet another 'third way.'"[35]

What is useful, Field argues, is that *Yuhi* resists a simple binary of a romanticized, essentialist Korea with a colonial-hypercapitalist Japan, and the highly charged but ambiguous homoeroticism between Onni and Yuhi hints at another paradigm that has yet to come into focus. Similarly, both Melissa Wender and Carol Hayes take issue with the reading of *Yuhi* as an exercise in ethnic identity acquisition. Instead, Wender reads Yuhi's lamentation of her inability to master Korean as a perennial condition that has no solution, only heartache: "It's not surprising, then, that what stays with me from her literature is not conclusions she comes to about what it means to be a Korean in Japan, but rather repeated motifs, fleeting images, and an intensity of emotion: self-hatred, terror, and irritations, mostly; but on occasion, joy. Her fiction is not so much about where the characters end up (which is not at any time Korean identity, strictly speaking), but about their journey to that point, about her feelings, their interpretations of images, their often frustrated attempts to communicate with others."[36] It is, in her assessment, a reflection of the unbridgeable gap between Zainichi and Korean as currently defined. The humanity is found in the journey and struggle rather than in meeting any arbitrary notion of linguistic fluency and acceptance by a distant Korean community. Hayes points out that Yi elides the matter of language and finds another means of self-expression to formulate a space between an either/or binary. "It was through her writing and her music that Yang-ji worked through this fantasy and finally achieved self-empowerment, letting go of the nostalgic identification with the myth of Korea and returning to a conscious self-location in Japan, as a Korean Japanese, proud of a selfhood which was neither purely Korean nor purely Japanese."[37] Field, Wender, and Hayes, through different modalities, gesture at a similar construction of a third-way construct beyond a reductive either/or binary. Also common in their assessment is the necessary collision and juxtaposition of anomalous forces and the discarding of a "pure" Koreanness. That critical discontent belies *Yuhi's* simplicity; it calls for another comparative framework that can account for the nuances of its mode of quietude and linguistic errata.

Presence/Absence

I follow the thread initially unspooled by Field, Wender, and Hayes in my reading of *Yuhi*. While I do not discount the importance of language in *Yuhi*, I am more interested in interrogating the mechanisms allowing for the exchange of students between Japan, Korea, and the United States. In other words, I am invested in studying the institutional and comparative structures framing Yuhi, Onni, and the absent presence of others in the novel—that is, the formulation of an implicit discourse involving colonial Japan and Korean America. In a text marked by silences and voids, critics appear to overlook absent figures that loom just as large, if not larger, than Yuhi, who has come to be a convenient stand-in for the narrator's fraught relationship with her family and her troubled sense of self. Instead of conceiving Yuhi as an ethnic sister who has returned to Korea to lay claim to her heritage, I suggest thinking through Yuhi's experience as sojournship, which accounts for an imperfect visit and return.

From the outset, Yuhi is described in terms far from the paragon of an ideology of return. She is an anomaly in a heavily regulated social and educational setting, a walking, talking body of contradictions that unsettles and defamiliarizes. Onni and her aunt have difficulty placing Yuhi in the neat categorizations occupying their minds. As mentioned, the first issue is linguistic; Onni is perplexed by Yuhi's stiff, stumbling Korean, in addition to her overall awkwardness. The second is institutional; while Yuhi attends the prestigious S. University—the most difficult university in the country to gain admittance to—her Korean is far from fluent. There is some recognition of the alternate means by which international students attend domestic universities, but her halting Korean belies the assumed fluency needed to successfully navigate her classes. At the same time, Yuhi purports to fulfill the socially acceptable (and neoliberal) archetype of the hardworking student, presumably on track to attain a salaried position in a large multinational conglomerate. University students, in the Korean context, are often perceived as destitute figures sacrificing creature comforts for the greater good of the family, company, and nation. However, Yuhi as an international student both fits and troubles that image—her arrival from the economically superior Japan intimates a degree of comparative wealth, yet at the same time she chooses to board with them, though the commute to campus is longer than normal.[38] Third, she is physically amorphous; androgynous in appearance, awkward in mannerisms and speech, she elicits in equal parts fascination and repulsion.[39] Yuhi is both premodern and modern, Korean and non-Korean, communicative and uncommunicative, ambiguously gendered—in short, almost human but not quite: "Whether just her personality, or because she was here in a country that—despite being her homeland—remained unfamiliar, Yuhi gave the impression that she was always tensed up as if she were nervous, wary of her surroundings while closing herself up. As I watched Yuhi's expression, I realized that in those moments the fragile, delicate aspect of Yuhi—similar to a young boy or girl who had yet to fully mature—suddenly appeared from within her nervousness as pain and apprehension" (276–77). Finally, Yuhi hints at a Korean familiarity, but her impenetrable Japaneseness reasserts itself to remind them that theirs is a kinship that is nearly but not quite whole. The result is that Yuhi embodies a patchwork of contradictory signifiers—physical, linguistic, ethnic, economic, social—and disrupts enough Korean conventions to recast her as a Frankensteinian bride groping her way back to Japan.

And yet, despite the enumerated abnormalities listed above, Onni finds herself drawn to Yuhi for reasons she cannot satisfactorily articulate: "Perhaps I saw something of myself in her. I feel that on first meeting her, I wanted only to see her reclusiveness (as well as her reluctance to open up to people) in a positive light, as somehow similar to my own" (273). In other words, Onni identifies with Yuhi along an undiscovered axis. What appears to be central to her attraction is a "reclusive aura"; that is, in Yuhi's resistance, Onni detects a negative capability that both enchants and confuses her. Yuhi's anomalousness reflects Onni's own sense of alienation, and it is only in their chance encounter that a constellation of absent/present archetypes and people come into view.

I want to pause and draw attention to this, for it is here that the crux of my argument intersects with my reading of the novel. Void of clear indicators of which categories she fits into, Yuhi is at once both present and absent, substantive and empty. The yawning chasms and silences of the novel define it, for it reflects dual pressures that the diasporic returnee student deals with in studying abroad in South Korea. Indeed, insists Sonia Ryang, absence is *the* defining shibboleth for the Zainichi; she posits that it is not a state of incompleteness or conditional acceptance but the utter exclusion of Zainichi by both Japan and Korea.[40] Yuhi desires to gain fluency and demonstrate her ethnic kinship, yet that is always beyond her reach—her slanted intonation will never align correctly. Yet if she remains silent, she can "pass" for Korean and belong. I suspect that it is for this reason that the author, Yi, eventually gravitated toward traditional forms of Korean dance as a means of expressing herself rather than through the written or spoken word—silence and physicality were alternate means of drawing closer to Korean acceptance that had always eluded her. The body, then, becomes the medium for accepted communication and kinship; but even that is denied to Yuhi, for her body is equally illegible and incomprehensible. In other words, silence and absence, the absent presence of the recently departed, shapes and influences the present and histories of those left behind.[41] It is here that the text points to the inadequacies of a postcolonial legacy of "return."

In its stead, *Yuhi* calls for a recognition of the diasporic minority sojourn. Onni narrates and chronicles Yuhi's time in Seoul, yet her interactions with Yuhi are defined more by what she does *not* say than by what she does. Yuhi, on reflecting upon her adopted *tong* (K: neighborhood), admits that she is attracted to its absence of noise, in contrast to the din of Seoul. "'It's a quiet *tong* [neighborhood], and just knowing that I could see the mountain every day, I completely fell in love with this place. Not only is the *tong* peaceful, I had a feeling that I'd finally be able to meet people leading quiet lives, and I was happy,' Yuhi explained. She had lowered her eyes and mumbled the last words as if she were embarrassed. Her pronunciation of the adjective *jo yon han* (silent) was perfect. Not only that, but even I could sense that Yuhi's thoughts were bundled up within that sound" (292). Though the neighborhood is a rather long commute to S. University, Yuhi is drawn to it for its silence and its proximity to a mountain. I would contend that that silence is defined, not wholly by absence, as Onni and the reader might assume, but by a presence of some kind. It is notable that on the rare occasion that Yuhi is not marked linguistically as Other, she pronounces "silence" in Korean perfectly. Yuhi, then, chooses to escape noise, sound, and speech to the point of retreating to her room in a suburban neighborhood, and eventually to the space in her mind, overflowing with Japanese, despite her arrival in Korea under the auspices of an international education program designed to impart an immersive fluency. Yet her taciturn nature belies an abundant inner life that remains impenetrable and inaccessible to Onni, both emotionally and linguistically.

Stepping back, if we were to examine the narrative's structure, we would note that it is framed, from beginning to end, by Yuhi's *absent presence*. That is, her departure leaves such a conspicuous gap in the home that it becomes something of substance, to the point of sensory tangibility. For example, after Yuhi has left, Onni enters Yuhi's abandoned room only to collide with the ghost of her presence:

> If anything, the room, deserted and completely empty of any trace of Yuhi's belongings, felt smaller than it did when Yuhi's luggage was there.
>
> She was still in this room.
>
> Her presence in the room was palpable, and I felt unsettled, as if it held me back when I tried to leave and made me sit in that spot. (262)

That tangible negative presence haunts Onni as she sifts through her recollections of Yuhi's time in the house and leads her to trace Yuhi's ghostly trail to her room, where she discovers her diary. Moreover, her absent presence does more than create an atmosphere of the house and transforms the living space in subtle yet obvious ways. "The difference in odor between the first and second floors was subtle; and yet the thickness and flow felt completely different. The Yuhi shown to Auntie downstairs and the Yuhi shown to me on the second floor—perhaps even her expression itself—were different" (255). Even within her absent presence are subtleties and differences that Onni detects: that is, Onni differentiates between the ghost of Yuhi that she knew in their more intimate moments and the Yuhi who interacted with her aunt, as evidenced by the thickness of the air and the shift in odors. Absent presence, then, has a shaping effect that goes beyond apparitional—it has a physical, concrete form that can be interacted with. Indeed, the entirety of the novel is a recollection of Yuhi through Onni's consciousness: Yuhi has already left Korea by the beginning of the novel, and she appears only through Onni's recollections. Yet Yuhi's sojourn in Onni's domestic space and her departure leave an indelible inscription on the parchment of Onni's being.

Here, we turn to the hollow, the negative, and the departed as a means of comprehending a transnational relationality between Zainichi Korea, South Korea, and the United States. The negative space that is Yuhi overwhelms Onni, and while it is the largest absence in the novel, it is one of several interrelated absences that define the house, including that of her uncle, who has passed away, and her cousin, who has emigrated to the United States, both of whom Yuhi seems to intersect with in meaningful ways.[42] For instance, her aunt recalls that it was Yuhi's uncanny alignment with her late husband through S. University that initially drew her to take Yuhi as a boarder:

The first time I considered renting out the room upstairs, she came along. What's more, she was a fellow Korean from Japan. By some kind of cosmic coincidence, she was a student at S. University, and if he were still alive, she would have been his junior. Because it was the first time we had a boarder, I tried to be especially attentive to her needs, but it ultimately ended up this way. No matter what happened, I had planned to go to her graduation. When she first came to this house, I talked with you about how we would definitely go to the ceremony. I wanted to go and see S. University—I haven't seen it since it moved from Tongsung-tong. . . . If your uncle were still alive, he'd call her his junior, and look after her like family. He'd have even gone to her graduation. He certainly wouldn't have let her drop out. . . . Surely, he would've been stricter with her than you or me, would've encouraged her and convinced her to stay in school. Your uncle loved S. University. He was so proud of it. (257–58)

Through Yuhi's institutional connection with S. University the aunt feels connected to her late husband. While Onni's relationship with Yuhi is defined by her absence, her aunt's relationship with her husband, Onni's uncle, is similarly defined. Auntie sees in Yuhi a kinship that could be described as a sort of slant rhyme—a similar but not quite same familiarity that connects her to her late husband. The alumni network at Seoul National University is reputed to be quite strong, and her uncle, acting as Yuhi's *sŏnbae* (K: senior), would have taken her under his wing as his *hubae* (K: junior).[43] Her aunt, therefore, perceives Yuhi as a stand-in connection to her late husband through her affiliation with S. University. More than a mere school, S. University is a cultural and social signifier of immense promise and social status—her uncle's passing denies her aunt access to those intangible benefits, and Yuhi's failure to graduate dredges up feelings of regret and mourning that she has not quite put behind her.

Korean America appears, obliquely, in the final panel of the triptych. Onni's cousin, her aunt's daughter, whose absent presence similarly defines her existence, is spoken about in vague terms, but she presents a contrast not only to Yuhi but to Onni, even though Onni does not willingly engage in the comparison. Yuhi, after all, takes Onni's cousin's place in the house by inheriting her room. It is hinted that Onni stands on the brink of illegibility according to Korean norms—she is in her late thirties, unmarried, with no prospects for settling into a socially acceptable coupling and/or employment. She notes that her cousin's departure created a rift in her relationship with her aunt.

> It was a little before my cousin married and left this house that Auntie started criticizing me.
>
> I didn't think my depression stemmed from the fact that my cousin married before me. Even so, Auntie had started to tell me with increasing frequency: "If you can find a nice man, you should hurry up and get married." Unable to feel better, I was mired in a constant, listless depression. I wondered what would become of me if I were to continue living without feeling or desire, unable to find something interesting in each passing day, and felt suffocated by my anxiety. Soon enough, I was becoming unable to escape from a relentlessly self-recriminating way of thinking about even the most minor of missteps in my daily routine. (270)

The departure of Onni's cousin creates a hole that neither she nor Yuhi can fill, as two women ill-fitted for the narrowly defined, strict social norms of South Korea. In contrast to the relative failures of Yuhi and herself, the cousin is perceived to be an emigrant success story who has mastered English, journeyed to America, and married a Korean American. "Six months before Yuhi came to live here, Auntie's daughter (my cousin) had been using this room. My cousin married and left for America. She was three years younger than me. For my cousin, who had a degree in English literature, traveling around America had been her dream. But once she met a fellow Korean, an accountant, and fell in love, her trip to America turned from vacation to a state of permanent residence" (264). There is some ambiguity as to whether the cousin's husband is a Korean national, using term *zaibei dōhō* (J: American resident compatriot [在米同胞]), but it is assumed that he is Korean American, as her trip is defined by its permanence. It is curious that Yi uses *nakaba towateki* (J: semipermanent resident [半ば永久的]) to describe her cousin's living situation, signaling the kind of stateless limbo that the Zainichi suffer, and further proving that Yi uses Zainichi politics as her frame of reference for comprehending Korean American subjectivity. Her cousin, then, succeeds where both Onni and Yuhi fail—in fulfilling heteronormative coupledom, conforming to feminine ideals, and emigrating from Korea to modernity.

Yet although the cousin wields all the signifiers of success, her absent presence continues to haunt Auntie and her relationship with the other members of her household. Overcome with longing, Auntie decides to call her daughter in the US, a connection that is defined by the ghost of her presence and inability to connect.

> After checking the number written in her address book, she began to dial her daughter's house in New York.
>
> It was apparent that someone had picked up the phone on the other line. Auntie, in a high voice, eyes wide, called my cousin's name as if her daughter were present with us in the room. Out of the blue she had said that she would call.
>
> I estimated the time in New York. It was probably around 7:00 or 8:00 in the morning. I told Auntie that this might be a busy time for her daughter, when she was making breakfast and seeing her husband off, but my

words seemed to fall on deaf ears. She had already reached the threshold and was in the process of picking up the phone.

The sound of rain and Auntie's voice as she called her daughter's name collided for a moment in the living room, then scattered. Auntie bent over, as if to cradle the phone above the floor. She continued, and as she wrestled with the sound of the rain, both the rain and her voice reverberated throughout the living room. (352–53)

Auntie's attempt to connect with her daughter is depicted as an act of mourning. Hers is a presence that is similarly defined by an absence that leaves a split in her Aunt's being. Her aunt, at different points, similarly speaks to her husband in the house as if he were present, just as she utters her daughter's name into the phone receiver.[44]

Moreover, if we contrast Yuhi and Onni's cousin directly, they are opposing figures on the Korean scale of successful international travel. Yuhi is the failed international student—she is unable to master Korean, falls short of rediscovering her kinship with her ethnic heritage, drops out of S. University, and retreats to Japan and the Japanese language. Onni's cousin, in contrast, succeeds on every front where Yuhi fails; she marries a Korean American, lives in the gleaming metropole of New York City, presumably masters English—she is the virtuous and successful immigrant. Still, they both leave behind a melancholy that is likened to death; and while Onni's relationship with her cousin is defined by her failure to live up to her example, her relationship with Yuhi is defined in terms of her own failure to surmount Yuhi's impenetrable wall. Yuhi leaves behind our unnamed narrator, who is left feeling ambivalent.

Yuhi complicates and problematizes the Korea-Japan and Korea-America binaries that often portray colonization and modernity in starkly simplistic terms. According to these binaries, Zainichi Koreans returning to Korea conform to a narrative of "return," with no room for preserving a Zainichi subjecthood; it is a consequence of a colonial narrative that leaves no room for an ethnic minor subjectivity like the Zainichi. While Zainichi intellectuals argue among themselves for a third or fourth way beyond a narrative of return, South Koreans blithely assume that return is always the goal because of the colonial origins of the separation. Likewise, Koreans emigrating to the United States fulfill a neoliberal fantasy of economic and social prosperity in claiming modernity; Koreans who succeed in the US cannot return and must cut off ties to those left behind, for there can never be a return to premodernity for the sake of the nation.

Yuhi resists that binary. For instance, there are hints of such gradients in Yuhi's refusal to conform to Onni's and her aunt's reductive terms. Auntie notes that she has long heard of rampant discrimination against Zainichi Koreans by the Japanese, whom she still despises for colonization. However, much to her surprise, Yuhi gently refutes her assumptions:

> "Yes, I was surprised when I first learned about that sort of thing, but I personally haven't ever been directly discriminated against or bullied or anything like that," said Yuhi.
>
> Her expression softened, and since she'd become more comfortable with us, her Korean also became smoother. To be honest, I had a good impression of Yuhi—she answered with such clarity. (281–82)

On two separate occasions, Yuhi claims that she has not faced discrimination. But she undermines her claims when she casually mentions that she and her family passed for Japanese and that she actively hid her Korean ethnicity. "Where I live, there were only Japanese around us. My mother and father are Korean, but we had so little interaction with other Koreans that it was almost nonexistent. I went to Japanese schools until college, and had only Japanese friends. Up to a certain point, I had been hiding the fact that I was Korean, so I suppose the fear that compelled me to hide my identity could be a form of discrimination, but, speaking for myself, I haven't grown up experiencing the kind of intense, direct discrimination that people in Korea talk about" (282). At the same time, the relative ease with which Yuhi passes for Japanese in Japan is something that eludes her in Korea. She cannot pass for Korean unless she remains completely silent—her accent gives her away—but a charade is unsatisfactory. An ungenerous reading might paint Yuhi's contradictions as evidence of racial self-hatred and perhaps her subscribing to the idea of Japanese supremacy, but I counter that her fumbling is the result of an instinctive resistance to a totalizing ideology of return.

After all, Yi herself felt conflicted and protective of her Japanese when she was in Korea. A long history of colonial subjugation created a narrative framework in which all Zainichi Koreans who came to Korean shores were presumed to have "returned" to their ancestral homeland to escape racial discrimination. Likewise, depicting America and English language acquisition as the final step toward modernity leaves no room for a return to

Korea. Instead, sojournship frames international study not only as a means of learning a language, acquiring a degree, or seeking modernity but as a meditation on departures. Yuhi and Onni's cousin are two sides of the same coin—one successful and the other not—but both leave behind a deep sense of melancholy. We are given a hint into Yuhi's predilection for complicating politics and national narratives in her discussion of a colonial-era writer:

> I read Yi Kwang-su. Because of Japan's imperial legacy in Korea, other students usually reject him as a puppet of the state, but for me, my feelings about him are a bit complicated."
>
> Yuhi lowered her voice. I'm sure she wasn't saying that Yi Kwang-su was good in front of other students.
>
> "Yi Sang and Yi Kwang-su are really different, aren't they," I said.
>
> "Yes, but for some reason I'm fascinated by Yi Kwang-su." (285)

The Korean disdain for Yi Kwang-su is reflective of Korean studies' longtime disavowal of colonial-era fiction, for it was verboten to study figures who dared to write in Japanese during the colonial period.[45] A totalizing ideology of return has little tolerance for those who would indulge in hybridity.

This particular form of international study—undertaken by the heritage returnee and modernity seeker—complicates the concept of the international student. It is often thought that study abroad as a mechanism for international exposure mainly benefits the international student, but it is also true that the journey itself, not the certificate of matriculation or graduation, leaves behind its absent presence. A theory of sojournship by second- and third-generation diasporic subjects creates room for the diasporic encounter without an obligation of return.

A Brawl in Yongin

In classic 1980s movie fashion, our *Seoul Searching* protagonists have their foil—their rival camp counselors, their ski academy villains, their troglodyte bullies—in this case, a hostile group of Japanese high schoolers on a parallel tour of South Korea. They encounter each other in passing on several occasions in the film. The presence of Japanese students is particularly offensive to a jingoistic Korean American who appears to be a member of the JROTC—buzz haircut, fatigues, and spit-polished boots. Several male Japanese students, wearing their military-inspired school uniforms and rockabilly hairstyles, make it clear that they are equally unamused by the presence of their American counterparts (figure 9).

When our Korean Mexican lead, overcome with romantic desire, cannot help but declare his love for a female Japanese student, a huge melee breaks out. After their Korean and Japanese teachers have separated the two sides and regained control, the film unveils its plot twist: the Japanese students are Zainichi Koreans, who have been on their own tour of their ethnic homeland. The two sides, chagrined at this case of mistaken identity, come to an understanding and shake hands (figure 10). In this third national

FIGURE 9   A JROTC Korean American confronts several Zainichi high school students in *Seoul Searching* (Mondo Paradiso, 2016).

FIGURE 10   The Korean American and Zainichi students reconcile in *Seoul Searching* (Mondo Paradiso, 2016).

space of South Korea, where they are ostensibly learning about their mutual heritage, the two factions misread each other as stand-ins for their respective national referents—an imperial United States and Japan—and, eventually recognizing their respective marginalization and racialization as minorities and diasporic subjects, embrace each other.[46]

Seoul Searching's plot twist is not without its problems, for the mistake would have likely been one-sided. It is entirely possible that the Korean diasporic students would have mistaken the Zainichi students for Japanese, since outside of Korea not much is known about the Zainichi. The Zainichi students, in contrast, would have likely recognized their American counterparts. That misrecognition is indicative of the asymmetry of this book's central argument—that if there is a transpacific channel of communication between Korean American and Zainichi minor literatures, it is relatively one-sided. International study is one possible conduit through which diasporic subjects may sojourn to Korea. By cultivating interminority contact zones, diasporic collisions—some oblique, others more direct, or even violent—may lead to a refining or complication of the Korean diaspora. As it stands, limited views devoid of the greater transpacific context in both *Seoul Searching* and *Yuhi* lead to myopic encounters. However, that asymmetry has slowly begun to balance out, even if the change has been decades in the making. In the following chapter, I show how two novels engage with their corresponding minority sites in the intertextual travels of Min Jin Lee and Kim Masumi.

CHAPTER 5

Los Angeles and Osaka Are Burning

Diasporic Minority Transpositions in
Pachinko *and* Moeru Sōka

> Nowhere is this more true than for the American humanist today, whose
> proper role, I cannot stress strongly enough, is not to consolidate and affirm
> one tradition over all the others. It is rather to open them all, or as many as
> possible, to each other, to question each of them for what it has done with the
> others, to show how in this polyglot country in particular many traditions have
> interacted and—more importantly—can continue to interact in peaceful ways.
>
> —Edward Said, *Humanism and Democratic Criticism*

IN MAY 2019, former US president Barack Obama posted a list of books
he found compelling and recommended to his considerable following on
social media. Included among them was an entry for Min Jin Lee's novel
about a Zainichi family:

> [*Pachinko*] is a captivating book I read at the suggestion of a young staffer
> on my team—a historical novel about the Korean immigrant experience in
> wartime Japan. Min Jin Lee draws you in from the first line, "History has
> failed us, but no matter." The book is named after a popular game in Japan
> that's a bit like a pinball machine—a game of chance where the player can
> set the speed or direction, but once it's in play a maze of obstacles deter-
> mines the outcome. Staying true to the nature of the game, Min Jin Lee's
> novel takes us through four generations and each character's search for
> identity and success. It's a powerful story about resilience and compassion.[1]

It is fitting that *Pachinko* would resonate with Obama, who has called himself "America's first Pacific president," with others going as far as referring
to him as the first "Asian American president."[2] He was born and raised in
Honolulu, Hawaii, an early transit station for trade, culture, and migra-

tion between the continental United States and Asia. Moreover, Obama's multiethnic background and multiply located identity as a Black American make him an ideal reader for Lee's novel, which intersects with much of the transpacific critical groundwork that this book and others before it have articulated. Its universalist themes of "resilience and compassion" would find an audience with the broader American readership, despite a minimal awareness of the colonial history between Korean and Japan. But *Pachinko*, I will show, was not the first direct transpacific literary gesture by or about Zainichi Korea—instead, it was a response to a call that preceded it by some twenty years.

The apex of this book's argument centers on Min Jin Lee's *Pachinko* (2017) and Kim Masumi's *Moeru Sōka* (The burning Grass House, 1997). The preceding chapters laid the groundwork for an argument that Zainichi Korea and Korean America demonstrate awareness of their respective political and racial discourses, refracted by the specificity of their mediating sites—the United States and Japan. This chapter underscores that dynamic by examining two direct literary overtures by each community to the other. Min Jin Lee, a Korean American author writing solely in English, writes about the Zainichi; conversely, Kim Masumi, a Zainichi Korean, writes in Japanese about Korean America. To be sure, the two books are quite different—*Pachinko* is a sprawling, multigenerational bildungsroman, spanning several countries involving a litany of characters, whereas *Moeru Sōka* takes place over the span of a single afternoon in Los Angeles within the circle of just a few characters and a solitary narrator. Yet they both center on sites of racialized trauma; both wrestle with questions of their population's place in the national imaginary and search for possible answers in an intersectional, transpacific context; and both revolve around a homegrown industry that has been racialized—Korean-owned pachinko parlors in one book, convenience stores in the other. Indeed, the titles of both works directly reference their similarly marginalized industries; *Pachinko* is obvious, but *Sōka* (Grass House) is the name of a convenience store around which the characters' lives revolve.

The two novels bring into stark relief a quandary for both Asian studies and Asian American studies. To which discipline does *Pachinko* belong? After all, the subject matter, on a superficial level, belongs to Japanese studies (or perhaps even Korean studies), which has a rich body of scholarship on Zainichi literature. However, the novel is written entirely in English by a Korean American author, whose first book fits squarely in the tradition of Asian

American literature.³ Nor is Lee interested in writing a novel restricted to national and cultural boundaries; she explicitly introduces characters and ideas from Asian America to Zainichi Korea. Similarly, *Moeru Sōka*, set against the backdrop of a distinctly American site of trauma and written in Japanese by a Zainichi Korean author, centers on the relationship between a Zainichi and her Korean American friends but is framed through an entirely Zainichi perspective. Her book is even more explicitly transpacific than *Pachinko*, with the novella's lines of tension expressly taut between Zainichi Korea, Korean America, Japan, and the United States. Yet for the vast majority of Asian American studies scholars, *Moeru Sōka* would fail to register because of the language barrier alone; and even then, there remains the question of which scholarly discourse would be best suited for its subject matter.

Diasporic Minority Transposition

I propose reading these novels as examples of *diasporic minority transposition*. Until recently, there have been few direct examples of dialogue between Zainichi Korea and Korean America—but these texts evince a fascination with their respective lived and imagined experiences that they attempt to occupy. While both novels take place in a displaced minority environment, they are ultimately explorations and negotiations of a global minority diaspora. That is, they are formations not of an origin diaspora (Korea and a target destination), but of a *minor* diaspora in which narratives of racialization are transposed upon one another through mediating national sites—in this case, Japan and the United States.

Diasporic minority transpositioning decenters the homeland-and-destination narrative, foregrounding instead a mutual engagement in several ways. First, these interwoven lines of tension are a by-product of history—the result of nearly a century of imperial ambitions gained, lost, and reconfigured. Imperial Japan and colonial Korea's intimacy eventually included the United States, and the flow of migration soon followed, along with the requisite discriminatory racialization that is so particular and unique to each respective landing site. Second, the novels are written in their adopted languages with a dual purpose—to introduce a "foreign" body of racial discourse to a domestic readership and to occupy that debate to explore a racial group's minoritization through that foreign body.

Third, they explicitly include representations of minority discourse from the domestic sphere to contrast with the aforementioned "foreign" racial discourse. *Pachinko* concerns a Korean American character who is thrust into the Zainichi sphere much to her bewilderment, and in *Moeru Sōka* the Zainichi protagonist must navigate a racial climate that is quite alien to her. Finally, these texts decenter racial dominants and move their respective medial sites to the background. Neither *Pachinko* nor *Moeru Sōka* has central characters who are White or Japanese—and even characters representative of modernity are some flavor of Korean. Instead, they choose to relegate that dominance to more structural forces. For example, no Japanese landlord or racist White policeman is central to the narrative; if present at all, such characters are rendered as fleeting background figures or abstractions. Taken together, these parameters making up a diasporic minority transposition signal, as Françoise Lionnet and Shu-mei Shih write, a "recognition of the creative interventions that networks of minoritized cultures produce within and across national boundaries."[4]

Two disciplinary phenomena present challenges in discussing *Pachinko* and *Moeru Sōka*. First, as implied in the structural argument of this book, the problematic consequences of the division between Asian and Asian American studies become clear with this chapter's comparative study of Zainichi- and Korean American–inflected narratives. Again, the division is not unique to this particular subdiscipline: it mirrors a larger divide that has haunted, as Ali Behdad notes, American studies and comparative literature.[5] A "traditional" American studies approach would be crippled by its monolingualism and predilection for the logic of exceptionalism; and its comparative literary analogue would likewise gloss over sociopolitical context. Given their histories, we can anticipate how these disciplinary boundaries do a disservice to Korean American and Zainichi literary fictions. Second, situating this study in an Asian American transpacific frame is not without its complications. With the transpacific turn, Asian American scholars began, belatedly, to question definitions of their discipline and its cultural objects of study. In a way, such questioning is a sign of the field's health and robust nature—these definitions were much easier to intuit when there were only a few scattered authors and texts. But, as Colleen Lye notes, with the field's broadening and the literary categories diffusing, its ontological assumptions needed refinement:

Recourse to the idioms of civil rights strategy and coalition-building by the field's most expert literary critics reflects a genuine fealty to the activist ancestry of ethnic studies—and the extraordinary difficulty of developing a historically self-reflexive model of textual selection. Not only has no one taken up the challenge . . . to develop a formal analysis that could supplement the sociological justifications . . . [but] the deconstructive critique of essentialism continues to underscore the social heterogeneity of Asian Americans to the point where the claim to Asian American identity can only be tendered on strategic . . . grounds.[6]

In other words, the diversity within "Asian America" as a racial category challenges the default impulse to anchor the field in social justice and civil rights political movements or in an uncritical reliance on an essentialist token such as ethnicity. However, the question remains: If an essentialist, biological through line is unsatisfactory, what is the intellectual justification for including both *Pachinko* and *Moeru Sōka* in transnational Asian American literary studies? As a possible answer, Stephen Hong Sohn, Paul Lai, and Donald Goellnicht speculate how to define Asian American literature beyond race:

Conceptualizing Asian American fiction as a chameleonic body is essential precisely because field organization has rested primarily on the unstable relationship between textual content and the writer's racial descent. The instability that exists at the juncture of authorial descent and textual content is exemplified by the variegated ways in which the field has been defined. For instance, texts that have been penned in languages other than English have been considered Asian American based on the setting of those texts in America. . . . One recalls the centrality of the Angel Island poets in positing that English may not always be the center from which Asian American literature grounds itself. Others . . . [offer] up the possibility that Asian American Studies advance[s] more productively its connection to textual landscapes that have not been imagined by those of avowed Asian descent. The continuing emergence of cross-minority and cross-racial representational critiques highlights the ways in which Asian American identity and cultural contexts might be explored from the vantage point of other racial communities.[7]

That is to say, if we are to reject an essentialist framework, how can we determine under what rubric Asian American texts might belong? As Sohn et al. note, "Authorial descent does not necessarily and solely determine the applicability of a particular text toward advancing Asian Americanist critique"; instead, "There has been a collective movement toward the importance of a content-centered literary approach."[8] The notion of a "content-centered" approach may be a bit vague, but it is helpful for theorizing cross-diasporic minority literatures in a way that avoids essentializing and foregrounds history, migration, and political structures to articulate a more sophisticated understanding of racialization.

Given these debates, we can anticipate some of the issues that might emerge from a less sophisticated comparative study of Zainichi and Korean American fiction in two dimensions. First, an Asian American studies approach that projects onto other cultural and national contexts in totalizing fashion occludes a comprehensive reading of *Pachinko*. Second, the challenge of defining Asian American literature makes it difficult to neatly categorize *Pachinko* and *Moeru Sōka*. If we define Asian American literature according to authorial descent, then do both novels qualify? What of content-dependent definitions? Or sociological contexts? Finally, there is a temptation to perceive the two components as part of the larger Korean diaspora, indelibly tied together by the persistent memory of the homeland, but that would underplay or elide the importance of historical and regional contexts in racializations—not to mention skirting dangerously close to essentialism.

If, however, we were to frame them as two sides of a cultural conversation—that is, a transposition of minority discourses—then we would be able to circumnavigate the aforementioned obstacle of disciplinary boundaries and a colonizer-colonized binary. Instead, we would be forced to build conduits that center race and racialization with the attendant considerations of history, empire, and migration. A look at the structurally similar body of comparative ethnic theory in a domestic context is instructive. In a vein analogous to this book's broader argument, David Vázquez posits that Latinx American writers navigate through triangulation between "two known identities (the meaning of Black and White racial identities in the United States, for example) and an 'unknown' one (the meaning of Puerto Rican, Chicana/o, or Latina/o subjectivities)" to "locate their own subject positions through an analogous triangulation of identity—often in terms of serial and progressive negation (not 'this,' not 'that,' but something other)."[9] Similarly, Claire Jean Kim's seminal essay "The Racial Triangulation of Asian Americans" traces how Asian American racialization must always be defined against a Black-White binary system, arguing that "group racialization processes are mutually constitutive and that they generate rankings along more than one dimension."[10] The closest American parallel might be the literary history of African American and Afro-Caribbean writers, pioneered by Paul Gilroy and extended by Brent Edwards, Marlene Daut, and others.[11] There is even a rich scholarly discussion of early Black racial transpositioning—African American intellectuals, for example, indulging in Japanophilia as a means of counteracting American racism, a stance that, while deeply misguided, led to a reworking of racial epistemologies that ultimately bore fruit.[12] Asian American literary scholarship is in the early stages of theorizing on specific bodies of transpacific literature, despite obvious connections—think of the fertile ground of possible connections between Vietnamese American and Vietnamese French literature, or Filipino American literature and the Filipino literature of the Japanese period, both of which deal with the consequences of colonialism, war, migration, and labor. They are both Asian and Asian American literatures, neither of which negates the other; both belong to American studies and comparative literary studies. I propose to place them, not in an either/or binary or a zero-sum scenario, but instead as part of a larger, fluid constellation of texts whose purpose is to engage with one another to push forward the epistemological conversation. To consider them only in isolation—*Pachinko* as Asian literature, and *Moeru Sōka* as Japanese literature—would be untenable.

If the two novels engage one another as literary bodies of racial discourse and migrant histories, then the family business is an active site of racialization and self-definition: for post-1965, merchant-class Korean American immigrants, the Korean-owned store, and for Zainichi Koreans, the pachinko parlor. As sites of racial formation, minority family enterprises deserve scrutiny. In her essay "The Asian-Owned Store and the Incommensurable Histories of War in Narratives of the City," Caroline Yang proposes that analysis of literary instantiations of the Asian-owned store can illuminate and critique the workings of American Empire: "We might think about how it [the Asian-owned store] is used to justify equating urban neighborhoods to war zones as a foregone conclusion. Doing this requires that we think about how space is racialized and broaden our scope to see the workings of the United States as an empire-state. . . . The Asian-owned store—run by immigrants and frequented by those who do not have the option or the means to go elsewhere—and the surrounding neighborhood stand as a testament to the organization and operation of the US empire-state."[13] Indeed, the titular convenience store of *Moeru Sōka* becomes the flashpoint for racial tensions—Black and Korean, Korean and Zainichi, Zainichi and Black—through the course of the novel; similarly, the family pachinko business's gravitational pull defines the orbits of a multitude of characters in *Pachinko*, despite their best efforts to escape. Both businesses are consequences of imperial policies and structural discrimination. They are sites for racial negotiation and the main conduits through which Zainichi Korea and Korean American speak to one another; they also serve as critiques of empire and push against boundaried thought.

Osaka Mon Amour

Two parallel threads in *Pachinko* question how to reconcile paradoxical impulses. The first is highly personal, embodied in the lives of Sunja, Isak, and Hansu, Noa and Mozasu, and Solomon and Phoebe as they attempt to navigate their complicated, contradictory existences using starkly simplistic frameworks. The second is more social and national in scope—determining how much of their lives should be governed by racialization and citizenship in an increasingly multinational environment. In this respect, Lee's novel does not tread new ground—Zainichi authors and intellectuals have wrestled with these ideas in their work long before *Pachinko*.[14] What is most germane to this study is an additional layer of complication that comes with Lee's Korean American authorial perspective, and the explicitly Korean American layer of racialization interwoven into the narrative.

A sprawling Dickensian tome, Lee's novel follows three generations of Zainichi Koreans beginning in colonial-era Jejudo (Jeju Island), Korea, and ending in contemporary Tokyo, Japan, with an offstage sojourn to New York City. The novel begins with Sunja, a young illiterate woman who encounters two young men inflected by Western modernity—a sickly Christian minister named Baek Isak and a glamorous, dapper gangster named Koh Hansu, a binary contrast that will subsequently define her family for decades. Those encounters eventually lead to her bearing two sons, the brash Mozasu and the intellectual Noa, who take separate, winding paths to the same destination—the shameful pachinko gambling industry. It will be Mozasu's son Solomon (Sunja's grandson) who, by going abroad to the United States and returning to Japan to take over the family pachinko business without any feelings of guilt or shame, ultimately breaks a cycle of tragedy.

The title *Pachinko* refers to the Japanese gambling industry's most popular gaming device. Originating in the early Shōwa period (1926–89), it is often described as a cross between a slot machine, complete with bright, flashing lights and a cacophony of bells and jingles, and an upright pinball machine, where a cascade of small silver balls bounce off various pegs and obstacles to descend to several chutes at the bottom of the machine. There is little control over the pachinko balls, as they appear to fall at random—with the exception of a hand dial that ostensibly controls the rate and initial trajectory of balls dropped. The goal is to win more pachinko balls by dropping them into the correct chute, where they are collected in large plastic trays. One of the absurdities of pachinko is that gambling is technically illegal in Japan, so amassed winnings are traded for "gifts" or cards inside the pachinko parlor, then traded for cash at a connected, but separate, "tuck store" nearby. Today, the pachinko industry is ubiquitous, hugging train stations and operating at all hours of the day and night.[15] As Lee explains in her novel, the pachinko industry is overrepresented by Zainichi Koreans, who, with few legal avenues for pursing employment because of discriminatory hiring practices, built a niche in gambling, which came with attendant associations of yakuza extralegality and industry racialization.[16]

Despite its illicit reputation, over the years the Baek family cannot help but be drawn back, time and again, to the pachinko industry. The game provides a means of fabricating a kind of structure and logic for the larger machinations of empire and war that have laid waste to their home lives. At different moments, characters attempt to rely on other frameworks—social standing, nationalism, market logic, Christianity, and global capital—but they all fall short; the pachinko business appears to be the only structure left standing. Beyond granting a livelihood, the game has a certain metaphorical appeal that encapsulates the arbitrary nature of geopolitics and its collateral damage: "His [Mozasu's] Presbyterian minister father [Isak] had believed in a divine design, and Mozasu believed that life was like this game where the player could adjust the dials yet also expect the uncertainty of factors he could not control. He understood why his customers wanted to play something that looked fixed but which also left room for randomness and hope."[17] The Zainichi characters do not necessarily play pachinko, but they work in an industry that feeds its customers the illusion of control and a grand design organizing randomness and chaos. That is, the Zainichi who survive choose not to play the game but acknowledge its nature, its rules, and adjust accordingly.

A Doubled Consciousness

Sunja and her family take a circuitous path to their eventual return to the pachinko industry. They first wrestle with reconciling their lives to simple binaries in relationships, social roles, race, theology, or nationalities. For example, Sunja's extramarital relationship with Koh Hansu and her survivorship are at odds with the rigid social norms of rural Korea. She works herself to the bone to ensure her family's survival and has little patience for high-minded ideals. Even as the Japanese discriminate against the Zainichi, the Koreans in Ikaino (a slum in Osaka) do the same to those who would dare to pollute their bloodlines by marrying Japanese.

> "Mrs. Kim next door told me about the quiet lady who lives at the end of the road who's Japanese and married to the Korean who brews alcohol in his house. Their kids are half Japanese!" This had shocked Sunja when she'd first heard of it, though everything Mrs. Kim, the lady who raised pigs, told her was shocking. Yoseb didn't want Kyunghee and Sunja to speak with Mrs. Kim, who also didn't go to church on Sundays. They weren't allowed to speak to the Japanese wife, either, because her husband was routinely sent to jail for his bootlegging. (129)

Despite occupying the same ghetto, Sunja and her family cannot help but be held under the thrall of Korean social norms that strictly enforce hierarchy. Mrs. Kim should be avoided because she does not share their Christian faith; and the Japanese woman who lives in solidarity with her Korean husband in Ikaino should likewise be ostracized because he engages in bootlegging, and their mixed-race children offend Sunja's family's sensibilities. There is no comprehension of the fact that these norms follow the same binaristic logic as the ones leading to discrimination against the Zainichi.

That dualism is underscored by two suitors, who mark divergent paths. Entranced by Koh Hansu's otherworldly charisma, Sunja becomes pregnant, compelling Baek Isak, out of a sense of Christian generosity and mercy, to spare her from public disgrace by marrying her. Suffering from tuberculosis, Isak is not long for this world, yet he adheres to an idealistic sense of justice, family, and the nation that compels him to consult with Pastor Shin about his plan to marry Sunja. Even Pastor Shin, however, has his limits: "Shin smiled at the young man, not knowing how to protect him from his wish to make such a grand sacrifice. More than anything, he was incredulous. If it hadn't been for the warm letters from his friends in Pyongyang attesting to Isak's intelligence and competence, Shin would have thought that Isak was a religious lunatic" (67). Isak's unwavering faith and probity, in this case, avert disaster. In contrast, Koh Hansu believes in no one other than himself and pledges no allegiances, whether in marriage or in nationalism. For him, there is only the market and trade, legitimate or not. In a conversation with Kim Changho, an associate who wants to repatriate to North Korea, Hansu lays out his philosophy:

> Here's the truth: There's no such thing as a benevolent leader. I protect you because you work for me. If you act like a fool and go against my interests, then I can't protect you. As for these Korean groups, you have to remember that no matter what, the men who are in charge are just men—so they're not much smarter than pigs. And we eat pigs. You lived with that farmer Tamaguchi who sold sweet potatoes for obscene prices to starving Japanese during a time of war. He violated wartime regulations, and I helped him, because he wanted money and I do, too. He probably thinks he's a decent, respectable Japanese, or some kind of proud nationalist—don't they all? He's a terrible Japanese, but a smart businessman. I'm not a good Korean, and I'm not a Japanese. I'm very good at making money. This country would fall apart if everyone believed in some samurai crap. The Emperor does not give a fuck about anyone, either. So I'm not going to tell you not to go to any meetings or not to join any group. But know this: Those communists don't care about you. They don't care about anybody. You're crazy if you think they care about Korea. (233–34)

His is a cynical, dangerous world, where ideals about the nation and greater good lead to an early death. Hansu has no use for nostalgic sentiments about the homeland, and his rejection of national labels liberates him to exploit conditions to turn a profit. Indeed, Changho leaves for North Korea and is never heard from again, presumably because he has been sent to a labor camp and has died there.[18] The stark contrast between Isak and Hansu creates friction enough to spark a conflagration that threatens to consume them all.

Sunja, faced with the mortal danger of poverty and starvation, straddles the two worldviews. She accepts Isak's proposal and rejects Hansu's offer to make her his mistress, but she is not exactly confident that she has made the right decision. While it seemed the correct choice in the short term, as time marches on, her uncertainty grows. Looking around her, Sunja sees how others who are similarly committed to social norms follow the rules but suffer a lifetime of unhappiness:

> Were you supposed to have only one person in your life? Her mother had her father and no one else. Was her person Hansu or Isak? Did Hansu love her or had he just wanted to use her? If love required sacrifice, then Isak had really loved her. Kyunghee had served her husband faithfully without complaint. There was no one as kindhearted and lovely as her sister-in-law—why couldn't she have more than one man love her? Why did men get to leave when they didn't get what they wanted? Or had Changho suffered enough waiting? Sunja wanted her sister-in-law to make Changho wait, but it wouldn't have been Kyunghee if she had made him do so. Changho had loved someone who would not betray her husband, and perhaps that was why he had loved her. She could not violate who she was. (278)

Following rules, then, does not guarantee happiness—indeed, it seems more likely to lead to misery. Moreover, that appears particularly true for women, whose lot in life, they are reminded, is to bear pain. This absurdity leads Sunja at times to disregard social norms—hawking kimchi at the train station, intervening in Kyunghee's husband's financial debts—but while they might bend, norms snap back into shape with surprising force. That tension is always at play; the novel's refusal to advocate for one side or the other is a tacit critique of reductive systems, be they moral or racial.

Sunja's children and grandchildren suffer from the same struggle. Their attempts to navigate a discriminatory Japan as Zainichi initially lead to only two options, exemplified by Sunja's sons. Mozasu, lacking aptitude for schoolwork, has little option but to enter the pachinko business and embrace the marginality of illicitness, whereas his brother Noa capitalizes on his intellect to earn a spot at the prestigious Waseda University to earn a degree in English literature so that he may one day become a teacher. Ironically, Mozasu's pachinko business thrives, resulting in his building a small empire and lifting him and his family out of the Ikaino ghetto and poverty. Meanwhile, Noa's noble aspirations come at a cost—he has internalized a strongly binary logic of purity and pollution, an amalgamation of his father's religious legacy, Korean social norms, and colonial racialization. Beginning in primary school, Noa secretly dreams of becoming fully Japanese, but he struggles through Waseda as Zainichi until he learns of the true nature of his parentage and how Koh Hansu, the Zainichi gangster, has funded his education. His pride and deep sense of shame lead to his dropping out of college, adopting a Japanese name, and hollowing out a surreptitious second life as a pachinko bookkeeper. When Sunja finally locates him after many years of his hiding out, they have a quiet confrontation in which Noa bitterly rails against the impossibility of his duality and denounces his heritage.

> Yakuza are the filthiest people in Japan. They are thugs; they are common criminals. They frighten shopkeepers; they sell drugs; they control prostitution; and they hurt innocent people. All the worst Koreans are members of these gangs. I took money for my education from a yakuza, and you thought this was acceptable? I will never be able to wash this dirt from my name. . . . All my life, I have had Japanese telling me that my blood is Korean—that Koreans are angry, violent, cunning, and deceitful criminals. All my life, I had to endure this. I tried to be as honest and humble as Baek Isak was; I never raised my voice. But this blood, my blood is Korean, and now I learn that my blood is yakuza blood. I can never change this, no matter what I do. . . . I am cursed. (315)

Noa's early ambition was to engage in a racial uplift project of his own: by observing the rules and being the best possible representative of his race, he hoped to redeem himself and the Zainichi. Yet when he learns how his education was funded, he realizes the futility of his project and flees; and when faced with the prospect of his being discovered by his wife and employer, who as a matter of policy does not employ "foreigners," Noa's despair over his inability to reconcile his two halves leads to his committing suicide. According to this rather simplistic binary, he can either be an angelic Zainichi or pass as a "pure" Japanese with the attendant privilege of working in a trade of ill-repute. He cannot, however, face being a stereotypical "bad" Zainichi. In such a rigid system, there is no room for the complexities of humanity.

American Modernity and Social Capital

For others, a possible solution—a means of "opting out" of the binary system—appears in the form of Western modernity (but not *White* Western modernity) that the Zainichi characters fetishize throughout the novel. It bears repeating that both Baek Isak and Koh Hansu are marked by modernity, though for very different reasons, in their Western-style dress and manners, to which a young Sunja cannot resist being drawn. For others, the United States begins to take shape in their minds as a kind of mythic fantasy. That fascination is inherited by Sunja's extended family. Before Yumi, Mosazu's wife, passes away in a tragic car accident, she became fixated with America:

> Images of her filled his mind, and even as the mourners spoke to him, all he could hear was her practicing English phrases from her language books. No matter how many times Mosazu had said he would not emigrate to the United States, Yumi had not given up hope that one day they would live in California. Lately, she had been suggesting New York.
> "Mosazu, don't you think it would be wonderful to live in New York City or San Francisco?" she'd ask him occasionally, and it was his job to say that he couldn't decide between the two coasts.
> "There, no one would care that we are not Japanese," she'd say. *Hello, my name is Yumi Baek. This is my son, Solomon. He is three years old. How are you?* Once, when Solomon asked her what California was, she had replied, "Heaven." (348)

The West is imprinted onto Yumi's consciousness as a fantastical alterity beyond the reach of the Ikaino ghetto and Japanese racism. Conspicuously absent from their respective fantasies is the presence of a benevolent White character who confers upon them the promise of modernity beyond the colonial metropole. Instead, Yumi's fascination is initially promulgated by her encountering a Korean American missionary, Pastor John, who leads free English language classes.

English, then, signifies an alternate means of gaining social capital beyond the reach of racialized discrimination. Pastor John teaches it not as a means of proselytizing but because he "loved the sound of English words, the sounds of Americans talking," and "wanted to give this to the poor Koreans in Osaka. He wanted them to have another language that wasn't Japanese" (301). Arriving under the appealing auspices of American Christianity and a shared ethnicity, Pastor John signifies to Yumi a heretofore unimaginable subjectivity that can be achieved through an American citizenship and language. Yumi's obsession is tragically cut short, but the fixation on English continues to live through Noa, whose dream is more pragmatic but similarly dependent on Western modernity: "It had been a private dream of his to be a high school English teacher. He'd thought that if he graduated from Waseda then it might be possible to get a good job at a private school. Public schools didn't hire Koreans, but he thought the law may be changed one day" (337). While he quits his formal education because of his rigid moral code, he continues his literary studies in the nooks and crevices of his fabricated second life; but he does not leverage his education in the way that his nephew Solomon does to utterly transform his relationship to Japan and Korea through the United States.

After Noa and Yumi's aspirations are abruptly dashed, Mozasu and Solomon pick up where they left off. Material goods make up the first half of their transition to modernity; Mozasu moves his mother Sunja to Tokyo and sets her up in a comfortable home in a fashionable part of town. Even Koh Hansu is impressed by Sunja's new environs: "The furnishings resembled sets from American films—upholstered sofas, high wooden dining tables, crystal chandeliers, and leather armchairs. Hansu guessed that the family slept on beds rather than on the floor or on futons. There were no old things in the house—no traces of anything from Korea or Japan" (356). Furnished entirely in the style of American movie sets, Sunja's new home acts as a protective third national space within Tokyo. Yet material culture is only part of the equation; the second half of their transition begins with Solomon's education, which he undertakes entirely in English, speaking Japanese at home and a smattering of Korean with his grandmother. This is by design, for Mozasu has adopted Yumi's and Noa's obsession with the West. "Mozasu had chosen the international school in Yokohama because he liked the idea of Westerners. He had specific ambitions for his son: Solomon should speak perfect English as well as perfect Japanese; he should grow up among worldly, upper-class people; and ultimately, he should work for an American company in Tokyo or New York—a city Mozasu had never been to but imagined as a place where everyone was given a fair shot. He wanted his son to be an international man of the world" (409). The United States is synonymous with a raceless, classless meritocracy—all that has been denied to the Zainichi is promised by American mythmaking. The tragedy is that their family falls into a similar trap of totalizing determinism; there is little room in that image for the distributed violence of late capitalism and the paradoxes of American hegemony. Pastor John, for example, is the product of transracial adoption as a consequence of Christian evangelizing efforts in the aftermath of the Korean War and its devastating human toll, but that inconvenient fact is lost upon them.

With Solomon studying abroad at Columbia University in New York City, the Baek family legitimation project appears nearly complete—he has mastered English, lives in New York, works in the knowledge industry, and is in a long-term relationship with a Korean American woman. He joins the finance industry, working for an investment firm that eventually transfers him to its Tokyo branch. His return, with all the attendant cultural, social, and economic capital of American modernity, should be triumphant, yet he still faces familiar barriers associated with foreignness. For example, upon their arrival, Solomon rents an apartment, but since he is technically considered an alien resident, he needs a guarantor on his lease. Phoebe finds this outrageous, all the more because of Solomon's blasé response. It is a salient image of the fact that his acceptance in Japan is conditional, and dependent on the largesse of his investment firm, not on his own personhood or citizenship. Even that relationship eventually sours, as Solomon is eventually fired over a real estate deal that his father's associates assist in procuring. Kazu, Solomon's team supervisor, appears sympathetic and understanding of Solomon's position as Zainichi. Yet when he is fired, Kazu cannot help but reveal that he is also ruled by the logic of racism. "You're a nice boy, Solomon, and you will have a future in finance, but not here. If you are trying to imply that you were being discriminated against, something that Koreans tend to believe, that would be incorrect and unfair to me. If anything, you have been preferred over the natives. I like working with Koreans. Everyone knows this about me. The whole department thought that you were my pet associate. I didn't want to fire you. I just don't agree with your father's tactics" (466).

Kazu does indeed go out of his way to articulate his opposition to the injustice of Japan's treatment of the Zainichi, but he toes the company line and trades in stereotypes when profit margins are affected. It is later made clear that nothing untoward occurred, but because of the implied criminality of the Zainichi, the firm cuts ties with Solomon because it is beholden to the fears of its skittish Japanese clientele. All of Kazu's lip service toward social justice, then, is revealed to be under the thrall of capital and racist discourse. Solomon walks away understanding that he cannot escape his racialization as Zainichi through or by American capital, which, though increasingly multinational, is still ruled by local constructs of race.

Korean American Japan

I alluded to the fact that the novel consciously avoids appealing to White Western modernity; this is symptomatic of a decentering imperative in both *Pachinko* and *Moeru Sōka*. Two differences set *Pachinko* apart from the existing body of Zainichi literature—both being related to the fact that it is a Korean American novel about Zainichi Koreans. First, Min Jin Lee writes in English for an English-speaking readership; that alone colors the nature and purpose of the text as quite different, even if the actual subject matter and plot points have been covered many times over by Zainichi writers. Second, the explicit, direct introduction of Korean American discourse intimates an engagement and dialogue between the two writing communities. In chapter 2, I discussed the postwar dynamic in which Zainichi groups appealed to universal humanitarian principles through the Supreme Commander for Allied Powers (SCAP); a similar dynamic is at play in *Pachinko*, but instead of appealing to military powers, the Zainichi explicitly engage with Korean America.

On the surface, Korean America comes to mean the perfect amalgamation of Western modernity, social capital, cosmopolitanism, and citizenship. That form is mostly embodied in Solomon's girlfriend, Phoebe, whom he meets during his time at Columbia University. Drawn to her brash confidence, Solomon convinces her to come with him to Tokyo, where his investment firm has placed him at a branch office. Phoebe is in a way all that his father, mother, uncle, and Koh Hansu have ever wanted for their descendants—fluency in English, a rightful claim of citizenship, and all the attendant privileges of modernity as a means of circumventing Japanese discrimination. Yet her integration into Solomon's life in Japan appears stunted and one-sided.

Phoebe suffers from a myopia that unfortunately replicates and reinforces an either/or logic that plagues the novel—a kind of Korean American hegemony. While Phoebe may understand on an intellectual level that Solomon's family history and the peculiarities of their colonial migration are quite different from her Korean American background, this does little to assuage her misgivings about Japan. She cannot help but be upset by her encounters with the wide array of discriminatory barriers against the Zainichi; moreover, she is unable or unwilling to make sense of Solomon's positionality:

> "In America, there is no such thing as a *Kankokujin* [South Korean] or *Chosenjin* [North Korean]. Why the hell would I be a South Korean or a North Korean? That makes no sense! I was born in Seattle, and my parents came to the States when there was only one Korea," she'd shout, relating one of the bigotry anecdotes of her day. "Why does Japan still distinguish the two countries for its Korean residents who've been here for four fucking generations? You were born here. You're not a foreigner! That's insane. Your father was born here. Why are you two carrying South Korean passports? It's bizarre." (441)

From her perspective, Solomon's conditional residency is utterly offensive. Her understanding of her lineage and citizenship has never been in question—not systemically, at least—and when faced with another paradigm that frames her as a Korean American outsider, she reacts with outrage and lashes out.

Upon meeting Solomon's family—his mother Sunja and aunt Kyunghee—Phoebe proudly, and blithely, enumerates the ways in which she and her family are not Korean. Having had two working parents, Phoebe reveals that she grew up eating fast food and ate Korean meals only at restaurants—her mother never learned to cook, much to Sunja and Kyunghee's dismay. Nevertheless, they are curious about her and quietly observant; to her credit, Sunja takes Phoebe's proclamations in stride, thinking to herself, "If she didn't cook, then so what? If she took good care of Solomon, then nothing else should matter, though she hoped that Phoebe wanted children" (457). Explaining further, Phoebe draws a portrait of her immediate and extended family's mixed-race marriages, as if to make a point about America's racial progressivism:

"My aunts and uncles are married to non-Koreans. My brother and sisters married ethnically Korean people, but they're Americans like me. My older brother-in-law, the lawyer, speaks fluent Portuguese but no Korean; he grew up in Brazil. America is full of people like that. . . . I have aunts and uncles by marriage who are white, black, Dutch, Jewish, Filipino, Mexican, Chinese, Puerto Rican, and, let's see, there's one Korean American uncle and three Korean American aunts. I have a lot of cousins. Everyone's mixed," she added, smiling at the older women wearing spotless white aprons, who were paying such careful attention to what she was saying that it looked as if their minds were taking notes. (456)

It is quite a utopic vision of multicultural America that she conjures, but she elides its complicated and painful struggles. And it goes unspoken that one of the structural factors that her relatives need not worry about is citizenship upon birth, a happenstance and fluke of history that the Zainichi do not take for granted. What is lost upon Phoebe is the fact that for the Zainichi, retention of their ties to their ethnic heritage was something that blood was spilled over. Without citizenship, all they had was their increasingly ephemeral and elusive sense of Koreanness, lest they be assimilated into Japan with nothing left of their ethnic heritage. Racialization still occurs, whether Phoebe recognizes it or not, but at different registers and by different mechanisms. The ease with which she can disavow her Koreanness is a consequence of a racialization system that does not seek to erase her ethnicity—a context that is completely at odds with that of Solomon's family.

Ultimately, Solomon and Phoebe go their separate ways. The final step in his transformation would have been to marry Phoebe and become an American citizen, thereby completing his family's intergenerational project. But he realizes that he does not want to give up on Japan:

Ever since they got here, either she had changed or his feelings for her had changed. Hadn't he been leaning toward asking her to marry him? Yet now, when she put forward the idea of marrying for citizenship, he realized that he didn't want to become an American. It made sense for him to do so; it would have made his father happy. Was it better to be an American than a Japanese? He knew Koreans who had become naturalized Japanese, and it made sense to do so, but he didn't want to do that now, either. Maybe one day. She was right; it was weird that he was born in Japan and had a South Korean passport. He couldn't rule out getting naturalized. Maybe another Korean wouldn't understand that, but he didn't care anymore. (477)

Here Solomon begins to claim Japan on his own terms rather than someone else's. Phoebe's Korean American entitlement and confidence intoxicate him while he in the United States, but when she is placed in Japan, her history is incongruous with his own. Instead, as Zainichi intellectuals have theorized, Solomon discovers a third way beyond the Korea-Japan binary and the US bypass: he decides to stay and enter the pachinko business, reversing the decades of shame and extralegal associations, to forge his own path.

Lee's interest in the Zainichi was always comparatively oriented. That is, she was fascinated by the respective racializations of Koreans in the US and Japanese contexts, which implicitly underscored the malleability of race. Indeed, in interviews she confesses that her interest in the Zainichi stemmed from her complete ignorance about their existence—they are not part of the Korean American diasporic consciousness even though there are intimately shared colonial and immigrant histories. A profile in the *New York Times* notes that the seed for *Pachinko* "was planted in 1989, when, as a student at Yale, she attended a talk by a Protestant missionary who had spent time among the zainichi. Until then, she said, she had never heard of this branch of the Korean diaspora. Growing up in the United States, she was used to Koreans being viewed as hardworking and upwardly mobile, a model American minority. But many zainichi, she was surprised to discover, languished at the bottom rungs of Japan's socioeconomic ladder."[19] In other words, Lee's "conventional" path toward upward mobility as the daughter of merchant class immigrants at an elite university was at odds with the reality of an entire subset of the same diaspora being relegated to the underclass in a similarly wealthy country. While Solomon's decision to return to the pachinko business may be read as a tacit critique—that the Korean American model is not a viable solution for the Zainichi—it also uncannily parallels the plot of Lee's first novel, *Free Food for Millionaires*, in which several Korean American characters in New York's finance industry spurn hypercapitalism for more fulfilling ventures. Solomon's turn could be read merely as his coming to terms with the unique history and situatedness of the Zainichi, but I suspect that it has another agenda: Lee's novel, while ostensibly centered on Zainichi history and discourse, explores and integrates Korean America as well. That is, *Pachinko* is the latest in a long line of Korean American texts to approach the legacy of Japanese colonialism—in this case, just more visibly and directly. It is, as I have argued in my discussions of *East Goes West* (chapter 1) and *A Gesture Life* (chapter 3), an effort to make visible that which has been rendered invisible by immigration history, strategic alliances, and pan-Asian American solidarity.

Lee's novel, introducing an entirely new world of the Korean diaspora to the general reading public, has had a meteoric ascent that appears unprecedented. But if we expand our outlook globally instead of restricting ourselves to an anglophone readerly world, *Pachinko* is the latest novel to dwell on the subject of Zainichi selfhood; its main contribution to the body of literature is its framing by a Korean American writer explicitly reaching outward to Zainichi Korea. But even as part of a dialogue, *Pachinko* is not the first. It is late to the conversation by some twenty years. The distinction of being first goes to Kim Masumi's *Moeru Sōka*.

Zainichi America

The 1992 Los Angeles Uprising casts a long shadow. In Asian American literature, the trauma of *Sa-I-Gu* would be reflected by Chang-rae Lee's *Native Speaker*, Nina Revoyr's *Southland*, and many other works. However, the Uprising was not just a domestic affair; its images multiplied and circulated globally. That narrative would wend its way from California over the Pacific to land in Zainichi Korea, where Kim Masumi, who had spent time in Los Angeles, would attempt to capture those tensions through a Zainichi perspective. *Moeru Sōka* integrates Korean American racial discourse into Zainichi Korea, by way of decentering both Whiteness and Japaneseness as social, cultural and political dominants. Instead, *Moeru Sōka* navigates thorny questions of race and racialization by foregrounding two very different contexts—Zainichi Korea and Korean America, complicated further by Black America against the backdrop of White supremacy.

Taking place over the span of a single day during the 1992 Los Angeles Riots, *Moeru Sōka* jumps back and forth between the United States and Japan, all the while traveling via that most Los Angelean of means—the car. The Zainichi Korean protagonist, Ryoko, drives with her Korean American friend Mi-ryon as they weave through traffic and rioters from Koreatown,

Little Tokyo, to a South Central convenience store, Sōka (Grass House), owned and operated by Mi-ryon's husband, Kim. Ryoko confesses to Mi-ryon that she thinks she is pregnant, and they discuss Ryoko's plans for naturalization so that she and her husband can access the privileges of Japanese citizenship, to which Mi-ryon and Kim object. Permeating the novel are reflections of the tensions between Korean Americans and Black Americans, who are represented somewhat two-dimensionally as rioters, homeless people, and store customers. The novella ends with the fiery destruction of the store, hence the title "The Burning Grass House."

Just as the pachinko game operates as a metaphor for the positionality of the Zainichi, the titular Sōka has a similar metaphorical function. It is no accident that Kim situates the narrative through a common first-generation Korean American merchant class experience; it is a phenomenon that was seared into the collective consciousness on a global scale by the mass media during the Los Angeles Riots. A running thread throughout the novel is Ryoko's question about the origins of the store name, since it recalls the instability of the straw house of the *Three Little Pigs* folktale. At several points she suggests changing the name to Brick House (J: *Renga no ie* [煉瓦の家]) to better signify stability. The store, then, can be read ambiguously as a site of opportunity and prosperity or as a fragile construction that is the object of hostility, mirroring Mi-ryon and Kim's place in the United States as Korean Americans and Ryoko's own conditional acceptance in Japan as a Zainichi Korean. But the store as a discursive site for racialization cannot ignore the forceful presence of Blackness, which is integral to Ryoko's self-signification. Located in South Central Los Angeles, the store underscores the dynamic leading to the eruption of tensions between the Korean and Black communities during the L.A. Riots. While the store is the couple's livelihood and the economic means for Kim's immigrating to the United States, it does not necessarily have the local Black community's best interests at heart, and that tension is felt most palpably in the events leading up to the novel's dénouement.[20]

Citizen Takamoto

Several modes of racialization bring into stark relief the difference between Zainichi Korea and Korean America. Ryoko's central preoccupation is with citizenship; she believes she may be pregnant, and she has filed the paperwork for naturalizing to Japanese citizenship, just as her husband has already done. As discussed in chapter 2, naturalization for the Zainichi is a freighted political matter; to many first- and second-generation Zainichi, who have resisted colonial-era and more insidious contemporary pressures to assimilate and erase their Korean selves, naturalization is tantamount to betrayal. The pressure to retain her South Korean passport comes not only from her friends but from her family as well. Her father initially opposed her marriage because her husband had already naturalized; her compromise is to wait until he passes away so that he will not have to witness his daughter's betrayal.[21] However, Ryoko has aspirations to teach at a national university, which will not hire noncitizens, and she worries that her remaining a foreign national in Japan may alienate her from her husband and unborn child. Given the fraught history of Zainichi in Japan, it would make sense for her Zainichi friends and family to have strong opinions, but the novel curiously has some of the strongest voices of opposition come from Kim and Mi-ryon, two Korean American characters who have already naturalized in the United States. In an exchange between Kim and Ryoko, he criticizes her decision to naturalize:

"I was back in Japan."
"What, again?"
Kim sliced meat and gestured with his chin at the chair at the back. I passed alongside the refrigerator and entered the deli. I took a deep breath. I wanted to calm the tiny storm brewing inside of me, swallow it down. Even though I felt like I had something caught my throat, I still felt that I would gain something here.
"I've got to change registration every five years. But this time was the last. I'm going to be Japanese like my husband."
The English word for "naturalization" didn't come to mind. Maybe I deliberately chose not to remember it. I tapped the back of my head twice but the word wouldn't come. Willie Nelson's "Georgia Oh My Town," drifted from the radio. I sat down on the black stool. Kim, silent, opened the refrigerator door and picked up a large piece of beef marbled with fat in a way that made it look like a map. He unfolded the cold meat over a white cutting board on top of a stainless-steel table in front of the display case. On the wall, posters with dozens of types of meat—cows, sheep, pigs, birds, and so on—flashed before my eyes.

"In other words, you've sold out your country."

I stared in surprise because Kim had used the English word "sold." Kim clenched his teeth and stabbed at the meat, center mass. (127–28)

The preceding exchange contains multiple layers of projection. First, Kim and Ryoko's discussion is mediated through the preparation of consumer goods—meat products. In a later passage, Kim awkwardly lays out a thesis on racial essentialism by remarking on the differences between beef and pork as metaphors for being Korean, Japanese, or American; the store and its products function as a discursive site for racial construction. Second, Kim and Mi-ryon's opposition to Ryoko's plan is clearly a projection of second-generation Zainichi attitudes toward naturalizing. In general, Korean American immigrants do not share similar sentiments regarding naturalization even if the country in question is Japan. It is an awkward license taken by the author, but it underscores the dynamic that the text builds between Ryoko and the Korean American characters. Kim and Mi-ryon's racialization is ever present because of their ethnicity; Ryoko has to deliberately choose to make an effort to preserve her racialization. Third, the entire exchange is conducted in English, for Ryoko does not speak Korean fluently, even if the text is in Japanese. Tellingly, she cannot seem to remember the English word *naturalization* (J: *kika* [帰化]). In fact, numerous occasions of linguistic displacement plague Ryoko, compounding and undergirding her inability to effectively communicate her positionality to her friends and strangers.[22] Their discussion of Korean and Japanese nationality and citizenship is mediated through a third language and national site that is undergoing its own racially inflected crisis—an environment that is rife with opportunities for miscommunication.

Passing for Japanese

This fear is made tangible at several points through the narrative when Ryoko, who presents as Japanese, has to correct people's assumptions or finds herself unable to articulate herself when the situation occurs. At multiple points throughout the text, Ryoko is mistaken for Japanese or Chinese, not only by African Americans, but by Koreans as well: "Pushed from behind, I ended up stepping on the foot of a woman in front of me. As soon I said, 'Excuse me,' another woman in front of me, this one with a purple scarf, turned and scolded me in Korean. Flustered, I apologized, '*mian hamnida*' [K: I'm sorry]. 'Oh—yes, that's okay,' she replied, nodding, and, staring at me from the corner of her eye, asked, 'Chinese?' A husky voice from the crowd asked again, 'Chinese?' I felt her voice expanding and reverberating, making its way through the crowd" (147). Ryoko's speaking English alienates her from the Korean woman whose foot she steps on, but the woman's demeanor changes when Ryoko switches to Korean to apologize. Even so, her accent betrays her, and the woman begins to interrogate her, assuming that she is ethnically Chinese rather than Korean. For her, it is a curious turn, for in Japan she can easily pass for Japanese. But in this third national space, she is misidentified time and again—she cannot even claim her Korean heritage adequately because in the US citizenship is not the primary qualifier for racialization; the entire citizenship apparatus that is so important in Japan is secondary in America. Therefore, Ryoko has to find another means of asserting her Korean identity—she has to forcefully verbalize and claim her Koreanness in English.

Speech and language, then, take an outsized role in Ryoko's navigating American racialization. It is a fraught medium, for each linguistic turn results in Ryoko finding others projecting onto her body. During an exchange with Kim and Tommy, an elderly Korean woman overhears Ryoko speaking Japanese and then confronts her, in the same language:

"You're Japanese, aren't you?" asked a husky voice from behind. When I turned around, I saw a small elderly Asian woman holding a blue basket.

She wore a faded orange T-shirt and a light brown visor. I couldn't see her facial expression because of the backlighting from the store entryway. The old woman seemed to live in the silence.

"You're Japanese," she repeated, her tone a bit sharper. "No, I—" I started to say, but the words stuck in my throat. How can I explain this in Japanese? An overpowering odor of Chinese herbs and fermented medicine pierced my nostrils. Her strong Japanese dialect and her countless clay-like brown winkles—they looked like they'd been carved by tiny knives—told her story. The woman looked at me, with shimmering black eyes contrasted against her white hair.

"Koreans my generation know Japanese. You know what I mean, right? A long time ago, in the next village over a young girl was taken to your country against her will."

> I tried to say something. But it was like there was a hole where my
> throat should've been. Only my breath went in and out from the back of
> my mouth. I search for words and my naked tongue wrestled with the im-
> possible from between my lips. "Su—," "ha—," I gasped meaningless noise
> from my cottonmouth. (153–54)

When accused, Ryoko finds herself paralyzed, unable to speak, and must
bear the burden of the old woman's animus. She cannot answer in Korean,
it is not clear English would be effective, and replying in Japanese would
only confirm the old woman's suspicions. The encounter underscores the
invisibility of citizenship and the determinism of language. What will happen when she cannot claim to have South Korean citizenship? If she speaks
Japanese—and not Korean—and also has Japanese citizenship along with
the rest of her family, is she not Japanese in every sense? Does that mean
she cannot credibly claim solidarity or kinship with the Korean woman
who still suffers from the trauma of colonialism? It is in this middle passage
while she transitions between nations that Ryoko suddenly finds herself
unable to deny Japan and claim Korea. Instead, she has to silently accept
the elderly woman's accusation on behalf of a country that also keeps her
at arm's length.

When interacting with her Black customers, Ryoko yearns for racialization without the option of passing. Absent phenotypical markers of difference, she concludes that to hold on to her ethnic sense of self she will have
to make a conscious effort, lest it slip through her fingers.

> I absentmindedly watched a black man with his daughter from behind bul-
> letproof glass. Her dad wore a white T-shirt and had a shaved head. He was
> small, but his muscular figure looked like a boxer's. Wearing tight jeans,
> he picked out this or that treat for his daughter. The daughter, who wore a
> pink ribbon in her hair and made one think of a peeled chestnut, happily
> bounced around her father. It's amazing that it's perfectly natural for black
> skin to bear black skin. They'll never doubt their genetics and bloodline.
> If the girl went to Japan and, for example, called herself Takamoto Ryoko,
> who would have any doubt of her lineage? That girl's daughter—no, grand-
> daughter's granddaughter. How many generations on Japanese soil would it
> take for her lineage to fade? I absentmindedly rested my chin in my hands
> and began to spiral downward. If your outward appearance is the same,
> then you have to deliberately preserve something like your ethnic blood.

The more you're not obviously foreign, the more important it becomes to
protect it. (151)

Faced with the American context of Black racialization, Ryoko comes to a
more comprehensive understanding of herself and positionality as Zainichi
in Japan. Yet her frame of reference is distinctly Japanese, importing discourse on generational bloodlines rather than phenotype to understand
Black racialization. She views African Americans through an assimilationist
logic, whether consciously or not; the hypothetical Ryoko in her scenario,
it is given, would eventually "dilute" into the general Japanese populace.
From behind the bulletproof glass, she spies on the Black customers as if
they were specimens, making little effort to conceptualize the Black experience in America. Thus even this moment of intersectional cognizance is
decidedly one-sided; she perpetuates the dynamic of incomprehension that
haunts the entire novel.

Passing is not without its advantages. In each case, her passing is something that is projected upon her, without a conscious decision on her part.
But Ryoko's ambivalence toward passing for Japanese comes to a head when
she and Mi-ryon are confronted by a young Black man who accuses them of
being in sympathy with White supremacy.

> The young man pulled out a gun with his right hand.
> "I won't let up on you Koreans. My brother was in one of your stores
> last week—"
> Mi-ryon interrupted him.
> "—*I'm* real *Korean but she is Japanese.*"
> She spoke quietly but clearly. I tried looking at her face. But my body
> wouldn't budge. The pounding of my heartbeat grew louder and louder
> until I heard a buzzing in my ears and all the noise of the outside world
> suddenly dissipated. The youth stood slack-jawed with a confused expres-
> sion on his face. . . .
> . . . I was determined to say something this time—what I couldn't say to
> the old lady in the store. I opened my mouth. Took a deep breath. But in
> the next instant, I found myself pulling back under his questioning gaze.
> "—Japanese?"
> He asked, furrowing his brow and turning his head. When I looked
> closely, I saw that the bluish whites of his eyes were startlingly clear. He
> turned the gun over in his hand, hunched his shoulders, and looked us

over. Behind him, I saw a large black cat running into the burning liquor
store.

I put on my clear raincoat and trembled in shame.

"Sometimes we went to a restaurant, Aoi, in Little Tokyo, and they always treated us well. They didn't treat us like criminals, like the Koreans."

He looked straight at me while he spoke. (168–69)

Their confrontation brings to bear simmering tensions in Los Angeles.
After Mi-ryon explains that Ryoko is Japanese, the young man recalls his
experience with Japanese Americans, who treated him and his friends well,
in contrast to Koreans, who looked upon them with suspicion. Ryoko,
who herself has been guilty of racial profiling in the store, chooses to pass
for Japanese to reap the benefit of their generosity. What is curious is that
White supremacy is largely absent in the form of White characters, with
the exception of police officers, who wander the periphery. Whiteness and
Japaneseness are decentered and relegated to the background, but they are
ever present, coloring each interaction. Mi-ryon's denial of Ryoko's Koreanness, in this case, could be read ambiguously—does she do so because
she wants to protect Ryoko, or is this simply a declaration of a belief she
has always harbored? Is this a moment of imperial Japan's triumph, or is it
White supremacy's?

Pachinko and *Moeru Sōka* occupy related but distinct histories and
contexts to step beyond what has become naturalized—what I mean by
diasporic minority transposition. In a way, they operate as works of speculative fiction, complete with intrepid explorers stumbling across an alien
landscape only to come to a greater understanding of themselves. Kim's
rendering of a distinctly American episode of national trauma expands the
scope so that Sōka's destruction not only operates as the site of racial animus
between Korean and Black Americans but defamiliarizes Japanese racial discourse as a means of reconceptualizing Zainichi Korean subjectivity. The
function of enterprise becomes all the clearer when we examine how these
sites are depicted. Whereas in *Pachinko* the Baek family business operates as
a redemptive scaffold, Sōka's fiery end bespeaks the tragedy of the American
experiment. The irony is rich; Min Jin Lee, who comes from a post-*Sa-
I-Gu* merchant class family, integrates a distinct optimism that stems from
a projection of Korean America's economic and racial recuperation onto
Solomon and the Zainichi. Kim Masumi, writing shortly after the Riots,

does not have the advantage of the same distance, and her more ambiguous conclusion reflects the calamity that defined the Zainichi for so long. Their respective renderings of the store and the pachinko parlor, then, in addition to acting as discursive sites of racialization, underscore the distinctiveness of Korean America and Zainichi Korea.

Considering two novels, published twenty years apart, in relation to one another uncovers a hitherto undiscovered channel of communication. There are major differences between the purpose and reception of the novels, of course. *Pachinko* stormed the American literary world with its 2017 debut and gained enough momentum to penetrate several layers of the American reading public. But much of the critical reception frames *Pachinko* as a largely Korean historio-ethnographic portraiture, with little commentary on the significance of a Korean American author engaging with Zainichi racial discourse and history, let alone its Asian American context. In contrast, *Moeru Sōka* did not receive similar levels of fanfare in 1997, and I suspect it was mainly absorbed as a literary witness to an American tragedy. Taken in isolation, the novels' respective misreadings are perfectly logical, despite American and Japanese racial discourse and history making disruptive, even violent defamiliarizing appearances. Their continued isolation is the consequence of disciplinary primacies and the disaggregation of transpacific minority discourses.

Described as diasporic minority transpositions, the two novels are in fact projections of each other. *Pachinko* and *Moeru Sōka* take liberties, whether consciously or not, that belie their conceits. They occupy another minor space made possible only by the intimacies of colonial history that gives room for imagining and wearing an entirely different racial history. And they do so, having shunted aside the majority dominants for an intimate portraiture of their appositional neighbor. They offer a kind of revisionist or speculative history that is not exactly fantasy or fantastical, but one that seeks to integrate and weave together despite a painful history of misreadings, misrecognitions, and clumsy assumptions. A slant rhyme. Repetition with a difference—or defamiliarization, to make visible those constructs that have been naturalized. These texts recognize that race is not constructed in isolation and is in a constant state of upheaval and change; most importantly, they engage with other sites of racial discourse to create a montage that they may introduce to a broader readership.

Zainichi, Korean, American

Beneath this image, it is possible to see Hiro's eyes, which look Asian.
They are from his mother, who is Korean by way of Nippon.

—Neal Stephenson, *Snow Crash*

ACTOR AND COMEDIAN Fred Armisen of *Saturday Night Live* and *Port-landia* was proud of his unique show business heritage. In interviews, he enjoyed sharing how his paternal grandfather, Masami Kuni, was a famous dancer in Japan who enjoyed a long, storied career as both performer and choreographer, traveling to perform in Italy and Germany during the 1930s and '40s. It was in Germany that Kuni had an affair with Armisen's grand-mother, who gave birth to his father, making Armisen one-quarter Japanese. But it wasn't until Armisen participated in Henry Louis Gates Jr.'s Pub-lic Broadcasting Service (PBS) television series *Finding Your Roots* that he learned the unsettling fact that his grandfather had volunteered to perform for the Nazis—the first in a series of startling revelations (figure 11).

While it was true, teased Gates, that Kuni had offered to entertain the German troops, according to a memo from the Office of Strategic Services he did so while operating as a spy for Japan. Furthermore, another layer of subterfuge was at play—Masami Kuni was not his grandfather's birth name; he was born Pak Yeong-in in Ulsan, Korea. Kuni, it turned out, had adopted a Japanese name during the colonial period after migrating from Korea to Tokyo to pursue his secondary and postsecondary education. Vis-ibly stunned, Armisen exclaimed, "I'm Korean? . . . I have so many phone calls to make."[1]

While novel to Fred Armisen and presumably much of PBS's viewership, the twists and turns of Masami Kuni's story should, by this point, strike the reader as remarkably familiar. For one, Kuni's migration from Korea to the metropoles of the Axis powers mirrors Younghill Kang's travels from Seoul to New York—also by way of Tokyo—driven by a hunger for modernity. Second, Armisen's surprise at learning of his ethnic heritage uncannily echoes the reactions of many second-generation Zainichi whose parents hid their ethnicity from their children. Recall, for example, Yi Yang-ji's similarly shocking discovery of her Korean heritage, which led to a lifelong search for kinship that would elude her, as evidenced in her novels. Third, Armisen's grandfather's adoption of a Japanese identity, lasting until his death in Los Angeles in 2007, parallels Doc Hata's journey in *A Gesture Life*. Even after liberation and a subsequent move to the United States, colonial logic was so all-encompassing that both Hata and Kuni preserved their Japanese identities in America. Interestingly, Kuni's Korean heritage was common knowledge in Japan and the broader art world, but he never saw fit to share that information with his son or his grandson; the US would be the final stage for the completion of Kuni's transformation. And the artifice would have held, were it not for PBS and Gates's work as a public intellectual.

Perhaps it's coincidental that Kuni went into a performance-related field, masquerading as Japanese and feigning alliance with Nazi Germany, all the while surreptitiously passing along intelligence to Japan as he practiced modern dance. Perhaps it's also coincidental that Armisen, who

FIGURE 11   Fred Armisen and Henry Louis Gates Jr. discuss his grandfather, Masami Kuni, in *Finding Your Roots* (Public Broadcasting Service, 2017).

presents as ethnically ambiguous, has similarly chameleon-like skills as an actor, having portrayed characters who were Black, Middle Eastern, Latinx, and White. Yet what makes their performances fascinating are the multiple levels of passing present in them—Kuni's performance being offstage and after the fact, and Armisen's work on *Saturday Night Live* being a comedic caricature. The tensions of their performing race make for complex, richer viewing—a tapestry that Kuni denied himself and that could be appreciated by the wider public only after those transpacific relationships had come into view.

This isn't to say that Fred Armisen presents or self-identifies as Asian American, let alone Korean American. But his connection to his grandfather was and is clearly important to his sense of self as an actor. And for much of his life, that relationship was uncomplicated—he shared Kuni's entertainment genes, he marveled at their physical resemblance, and, in his mind, their connection even explained his affinity for Japanese cuisine. But Gates's revelation, in Armisen's words, "changes everything" and makes his story all the more textured, a fascinating tale long hidden because of the disconnect between Asian American and Asian bodies of discourse. It's easier and simpler for Asian American literary subject formation to rely on a clear delineation between departure and arrival. But that effectively effaces an entire historical and artistic dimension that sacrifices nuance for the sake of expediency.

After Kuni ascended the American stage, his unwieldy colonial history was molded into a familiar, even comforting, immigrant narrative of arrival. But all three dimensions of Kuni's self-transformation are equally important—Korean, Japanese, and, later, Asian American.[2] The most fascinating—and mystifying—part of the story, to me, is how easily Armisen and his family could have learned about Kuni's ethnic heritage had they the will or inclination. But there was no impulse to revisit that history from the American side; and until Gates intervened, the story would have remained half complete. The family's lack of curiosity was determined by the narrative of forward momentum and finality of the United States as the site of modernity. If, instead, the US is resituated as one panel in our migratory triptych with its delightfully kaleidoscopic colors, we may more easily glean how it mediates minor subject formations. Thankfully, Gates's intervention afforded Armisen the chance to reconfigure his relationship with Japan and Korea, as well as Korean America, for a more expansive dialogue—in much the same vein as the minority transpositional conversations in *Pachinko* and *Moeru Sōka*. Liberated from a homeland-destination binary, Armisen could revel in his grandfather's multiple dimensions—and, by extension, his own.

At their best, art and literature metonymically echo the complexities and contradictions of a chaotic and nebulous life lived to challenge axioms that have ossified over time. Yet when their contours become familiar and disciplinary borders harden, there is a temptation, as the prism through which history is viewed, for them to operate as reductive metanarratives, smoothing out the jagged edges and splinters of life. The rift between Zainichi and Korean American literature perpetuates a parallel simplification and incompleteness. Instead, Asian American literature should interrogate its past and present intertexual and intersectional relationship with Asian and American colonial and postcolonial literatures and legacies. I would contend that the intimacy between the United States, Japan, and Korea in the formation of Zainichi and Korean American literature is made all the richer for their tensions and relationality, which deserve a full account.

I began this book with a somewhat misleading assessment—that Asian American studies has lacked engagement with Asian studies. Recently, the transpacific turn has produced a body of work that is increasingly inclusive, including Denise Cruz's *Transpacific Femininities*, Crystal Baik's *Reencounters*, and Jinah Kim's *Postcolonial Grief*, which are part of a conversation that interrogates the lasting effects of war and trauma from an Asian American perspective. My contribution to that conversation is the formulation of a structured means to pair literary traditions through mediating sites, for which there is increasing demand. For example, Viet Thanh Nguyen's *The Committed* takes place in France, after his protagonist has journeyed from Vietnam to the US and back to Vietnam again—a direct overture to the Vietnamese French diaspora. There are opportunities here for growth in comparative literary studies in English and French of Vietnamese American fiction and Vietnamese French authors such as Linda Le.[3] There's also opportunity for that work to be gathered—at the risk of fabricating another disciplinary barrier—under the banner of a mediated and minor transpacific studies that employs a conscious triangulating of imperial literary legacies, coming from Asian American and ethnic studies writ large, and their minor subjects. The US-Vietnam-France formulation is the most intuitively analogous construction, but I speculate that there are connections to be made with a US-Japan-Brazil comparative study through the works of Karen Tei Yamashita. Area studies scholars may be working to introduce minor literatures to anglophone readership, but Asian American studies has an opportunity to take the lead and round out the conversation to make the minor transpacific.

What I've constructed in this book is a framework in which these literary bodies and sites are compelled to consider one another in a structured— perhaps even overdetermined—manner to compensate for disciplinary and structural neglect. It's this framing that demands us to reconsider Younghill Kang's work in light of his complicated, paradoxical relationship to Japan and Japanese culture in his Americanization project, and to explore how the intergenerational trauma of war and colonialism haunts contemporary Korean American fiction vis-à-vis Chang-rae Lee's *A Gesture Life*. Moreover, where it may not seem obvious, the same framework calls on scholars to meditate upon Asian American and African American racial discourse and racialization through transpacific cultural mediation in Zainichi literature such as Kaneshiro Kazuki's *GO*, or to interrogate how the diasporic sojourn in Yi Yang-ji's *Yuhi* creates space for a comparative minority identity. Perhaps those intersecting lines will become self-evident and obvious, as works such as Min Jin Lee's *Pachinko* and Kim Masumi's *Moeru Sōka* begin to reach out more explicitly to transpose and occupy minority positions and to demand critical reckoning—and I imagine that call will be even more explicit with the *Pachinko* television adaptation.[4] Until then, this book pauses at moments of transition to self-consciously dwell on the inarticulable and ineffable, and to make the invisible visible, for richer consumption and inquiry.

Notes

Introduction: Triangulating Fictions

Epigraphs: Supreme Command for Allied Powers, "Status of Koreans in Japan," 3; Y. Kang, "Memories of a Zainichi Korean Childhood," 8; Chuh, *Imagine Otherwise*, 9.

1. This list is by no means exhaustive. Comfort women memorials exist in Hong Kong, Canada, Australia, and Germany, with more planned.

2. A. Nguyen, "Supreme Court Declines Case."

3. A prototype of the statue was displayed in an exhibit, *Hyogen no fujiyu ten* (Exhibition of unfreedom of expression) at Gallery Furuto, which was designed to test freedom of speech. All pieces in the exhibit had been previously removed or censored. See Yoshida and Nagata, "Self-Censorship Is Biggest Threat."

4. In *Hiroshima Traces*, Lisa Yoneyama performs an incisive reading of the memorial's politics and history as a discursive national site interpolating national, international, ethnic and racial tensions.

5. Numerous scholars and writers have tackled the subject of comfort women at length, including Nora Okja Keller, Chang-rae Lee, Kandice Chuh, and Lisa Yoneyama. My discussion of the memorials concentrates on their straddling multiple lines of political tension in locations that are geographically illegible.

6. For a more expansive political and performative reading of comfort women statues, see chapter 4, "Performances of Care," in Son, *Embodied Reckonings*, 147–75.

7. Yoneyama, *Hiroshima Traces*, 153.

8. Yoneyama, *Hiroshima Traces*, 158.

9. The site is not without its contradictions. Yoneyama writes,

Yet at the same time these narratives and practices of memorialization constitute contradictory elements in the production of subjectivities, thereby making distinctions within the group as well as within each individual. On the one hand, the Korean memorial and its discursive processes differentiate nationally and ethnically those who claim ownership to the memories specific to this icon and those who feel a sense of belonging to the mnemonic community built around the history shared specifically as Koreans. On the other hand, the narratives and practices of memorialization inevitably shape diverse *zainichi* consciousness about history, ethnicity, and nationality—in other words, about those elements that cannot be entirely subsumed by the totality of collective identity or by what are imagined to be shared communal experiences. (*Hiroshima Traces*, 154)

10. Authored by Rep. Honda, House Resolution 121 explicitly calls for the Government of Japan to take action on four points: it

(1) should formally acknowledge, apologize, and accept historical responsibility in a clear and unequivocal manner for its Imperial Armed Forces' coercion of young women into sexual slavery, known to the world as comfort women, during its colonial and wartime occupation of Asia and the Pacific Islands from the 1930s through the duration of World War II;

(2) would help to resolve recurring questions about the sincerity and status of prior statements if the Prime Minister of Japan were to make such an apology as a public statement in his official capacity;

(3) should clearly and publicly refute any claims that the sexual enslavement and trafficking of the comfort women for the Japanese Imperial Armed Forces never occurred; and

(4) should educate current and future generations about this horrible crime while following the recommendations of the international community with respect to the comfort women. (Honda, "H.Res. 121")

11. While in interviews Representative Honda explicitly has drawn parallels between the abuses of state-sanctioned violence and involuntary confinement to his experience in a Japanese internment camp during World War II, Lisa Yoneyama critiques his disavowal of Japan as a performance of White orthodoxy: "Similarly, to publicly disavow suspect Asian origins through the reiteration of the nation's orthodox Cold War American war memories—of not only the war against imperial Japan but the hot wars the United States has waged in and against different Asian countries—has been one intelligible gesture available to anyone in this precarious position to effectively prove Asian 'assimilability' to America. In this regard, Mike Honda's initiatives for California's Joint Resolution and related bills in the Congress

pertaining to Japanese war crimes can be read superficially as yet another rehearsal of a very familiar performance." Yoneyama, *Cold War Ruins*, 164. See also Honda, "Time for Abe to Apologize."

12. Yoneyama, *Hiroshima Traces*, 163.

13. *Zainichi* is shorthand for "Resident Korean in Japan," or "Korean Living in Japan." The complete term is *zainichi chōsenjin* or *zainichi kankokujin*, depending on citizenship (North or South Korean).

14. This study is by no means novel in that regard. King-Kok Cheung's *Chinese American Literature without Borders* takes a similar approach, which she herself explicitly characterizes as an answer to Ali Behdad's critical call: "In bridging the two disciplines through an inter-cultural and bilingual approach to Chinese American writing, this book follows Behdad's recommendation (in "What Can American Studies and Comparative Literature Learn") and answers the call for American studies to become newly transnational. It looks to and from both the United States and China to reveal the multiple engagements of American-born and Sinophone writers." Cheung, *Chinese American Literature*, 1.

15. I borrow "minor transnationalism" from Françoise Lionnet and Shu-mei Shih's book with that title. Moreover, this is an extension of a turn in Asian American literary studies that has been under way since the 1990s. Specifically, critics recognized the importance of Asia in Asian American literature to circumvent scholarly provincialism. Kandice Chuh writes: "Critically acknowledging the material effectivity of multiply located histories and chronologies . . . means recognizing the limitations of knowledge produced by distancing 'America' from 'Asia' as limitations that do ideological work." Chuh, *Imagine Otherwise*, 111.

16. In *Cold War Ruins*, Lisa Yoneyama notes that the construction of a monolithic Asian America serves a broader, conventionally nationalist narrative about "modernity, liberalism, colonialism, and postcoloniality that are embedded in Cold War epistemologies." However, if we were to resist and disaggregate Asian America, we might find the space for "Asian/Americans as new subjects of justice animated by the power invested in them as American citizen-subjects" to "illuminate contradictions of transnationality within the American civic sphere in such a way that they hold out the possibility of a radical politicization of justice and a critique of Americanization." Yoneyama, *Cold War Ruins*, 152. Similarly, I argue that articulating an Asian America that can account for internal tensions can help in producing a more comprehensive picture.

17. *The Intimacies of Four Continents*, Lisa Lowe's ambitious and far-ranging study, similarly recognizes the disciplinary traditions that have occluded the potential for interesting work recuperating neglected connections: "What we know of these links and intimacies is shaped by existing fields and by our methods of

disciplinary study. Europe is rarely studied in relation to the Caribbean or Latin America, and U.S. history is more often separated from studies of the larger Americas. Work on comparative U.S. racial formation is still at odds with American history, which disconnects the study of slavery from immigration studies of Asians and Latinos; the histories of gender, sexuality, and women [are] often separated from the study of race." Lowe, *Intimacies of Four Continents*, 37. In answer, she is chiefly concerned with tracing, through archival study, the formation of liberal humanism and the various forms of cultural and political imperialism that carried ideas through different geographic sites and their people in Europe, Asia, the Caribbean, and the Americas. A mediated minor transpacific, while specific to the histories and artifacts in the US, Japan, and Korea, is broadly allied with her formulation of "intimacy."

18. Numerous scholars have noted the structural tensions between Asian and Asian American studies. Asian American studies emerged largely from student activism and inclusionary social justice movements (Chuh, *Imagine Otherwise*, 5), whereas Asian and area studies were a Cold War response by the state; and increasingly, both disciplines are being funded by corporate interests. Benitez and Sears, "Passionate Attachments," 153; Chuh and Shimakawa, introduction to *Orientations*, 7–9.

19. V. Nguyen and Hoskins, introduction to Hoskins and Nguyen, *Transpacific Studies*, 19.

20. Asian American literary scholars Elaine Kim and Lisa Lowe call for dialogue, writing that they "believe there will need to be a variety of connections between Asian studies and Asian American studies." Elaine Kim and Lowe, *Positions*, viii. In a similar vein, Asian studies scholar Leo Ching argues that area studies suffers from rigid disciplinary boundaries, occluding meaningful dialogue, as "specialists in each field barricade themselves with venerable national languages and literature, paying scant attention to each other and their works." Ching, *Becoming Japanese*, 30. He writes of the dearth of scholarship crossing national borders and traditions (e.g., multilingual studies of Chinese, Korean, and Japanese literatures), but that observation likewise applies to the critical gap between Asian studies and Asian American studies. Recent work, such as Fujitani's *Race for Empire*, Bascara's *Model-Minority Imperialism*, and Cruz's *Transpacific Femininities*, as well as journals such as *positions* and *Verge,* consciously engages both fields.

21. In their introduction to *Transpacific Studies*, V. Nguyen and Hoskins point to the early binary that took hold of Asian American studies:

Asian American studies' historical focus on immigration, with the United States as the destination, meant that Asian American studies was generally reluctant to consider the importance of Asia or countries of origin. Throughout the end of the twentieth century, Asian American studies was focused mostly on issues within American borders. But its concern with immigration meant that it was at least conscious of the role of the United States overseas in the Asian wars that created the conditions of immigration for many populations. Transpacific history was already a structuring factor in the constitution of Asian American populations, but Asian American studies neglected the transpacific nature of these populations because of its imperative to "claim America," in Maxine Hong Kingston's words. (V. Nguyen and Hoskins, introduction to Hoskins and Nguyen, *Transpacific Studies*, 19)

22. Implicit in the transnational turn in Asian American studies is a repudiation of critics and activists such as Frank Chin, Jeffery Paul Chan, Lawson Fusao Inada, and Shawn Wong, who organized Asian American literature in their groundbreaking *Aiiieeee! An Anthology of Asian American Writing* (1974) and its follow-up, *The Big Aiiieeee!* (1991) but have since been critiqued for a hypermasculine and UScentric bent.

23. Elaine Kim and Lowe, *Positions*, vi–vii.

24. They write: "To account for the historical pasts and presents of these new immigrants, we believe there will need to be a variety of connections between Asian studies and Asian American studies, though these encounters will surely have to take account of the long history of dissymmetry between the two fields, the differences in their disciplinary imperatives and in the privileges of their institutional locations, and the large gaps between the subjects and knowledges posited by each field." Elaine Kim and Lowe, *Positions*, viii.

25. Lowe, *Immigrant Acts*, 63.

26. Lowe, *Immigrant Acts*, 67.

27. Huang writes: "On the other hand, the history of transpacific displacement, especially the history of textual migration, which involves not just exercising Orientalist fantasies but also acquiring actual knowledge of the Other, including appropriating or mimicking the Other's way of speaking, writing, seeing, and knowing, will provide the most meaningful background for the deepening and expansion of Asian American literature." Huang, *Transpacific Displacement*, 6.

28. J. Park, *Apparitions of Asia*, 19.

29. Working on a parallel track in comparative literary and postcolonial studies, Françoise Lionnet and Shu-mei Shih's *Minor Transnationalism* extends the decentering project in bypassing the colonial metropole; they critique a tendency in transnational and postcolonial studies to revolve around imperial, usually Western, powers. This, they lament, has the unfortunate effect of creating a structural barrier to interdisciplinary work: "Scholars in ethnic studies very rarely communicate or collaborate with scholars in francophone studies, although there are many geo-

graphical and cultural points of convergences between the two. Likewise, ethnic studies and area studies continue to be caught in a fraught relationship. . . . Ethnic studies remain an American domestic paradigm, while area studies continue to subscribe to an outmoded view of continental territories. National-language departments rarely question the metonymical relationship between language and nation." Lionnet and Shih, introduction to *Minor Transnationalism*, 4.

Disciplinary silos, stubbornly rooted in institutional legacies, preclude meaningful exchange; moreover, the constructed nature of their boundaries is rarely challenged. That, they assert, leads to an uncritical acceptance of domestically framed minority politics blithely projecting racial theory outward with little consideration of nuanced differences and complex histories.

> The formulation of "minority discourse" emerged within American studies as a way of theorizing diversity. But this approach to diversity remains largely monolingual, even though multilinguality is a given within minority communities. When non-U.S. forms of transnationalism and transcolonialism are brought into play, the "minority discourse" model is helpful only to a limited extent. Not all minorities are minoritized by the same mechanisms in different places; there is no universal minority position as such. By looking at the way minority issues have been formulated in other national and regional contexts, it is possible to show that all expressive discourses (such as music, cinema, autobiography, and other literary genres) are inflected by transnational and transcolonial processes. (Lionnet and Shih, *Minor Transnationalism*, 11)

In other words, Lionnet and Shih stress the importance of comparative studies of minor literatures in a context that gives the scholar pause and prevents her from uncritically and indiscriminately replicating domestic ontologies of power. A minor transnationalism, then, is multilingual and rejects monolingualism as the primary mode of inquiry; it is built on the premise of hybridity and exchange; and it is decoupled from the colonial center and outside the colonizer-colonized binary: "Most importantly, postcolonial studies fails to foreground the productive cultural work of minorities resulting from their transcolonial and transnational experiences. Postcolonial cultural studies has been overly concerned with a vertical analysis confined to one nation-state, such as the effect of British colonialism in India, where the vertical power relationship between the colonizer and the colonized is the main object of analysis. Finally, it reinforces the hegemony of English as the language of discourse and communication." Shih and Lionnet, *Minor Transnationalism*, 11.

30. Hoskins and Nguyen's *Transpacific Studies* attempts to coalesce some of the discussion that has been moving in this direction for some time. In their view, it is

necessary to acknowledge (and theorize) the cross-pollination that occurs in Asian and Western constructions of the Pacific: "In the context of the 'politics of imagining Asia,' as a parallel example, Wang Hui argues that Asian intellectuals cannot (re) imagine Asia without taking into account the history of European intervention in, and construction of, Asia, which has shaped the Asian nationalisms, internationalisms, and revolutions that have produced contemporary Asian nation-states and intellectual formations. Likewise, considering the Pacific, or transpacific relations, without grappling with the way those have been shaped by European and American interventions and intellectual traditions that have influenced Asian thinking and responses would be a mistake." V. Nguyen and Hoskins, introduction to Hoskins and Nguyen, *Transpacific Studies*, 4.

31. Chuh and Shimakawa, introduction to *Orientations*, 7.

32. In a subsequent chapter, Chuh describes her method in more detail: "This is a transnationalism that refutes any notions of a natural and wholly bounded national identity while simultaneously iterating the historic and material power of the nation-state. Transnationalism in this sense is a critical methodology that mediates interpretation, counseling deliberate disruption of normative understandings of nationhood and social subjectivity, and that insists on recognizing the ideologies conditioning national identity formation." Chuh, "Imaginary Borders," 280.

What is important to note is that Chuh advocates a critical self-awareness that highlights the ideological formation of nationhood both as an object of study and as a market of self-identification and a scholarly vantage point. With that in mind, a transnationalist approach can avoid a hegemonic projection of the Western subject onto any given site of inquiry.

33. Chuh expands upon this in "Imaginary Borders." I should also stress that Chuh does not advocate ignoring social justice in Asian American studies but pushes for acknowledging it as one of multiple lines in the field:

> Discourses like Asian American studies that are engaged in and indeed motivated by social justice, by the desire to correct inequities in the distribution of power and resources, cannot but unfold in the context of the unavoidable problematics that inhere in epistemological objectification. A certain watchfulness is necessary to avoid the pitfalls of what Rey Chow has called "self-subalternization," a process by which the critic identifies with a position of powerlessness in order, paradoxically, to claim a certain kind of academic power. Like minoritized discourses generally, Asian American studies' genealogy includes the language of powerlessness and victimization, a rhetoric that has participated in the institutional growth of Asian American studies and the establishment of its practitioners. (Chuh, "Discomforting Knowledge," 8)

34. For example, Leo Ching (*Becoming Japanese*) investigates colonial Taiwanese discourses of Japanese citizenship, and Nayoung Aimee Kwon (*Intimate Empire*) recovers Korean authors writing in Japanese during the occupation, largely ignored by Korean studies because of their being impugned as collaborators.

35. Hanscom, Washburn, and Fujitani apply racial formation theory according to the particular and unique circumstances of Japanese imperialism, which was built in part on the basis of its studies of other colonial models, including the United States. Fujitani's *Race for Empire* draws from both Asian and Asian American studies to reconstruct parallel racial projects in Japan's exploitation of Koreans and the United States' exploitation of Japanese Americans. Part of the project of incorporating Korean subjects into the colonial body was to construct an ideology of inclusion that simultaneously enforced exclusion—a move from "vulgar" to "polite" racism, one that "insisted upon the illegitimacy of formal racial discrimination, even as it reproduced a racist logic through a discourse of differential histories, lagging development, and culture." Fujitani, *Race for Empire*, 60. Hanscom and Washburn's *Affect of Difference* explores how affect actualizes race and racialization ideology in materiality—permeating the porous banal and mundane.

> An affect is something that must be present for one to invest in ideology—that is, ideology has to be affectively charged for it to constitute individual experience. Affect exists at the intersection of ideology and the experience of social, political, and everyday realities; it is through the production of affect that an easy division between the material and discursive is complicated. To put it differently, affect makes matter (or matters) matter—it sentimentalizes the material but also makes that matter count for something. Neither mere 'feelings' nor the product of ideological machinations, affect mediates the subjective experience of the social and provides fruitful and complex category by which to approach studies of race under empire. (Hanscom and Washburn, introduction to *Affect of Difference*, 6)

36. Cheung, *Chinese American Literature*, 4.

37. Cheung, *Chinese American Literature*, 1.

38. Cruz, *Transpacific Femininities*, 6.

39. A. Lee, *Mandarin Brazil*, 37.

40. Cheung, *Chinese American Literature*, 8–9.

41. Nakamura, "What Asian American Studies Can Learn," 263.

42. Ueki, "Past, Present, and Future," 57.

43. My approach, in a manner, expands upon Claire Jean Kim's notion of racial triangulation. In her seminal paper, she posits that "Asian Americans have not been racialized in a vacuum, isolated from other groups; to the contrary, Asian

Americans have been racialized relative to and through interaction with Whites and Blacks. As such, the respective racialization trajectories of these groups are profoundly interrelated." C. Kim, "Racial Triangulation," 106. However, whereas Kim focuses on domestic racial politics, my study widens the scope to include multiple national and international sites of racialization.

44. Yoneyama effectively triangulates Asian America in her reading of American legal and cultural discourse of redress for Japanese war crimes in *Cold War Ruins*: "At the same time, it [the Americanization of justice] consists of multifold dimensions of transnational and national processes that involve actors and institutions at multiple levels both within and outside U.S. state interests and interpellations. By deploying the analytic of Asian/Americanization, this chapter hopes to capture the multivalent meanings of seeking truth and justice for Japanese war crimes in the United States. The contradictory effects the Asian/American critique may bring to that process raise a number of key issues regarding violence and historical justice." Yoneyama, *Cold War Ruins*, 152–53.

45. In an early issue of *Verge: Studies in Global Asias*, Andrew Way Leong welcomes the disciplinary move toward a broader scope but cautions against replicating an imperialist mode of inquiry—what he calls the "possessive individualist" approach to criticism, in which a scholar gathers artifacts in a "collection" to be harvested and, ultimately, claimed. "In the context of these reflections, the recent emergence of this journal—*Verge: Studies in Global Asias*—can be read as a move beyond the mere collections and local horizons of Asian and Asian American studies toward a global plurality. As well intentioned as this expansion to 'global Asias' might be, to the extent that it proceeds in a possessive individualist mode that goes beyond the merely collective, the shift to 'global Asias' risks becoming yet another vehicle for extending disciplinary authority over ever-larger domains." Leong, "Pocket and the Watch," 77.

Instead, he posits a "collective individualist" mode that distinguishes between collection and possession, to circumvent creating a "a fixed group that is inherently opposed to the individual" (76). This study sympathizes with Leong's construct for decidedly banal reasons—in addition to a decentered mode of inquiry, venturing into a well-established discipline, Asian studies, requires recognizing an inherently limited mastery.

46. V. Nguyen and Hoskins call for a decentralized framework that acknowledges its artificiality, one made up of linkages and connections rather than naturalized sites of power: "In the twenty-first century we may be moving to a period that will emphasize other linkages, connections, and transnational processes. We see the transpacific as one of those 'spaces of interaction,' which is not itself a 'region' . . . but which does define flows of culture and capital across the ocean." V. Nguyen and Hoskins, introduction to Hoskins and Nguyen, *Transpacific Studies*, 7.

47. A few necessary caveats. I write from a Western intellectual tradition whose structural influence on attendant politics cannot be denied. Indeed, I recognize that the critical framework I employ has its own assumptions and preconceptions that are inexorably US-centric, as Hoskins and Nguyen have noted: "Asian scholars in Asia who also study Asia reasonably look with suspicion on both the western area studies tradition and its debates about the complications of area studies, as well as the nationalist assumptions of U.S.-based Asian American and American studies. But the field questions and methodological problems that U.S.-based scholars have been discussing also have relevance for Asian-based scholars because the academic industrial complex within which U.S. scholars work has trained many Asian scholars and is also being adopted by Asian countries." V. Nguyen and Hoskins, introduction to Hoskins and Nguyen, *Transpacific Studies*, 17.

Moreover, I do not pretend that I am fluent in the Asian studies tradition; I write from a distinctly Asian American disciplinary vantage. Moreover, my limited Japanese- and Korean-language abilities have considerably slowed down access to primary and secondary materials; all translations and mistakes are of my own making.

48. Lie, *Zainichi*, 134.

49. Fukuoka, *Lives of Young Koreans*, xxxviii.

50. There is some movement within the Zainichi community toward claiming a term to better reflect their identities as Japanese citizens, but this is not without conflict. First-generation intellectuals like Kim Sok-pom refer to themselves as *chōsen seki* ("Korean Family Register," which bypasses the choice between North or South Korean nationalities), while younger generations have adopted terms like the English moniker "Japanese Korean."

51. The Treaty of Kanghwa in 1876, which was forced upon Korea by Japan, marked the beginning of a path toward colonization. In 1910, Japan formally annexed Korea and began an economic, cultural, and political campaign to enfold Korea in its empire. Beginning with two agricultural policies termed "Land Survey Enterprises" (*tochi chōsa jigyō*) and "Rice Production Increase Plan" (*sanmai zōshoku keikaku*), Japan stripped Korea of the bulk of its crop production so that it was left with very little.

52. Fukuoka, *Lives of Young Koreans*, xxxviii.

53. Fukuoka, *Lives of Young Koreans*, xxxviii.

54. Ryang, introduction to *Koreans in Japan*, 3.

55. Lie, *Zainichi*, 33.

56. North Koreans were given the status of *chōsen*, which could mean North Korea, but as Japan and North Korea do not have diplomatic relations, it is essentially a placeholder.

57. Wender, *Lamentation as History*, 6.

58. Quoted in Patterson and Kim, *Koreans in America*, 20.

59. Hurh and Kim, *Korean Immigrants in America*, 39.

60. Because of the Chinese Exclusion Act of 1882, Hawaiian sugar plantation owners found themselves in need of replacing their Chinese workers. Japanese workers were quickly falling out of favor because of their predilection for organizing and demanding better working conditions (Jo, *Korean Immigrants*, 2). So they began to look to the small country in between China and Japan. With the cooperation of a US ambassador to Korea and an entrepreneur, they managed to procure permission from the emperor of Korea, Kojong, to hire Koreans for emigration. The first boatload arrived in Hawaii on January 13, 1903.

61. The year 1905 saw emigration channels close after Japan had annexed Korea. Because of negative reports of slave-like working conditions in Mexico and Hawaii, Korea demanded that their citizens be allowed to return home. Patterson and Kim, *Koreans in America*, 16. Of the seven thousand Koreans who emigrated from Korea, two thousand returned while the rest stayed behind. Patterson and Kim, *Koreans in America*, 27. Some moved into the cities of Hawaii, while others moved to the mainland to California, Oregon, and Washington in search of better opportunities. Patterson and Kim, *Koreans in America*, 33.

62. After the Korean War, another small influx of immigrants came to the US, dubbed the "second wave" by Asian American scholars. Mostly students, adopted children, or wives of American soldiers, the second wave began after the cessation of hostilities between the two Koreas in 1951, increasing the number of Korean immigrants to 15,050 in 1964. Jo, *Korean Immigrants*, 6. Images of orphaned children and students' lives destroyed by war led to a trend of sympathy that allowed more Koreans to enter the US. In conjunction with public opinion, the McCarran-Walter Act of 1952 abolished racial and ethnic bans on immigration (but not national origins). GIs who married Korean women while stationed abroad came home to stringent laws prohibiting their wives to join them in the US. In 1952 only one Korean woman was allowed to enter, but that number jumped to 1,340 in 1964, and leaped again to 3,000 in 1971. Jo, *Korean Immigrants*, 7. Immigration quotas kept more at bay until 1965 and 1968, when they were loosened to allow more Koreans to enter. Since then, about 15,000 Koreans have left Korea for the US. More wished to emigrate but were prevented by the South Korean government, which feared a "brain drain." By 1966, 250,000 Koreans were living in the US, more than half of them in California. Patterson and Kim, *Koreans in America*, 49.

63. Jo, *Korean Immigrants*, 13.

64. US Census Bureau, "Asian Population," 14.

65. Pew Research Center's Social and Demographic Trends Project, "Koreans in the U.S. Fact Sheet."

66. Wender, *Lamentation as History*, 12–13 (my italics).

67. Important symbolically, for Japanese rule over Korea did indeed end, but as many modern scholars will point out, it took decades for Korea to regain true sovereignty after the United States stepped in once Japan had left.

68. For a detailed study of Korean racialization, see Fujitani's *Race for Empire*.

69. "Neither South, North, nor Japan."

70. Kim deliberately uses the word *chōsen* as a political statement to deny the present division between North and South Korea.

71. Wender, *Lamentation as History*, 32.

72. S. Kim, "Kyomutan," 203. Subsequent page citations are given parenthetically in the text.

73. The nape of the neck, as one of the very few exposed areas when one wears a kimono, has been eroticized in Japanese culture.

74. Bascara, *Model-Minority Imperialism*, xxv.

75. For example, V. Nguyen and Hoskins point out the dangers of minor Asian nations replicating imperial hostilities as minor support players, as in the case of South Korean auxiliary military support of the United States in Vietnam. Some of the atrocities executed by South Korean soldiers in Vietnam are little commented upon in Asian American history. V. Nguyen and Hoskins, introduction to Hoskins and Nguyen, *Transpacific Studies*, 14.

76. Far, "Leaves from the Mental Portfolio."

77. Yamamoto, *Seventeen Syllables*, 36.

78. Hagedorn, *Dogeaters*, 161.

79. Hagedorn, *Dogeaters*, 161.

80. Choi, *Foreign Student*, 243.

81. Moreover, Theresa Kyung Hak Cha's *Dictee* meditates on the legacy of Japanese colonialism as a means of working through Korean American linguistic subjectivity. And Richard Kim's *Lost Names* catalogs various injustices suffered by his protagonist at the hands of Japanese colonial powers.

Chapter 1: The Japanese Empire, American Industrialism, and Korean Labor

Epigraphs: Ueno, *Ueno Yōichi den*, 187–89; Taylor, "Principles of Scientific Management," 7; Nevins and Hill, *Ford*, 461.

1. Y. Kang, *East Goes West*, 245. Subsequent page citations to this work are given parenthetically in the text.

2. Part of the Japanese Empire's project was the modernization of its colonies to

provide the industrial labor and products needed for total war. However, the term *modernization* has recently been complicated, for it has been accused of reductively assuming that colonial sites are always backward and external forces are always "modern." See Barlow, *Formations of Colonial Modernity*.

3. In a series of articles designed to turn public opinion against Japan, Kang outlined scenes of cruelty against the Korean people during its colonial occupation. He was also the acting chief of publications for the American Military Government in the Far East, a military public information operation. See Y. Kang, "Prelude to Korean Independence," 9–13; Y. Kang, "Japan's Secret Plans," 27–30; Y. Kang, "Japanese Mind Is Sick," 39–41; Y. Kang, "When the Japs March In," 110–11.

4. Koshy, "Fiction of Asian American Literature," 338.

5. Arguing that a consideration of Japan is necessary for a comprehensive analysis of Korean America, or Asian America in a larger context, can be a thorny proposition. For example, Korean studies scholars (in Korea) largely ignored colonial-era writers who wrote in Japanese—they were condemned as traitors and collaborators—partly because of the fresh wounds of colonial trauma. Only recently has there been a rising interest in Japanese-language colonial Korean writers, but considering the sensitivity of the area, I take pains to point out that my reading of Japan complicates and enriches Korean America but by no means defines it.

6. Elaine Kim, *Searching for a Door*, 39.

7. Kyhan Lee, "Younghill Kang," 74.

8. J. Kim, "Mediating Selves," 55.

9. Lew, "Grafts, Transplants, Translation," 182.

10. Palumbo-Liu, *Asian/American*, 123.

11. Chu, *Assimilating Asians*; Kuo, *East Is West*.

12. Knadler, *Fugitive Race*; J. Lee, *Interracial Encounters*; Kun Jong Lee, "African-American Presence."

13. Sorensen, *Ethnic Modernism*, 51.

14. Jeon, "Koreans in Exile," 127.

15. By the early 1900s, Henry Ford and Frederick Taylor heralded parallel manufacturing philosophies driven by the promise of efficiency, speed, and economy. A booming market and a rapidly transforming urban population demanded tremendous output from manufacturing centers, and the existing sluggish, craftsman-based mode of production simply proved insufficient. Ford and Taylor respectively formulated systems focusing on manufacturing and management; these new modes of industry would revolutionize the industrial world and would even make inroads into culture at large before falling out of vogue.

16. Four core principles drive Taylor's method: first, the designing of management as a true science; second, the scientific selection of the workman; third, the

scientific education and development of the workman; and fourth, intimate and friendly cooperation between management and labor. Taylor, "Principles of Scientific Management," 36–37.

17. In his expansive study *From the American System to Mass Production, 1800–1932*, David Hounshell outlines the rise of Fordism as a long march culminating with the Model T after much experimentation. While Fordism was successful in its endeavor to reduce manufacturing costs and increase output, it had significant drawbacks. First, laborers openly rebelled against its dehumanizing aspects, and turnover soared, surpassing 380 percent. Factory workers despised their reduction to caretakers of machines and the mechanization of their bodies. Management compensated by establishing incentives and raising wages, which stanched some of the bleeding, but turnover remained relatively high, and these measures did little to address other labor-related problems. Second, the assembly line system, while streamlining the manufacturing process, became an unanticipated bottleneck in matters of adaptation and innovation. To alter a product necessarily entailed disrupting a well-oiled process, which meant slowed productivity and higher costs—anathema to the Fordist creed. Thus producing upgraded versions of the Model T was a slow process; this would later turn out to be Fordism's downfall, for it had failed to account for consumers' desire to trade up their vehicles.

18. Hounshell notes that cultural critics excoriated Fordism, which they considered to be anathema to individuality, intellectual freedom, and democracy. Aldous Huxley, of course, satirized Fordism in *Brave New World*, casting Ford as a mythical god and Fordism as the dominant religion in a moribund society full of incurious workers. After touring a few Detroit automotive plants, Charlie Chaplin starred in a critique of the tyrannical assembly line in *Modern Times* (1936), perhaps playing off Charles Dickens's own critical commentary on industrialism, *Hard Times*. Upton Sinclair's *The Flivver King* directly examined Henry Ford and his relationship to the workers, ultimately portraying him as part of a larger system that devours Detroit and the protagonist's family. Hounshell, *From the American System*, 316–19.

19. Montgomery, *Fall of the House of Labor*, 220–21. The quoted worker may be playing on Tennyson's "The Charge of the Light Brigade" ("Cannon to right of them, / Cannon to left of them, / Cannon in front of them").

20. Montgomery, *Fall of the House of Labor*, 247.

21. Koizumi, "In Search of Wakon," 29–49.

22. In his excellent study *Manufacturing Ideology*, William Tsutsui notes that nineteenth-century America and Japan had been developing along remarkably similar lines when Taylorism was introduced, with both struggling to find more efficient alternatives to craftsman-based modes of production; at that time, Japan

relied largely on contracted *oyakata*, or skilled foremen, who determined the pace and tenor of the work—an indirect means of management. When *The Principles of Scientific Management* was published in 1911, it found a ready and willing audience in Japanese industry.

23. Quoted in Tsutsui, *Manufacturing Ideology*, 19.

24. Tsutsui, *Manufacturing Ideology*, 24.

25. Japanese intellectuals (the Kyoto School) argued that a synthesis of the Japanese spirit (a vague, inchoate term) and Western technology, guided by the Japanese spirit, allowed the Japanese to transcend the West by using Western technology even more effectively than the West. Koizumi, "In Search of Wakon," 39–40.

26. Koizumi, "In Search of Wakon," 30.

27. Y. Kang, "When the Japs March In," 110.

28. Tsutsui argues in *Manufacturing Ideology* that Japanese Taylorism integrated a tradition of *onjoshugi* (paternalism) but that analogous developments in America were contemporaneous and not at all unique or distinctive to the Japanese.

29. Furthermore, Kang opens the novel with a comparative portrait of Korea and America to highlight the din of grinding gears underneath the city. He describes Korea as a city of organic tradition, ancient in its history and, while materially poor, rich in soul. America, on the other hand, stands tall and erect, "a city of Babel towers," a testament to the fact that "there was no monument to the Machine Age like America" (6).

30. New York City is referred to several times as a metonym for technology, modernity, and machinery in *East Goes West*. For example: "I looked an alien to the Machine Age and New York" (12); "I had not yet known New York, or penetrated beyond the merest outskirts of her impregnable treasure, her fuller expanding life of the Machine Age" (87); "Again I had the Great City to wander in. Again I breathed the air of the Machine Age" (151).

31. Koizumi, "In Search of Wakon," 33–34.

32. As Japanese historians have shown, the Meiji Restoration and Meiji period (1868–1912) witnessed the bulk of Japan's rapid modernization and adoption of select Western sciences, but cross-pollination with Western forces began much earlier. See Jansen, *Making of Modern Japan*, 264–70; Gluck, *Japan's Modern Myths*, 18–19.

33. Smith, *Harpers Ferry Armory*, 225–30.

34. Tsutsui, *Manufacturing Ideology*, 32.

35. Y. Kang, "Prelude to Korean Independence," 11.

36. S. Park, *Colonial Industrialization*, 16.

37. Hori, *Chōsen kōgyōka no shiteki bunseki*, 114.

38. Hori, *Chōsen kōgyōka no shiteki bunseki*. 116.

39. S. Park, *Colonial Industrialization*, 89.

40. S. Park, *Colonial Industrialization*, 99.

41. S. Park, *Colonial Industrialization*, 90–91.

42. Foucault writes,

This bio-power was without question an indispensable element in the development of capitalism; the latter would not have been possible without the con-
trolled insertion of bodies into the machinery of production and the adjustment
of the phenomena of population to economic processes. But this was not all it
required; it also needed the growth of both these factors, their reinforcement as
well as their availability and docility; it had to have methods of power capable
of optimizing forces, aptitudes, and life in general without at the same time
making them more difficult to govern. Foucault, *History of Sexuality*, 1:141.

43. Koreans fluent in Japanese were common by this point, since the Japanese
had forcibly installed the Japanese language in the education system and outlawed
the Korean language. Chinwan's linguistic dexterity was therefore unremarkable,
but what was unusual was his rejection of a singular national identity.

44. I stipulate that it would be reductive to claim that capitalism is solely responsible for constructions of race and qualify my argument by claiming capitalism
as an important facet—but not the whole—of the social construction of race, but
for the purposes of this chapter I bring its role to the fore. See Omi and Winant,
Racial Formation.

45. Holt, *Problem of Race*, 35–36.

46. It is interesting to note that common tropes of racial difference in Japanese
discourse regarding Koreans center, besides language, on the literal stench of Korean culture. Japanese guards encountering family members bringing meals to factories would complain about the distinctive smell of *kimchi* (fermented cabbage),
a staple of Korean food. Since Koreans and Japanese are phenotypically similar, a
discourse of difference based on smell would take root; Japanese would swear they
could sniff out racial difference.

47. S. Kim, *Zainichi no shisō*, 24; Lie, *Zainichi*, 9.

48. Laurenzo may well be a rough sketch of W. E. B. Du Bois's concept of double consciousness. Kang depicts how the requisite dualism can be psychologically
unendurable. Also, if Laurenzo represents Du Bois, Wagstaff may be an example of
Booker T. Washington's "uplift" project, complete with the larger problem of self-
segregation. See Du Bois, *Souls of Black Folk*, 5.

49. See Takaki, *Strangers from a Different Shore*, 132–76; Chan, *Asian Americans*,
3–23.

50. That is not to say that a certain degree of labor racialization did not occur.
Patterson, *Korean Frontier in America*, 15.

51. Late nineteenth-century American literature contains ample evidence of Japan's rise as a world power. In William Dean Howells's meditation on material-ism in America, *A Hazard of New Fortunes* (1890), there are numerous references to Japan as a desirable site for cultural commodities and as a tourist destination on par with Europe. As noted in the Introduction, two early Asian American writers who were sisters, Edith Eaton (Sui Sin Far) and Winnifred Eaton (Onoto Watanna), both betray a cognizance of Japan's rank in the Anglo-Asian hierarchy. Edith Eaton's semiautobiographical "Leaves from the Mental Portfolio of an Eurasian" (1909) depicts an incident in which a White male suitor asks his half-Chinese, half-White betrothed to pass as Japanese. Winnifred Eaton's entire professional life evinces the same anxiety, given that she concocted a Japanese (nonsensical) nom de plume and persona to write about Japan, a country where she had never set foot. See Howells, *Hazard of New Fortunes*; Far, "Leaves from the Mental Portfolio"; Watanna [Win-nifred Eaton], *Wooing of Wistaria*; Watanna [Winnifred Eaton], *Heart of Hyacinth*.

52. Kun Jong Lee, "African-American Presence," 344.

53. Knadler, *Fugitive Race*, 104.

54. Fanon, *Wretched of the Earth*, 152.

55. Knadler, *Fugitive Race*, 104.

56. Palumbo-Liu, *Asian/American*, 122.

57. Palumbo-Liu, *Asian/American*, 119.

58. Y. Kang, "When the Japs March In," 110.

59. Y. Kang, "Prelude to Korean Independence," 12–13.

60. Y. Kang, "Prelude to Korean Independence," 12.

61. Lew, "Grafts, Transplants, Translation," 182–83.

62. Y. Kang, "When the Japs March In," 43. Interestingly, Kang was a stalwart critic of Buck's *The Good Earth*, which he criticized for its perceived erroneous take on Chinese culture. Y. Kang, "China Is Different," 185.

63. Y. Kang, "When the Japs March In," 43.

64. Y. Kang, "Japanese Mind Is Sick," 39.

65. Y. Kang, "Prelude to Korean Independence," 13.

66. Y. Kang, "Prelude to Korean Independence," 30.

67. Koshy, "Fiction of Asian American Literature," 316.

68. Chuh, *Imagine Otherwise*, 111.

Chapter 2: American Racial Discourse in Zainichi Fiction

Epigraph: Field, "Beyond Envy," 643.

1. Kitano, "Chunen josei ga nekkyō suru 'Yon-sama bumu,'" 78.

2. Hanaki et al., "*Hanryu* Sweeps East Asia"; Brasor, "Korean Wave."

3. I do not mean to characterize Kaneshiro's 1996 novel as necessarily represen-

tative of the tradition of Zainichi fiction that has preceded him; indeed, his work has been criticized for its problematic depictions of nationality and gender.

4. I use several terms that need clarifying. *Nationality* refers to citizenship of the state; *ethnicity* refers to a cultural lineage usually associated with a geographic location; and *race* refers to a power inequality based on socially constructed differences mapped onto bodies.

5. Ching, *Becoming Japanese*, 30.

6. Elaine Kim and Lowe, *Positions*, viii.

7. Koshy, "Fiction of Asian American Literature," 338.

8. Lionnet and Shih, introduction to *Minor Transnationalism*, 11.

9. Chuh, "Imaginary Borders," 280.

10. Ryang, introduction to *Diaspora without Homeland*, 2.

11. See also Bhabha, *Location of Culture*; Tölölyan, "Contemporary Discourse," 647–55.

12. Ryang, introduction to *Diaspora without Homeland*, 2.

13. Lowe, *Immigrant Acts*, 6.

14. Lowe, *Immigrant Acts*, 6.

15. Lowe, *Immigrant Acts*, 2–3; emphasis in original.

16. Yoneyama, *Hiroshima Traces*, 183.

17. Indeed, John Lie protests that the search for a universal definition is futile, for the Zainichi are too fractured and fragmented. "The persistent flaw," he writes, "of essentialism—seeking the least common denominator, or essence of a group—is that its presumption often turns out to be empty." Lie, *Zainichi*, xi.

18. For example, first-generation Zainichi intellectuals like Kim Sok-pom refuse to acknowledge the bifurcation of North and South Korea and instead adhere to a prewar imaginative citizenship—*chōsen seki*.

19. Lie, *Zainichi*, 177–78.

20. Lie, *Zainichi*, 116.

21. While Koreans were technically considered "citizens" of Japan, the reality was more complicated. Richard H. Mitchell notes that "few Koreans in the peninsula gained full equality as Japanese citizens. Koreans in Japan were in a more favorable position, but even they had attained only semicitizen status. Koreans were sometimes paid less than Japanese, barred from certain Japanese schools, and forbidden to serve in the military." Mitchell, *Korean Minority in Japan*, 93.

22. Chung, "Politics of Contingent Citizenship," 153.

23. Mitchell, *Korean Minority in Japan*, 107–8.

24. Chung, "Politics of Contingent Citizenship," 155.

25. Chung, "Politics of Contingent Citizenship," 156.

26. Ching, *Becoming Japanese*, 21.

27. Unlike European imperial powers, Japan had just recently modernized and did not accrue enough capital to facilitate expansion. Marxists argue that empire is the logical outgrowth of capitalism—as a nation reaches a maturity, it will reach outward for resources. However, Ching contends that Japan actually expanded rapidly to compete with other developing nations for its "place in the sun." Ching, *Becoming Japanese*, 23.

28. Ching, *Becoming Japanese*, 27.

29. Caprio, *Japanese Assimilation Policies*, 17.

30. Kuraishi, "*Pacchigi!* and *GO*," 117.

31. Zainichi Koreans were encouraged to assimilate by adopting Japanese names to erase their ethnic difference.

32. Noboru Tomonari argues that the works of Kaneshiro and fellow Zainichi author Yan Sogiru highlight the physicality of the body as a reflection of the consequences of colonial trauma on Zainichi male subjects, a theme that was once prevalent in Japanese fiction writ large and that denies female Zainichi subjectivity. Tomonari writes, "His [Kaneshiro's] resort to the conventional notions of masculinity perpetuates them, thereby strengthening the perceptions of masculinity and gender divisions that are still hegemonic in Japan today. . . . Kaneshiro's stories do not necessarily support [Zainichi women's] empowerment." Kaneshiro's adherence to heteronormative patterns, then, not only glorifies violence but "enables Sugihara to construct a common ground with the heterosexual, non-Zainichi Japanese men who share a similar view of gender, while keeping this world of masculinity off-limits to women." Tomonari, "Configuring Bodies," 262.

33. Wender, *Lamentation as History*, 200. See also Tomonari, "Configuring Bodies," 262.

34. See Scott, "Invisible Men."

35. Chapman, "Third Way and Beyond," 34.

36. Chapman, "Beyond the Colonised," 354–57.

37. Hester, "Datsu Zainichi-Ron," 144–45.

38. Sugihara recalls a traumatic encounter with a prejudiced South Korean taxi driver who treated him in a brusque and gruff manner for being Zainichi. Kaneshiro, *GO*, 88–90. All subsequent page citations to this work are given parenthetically in the text.

39. All translations are mine.

40. I use *citizenship* loosely in this context; North Korean "citizenship" in Japan does not truly exist, since Japan and North Korea do not have a normalized relationship. It would be more accurate to say that North Koreans in Japan are stateless peoples, with citizenship largely in their imaginary.

41. North Korean schools were not recognized or accredited, although graduates currently have more opportunities than before.

42. Scott, "Invisible Men," 175.

43. For a thematic reading of Springsteen's song, see Cowie and Boehm, "Dead Man's Town," 352–78.

44. Chung, "Politics of Contingent Citizenship," 153.

45. Paul Sminkey reads Tawake and Wonsoo as representative of "two possible responses to discrimination: escaping the problem by running away or attaching one's self to a group that defends one from the discrimination." Sminkey, "Korean-Japanese Identity," 16.

46. Though not quite beyond the Korean-Japanese dialectic; Miyamoto declines to procure Japanese citizenship, which he sees as defeat (212).

47. Isogai Jirō argues that *GO* functions as a springboard for the articulation of a "Korean Japanese" (spelled phonetically in Japanese katakana as コリアンジャパニーズ [*korian japanizu*]) subjectivity that mirrors much of the tertiary occupational modus operandi of the novel. Isogai, *Zainichi bungaku ron*, 242.

48. Sminkey notes that

> intelligent and physically powerful, he is portrayed as a superhuman hero doing solitary battle against all odds. Indeed, one might argue that such an approach is beyond ordinary Korean-Japanese, and that Kaneshiro's apparent rejection of the group in favor of the individual is mistaken: socially active groups are needed, not for people like Sugihara, but for ordinary people incapable of fighting on their own. Kaneshiro's response to this criticism is that "I am a novelist, not an activist, and it is my job to give illusion" (*Chuokoron* 329–330). In other words, he hopes to inspire ordinary Korean-Japanese through his portrayal of Sugihara. ("Korean-Japanese Identity," 14)

Chapter 3: Korean American Literature Has Always Been Postcolonial
Epigraphs: Chuh, *Imagine Otherwise*, 88; Caruth, *Trauma*, 4.

1. Han, *Unsung Hero*, 30.

2. Macmillan, "Unwanted Allies," 183–85.

3. Nayoung Aimee Kwon writes that "such entanglements were difficult to untangle even at the time they were unfolding, and were further muddled by later postcolonial erasures that too often projected and reinforced simple binary oppositions such as that of resistance and collaboration." Kwon, *Intimate Empire*, 199.

4. Kwon, *Intimate Empire*, 5–6.

5. Chuh, "Discomforting Knowledge," 9–10.

6. Yoneyama, *Cold War Ruins*, 152.

7. Chuh, "Discomforting Knowledge," 8.

8. As problematic as it may be, Norman Finkelstein's criticism against those who exploit the Holocaust for their own ends is our most salient point of comparison. Finkelstein, *Holocaust Industry*.

9. This is perhaps most concretely acknowledged in Filipino American literature, where colonization and its relationship with the United States are direct and tangible. See Bascara, *Model-Minority Imperialism*; Cruz, *Transpacific Femininities*.

10. Chuh, *Imagine Otherwise*, 91–92.

11. Espiritu, *Asian American Panethnicity*, 10.

12. Kauanui, "Asian American Studies,'" 129.

13. See Simeon Man's 2018 *Soldiering through Empire,* particularly chapter 2, "Working the Subempire: Philippine and South Korean Military Labor in Vietnam," 103–34.

14. For example, as discussed in chapter 1, Korean American writer Younghill Kang penned anti-Japanese screeds; during the height of the Japanese Empire, Kang took pains to write in popular journals to influence American public opinion against Japan and to galvanize the United States into entering a war that would hopefully lead to Korea's liberation.

15. R. Kim, *Clay Walls*, 76. Subsequent page citations to this work are given parenthetically in the text.

16. Among the numerous scholars who have written on *Clay Walls* from various perspectives, see Pamela Thoma and Shirley Geok-lin Lim's respective feminist readings of Haesu's resistance to Korean patriarchy and American racism: Thoma, "Representing Korean American Female Subjects," 265–94; Lim, "Feminist and Ethnic Literary Theories," 586–88. Seiwoong Oh notes the Japanese presence as plot device in "Cross-Cultural Reading," 4. Jane Phillips dwells on the Ronyoung Kim's ethnocentrism with respect to her portraiture of the Japanese in "We'd Be Rich in Korea," 177–78, 182–83. Duckhee Shin contextualizes Haesu's class consciousness within Korea, the US, and Japan in "Class and Self-Identity,'" 131. The most extensive meditation on the role of Japanese colonialism comes from Sae-a Oh, who takes pains to demonstrate the importance of colonialism in Haesu's attempt to build a life in the United States—it is not something she can ever escape. Sae-a Oh, "Precious Possessions Hidden," 31–49.

17. One exception is John Lie's excellent *Zainichi*, which briefly references *A Gesture Life* as a point of contrast between Korean American fiction and Zainichi fiction: "It is the thematic of Korean-American literature to dwell on the past—such as Japanese colonization of Korea in general or the problematic of *ianfu* in particular. . . . One doesn't find the same sort of obsession in the best-selling novels of Yū Miri or Kaneshiro Kazuki." Lie, *Zainichi*, 191–92.

18. For instance, while Chang-rae Lee's first work, *Native Speaker*, touched upon recognizably Asian American themes of assimilation, immigration, language, and identity, *A Gesture Life* must have initially confounded critics who sought more of the same.

19. In contrast, Kandice Chuh casts the novel as a squarely Asian American text: "What marks *A Gesture Life* as a specifically American novel is, I think, precisely that it conceptualizes Korea as postcolonial rather than neocolonial." Chuh, *Imagine Otherwise*, 107.

20. Carroll, "Traumatic Patriarchy," 595.

21. Y. Lee, "Transcending Ethnicity," 74–75.

22. Jerng, "Recognizing the Transracial Adoptee," 52.

23. Chuh notes that "*A Gesture Life* clearly takes interest in these factors, deploying the figure of the 'comfort woman' as a critique of Japanese colonialism." Chuh, *Imagine Otherwise*, 106–7. But that is only half the story—the concept of Zainichi subjecthood is missing from her study.

24. Chuh, *Imagine Otherwise*, 107.

25. Chuh, *Imagine Otherwise*, 100.

26. Chuh, *Imagine Otherwise*, 107.

27. Hata's reluctance to reflect upon his own hybridity and the problematic identity politics of his being raised as a Japanese citizen in a society that openly discriminated and subjugated his ethnicity goes largely unmentioned in scholarly discussions of the novel. To be sure, there is an awareness of his colonial condition, but that is largely in service to reading the brutal abjection of the comfort women. Absent from the conversation, which this chapter attempts to rectify, is the fact that he would have been considered a second-generation Zainichi—that is, a Resident Korean in Japan.

28. Chuh, "Discomforting Knowledge," 15.

29. The problem with this line of argument emerges only through a thought experiment: imagine for a moment, if you will, a Japanese studies scholar, in Japan, studying a Zainichi writer's novel about a Zainichi immigrant who spent half his life in the United States. Our hypothetical Japanese studies scholar completely ignores the history of Korean America—she views the text only through a domestic Japanese studies framework—and elides the character's American history as mysterious or unknowable. I imagine that the glaring absence of Asian American context would be noticed by American studies scholars. Similarly, because Chuh writes unaware of the Zainichi, she is unable to articulate the broader context of Hata's hybridity—disciplinary boundaries preclude meaningful engagement. It is, I contend, only through disciplinary crossings that *A Gesture Life* comes into full view.

30. That is, as Françoise Lionnet and Shu-mei Shih define it, a minor transnationalism takes into consideration how minority formation in other "national and regional contexts" is "inflected by transnational and transcolonial processes." Lionnet and Shih, introduction to *Minor Transnationalism*, 11. In this case, I not only take Hata's minority formation in Japan into consideration but demonstrate how that mode is transported and integrated into a heterogeneity with an American form of racialization.

31. Ching, *Becoming Japanese*, 95.

32. Ching, *Becoming Japanese*, 105–7.

33. Quoted in Ching, *Becoming Japanese*, 108.

34. Consequently, the majority of adoptions in contemporary Japan are of adult men, who are adopted by families to continue the family line and/or take over an existing business in the absence of a suitable heir.

35. Ching, *Becoming Japanese*, 108.

36. C. Lee, *Gesture Life*, 72. Subsequent page citations to this work are given parenthetically in the text.

37. In *Becoming Japanese*, his study of colonial Taiwan, Leo Ching notes that the instrumentality of *dōka* and *kōminka* is exemplified in the enshrinement of Taiwanese aborigines at Yasukuni (a shrine for war heroes in Tokyo), who died as Japanese subjects but whose families are denied reparations or redress as citizens of Japan because after the war they were no longer Japanese. Japaneseness functions as a performance so that the body can perform, but once that category has outlived its usefulness, it dissipates. Takashi Fujitani notes that in addition to the 28,863 Taiwanese, 21,181 Koreans were interred at Yasukuni—evidence of Japan's multiethnic empire. Fujitani, *Race for Empire*, 4.

38. Ching, *Becoming Japanese*, 95.

39. Ching argues that *kōminka* was not simply an extension or intensification of *dōka*: "I consider that *kōminka* must be historicized in its own right, in both its identity with and *difference* from *dōka*. The conflation of the two colonial ideologies, I maintain, only reiterates the official discourse of a consistent and continuous colonial policy of equality and benevolence." Ching, *Becoming Japanese*, 91.

40. Fujitani, *Race for Empire*, 40.

41. For example, Hata suspects that his commanding officer, Captain Ono, holds him to impossible standards because of his ethnic heritage.

42. Fujitani, *Race for Empire*, 60.

43. Ching, *Becoming Japanese*, 37.

44. Caprio, *Japanese Assimilation Policies*, 9.

45. Rhee, "Consumable Bodies," 106.

46. This scene may be a reference to the infamous Unit 731, Japan's secret biological warfare and human experimentation research unit, which committed innumerable atrocities on live human subjects of Chinese, Russian, Mongolian, and Korean descent. See Nie et al., *Japan's Wartime Medical Atrocities*.

Chapter 4: International Study and Sojournship

1. B. Lee, *Seoul Searching*.

2. *Gyopo* may literally mean members of the Korean diaspora, but colloquially it is used as a slightly pejorative shorthand for Korean American.

3. Recent instances include Tao Lin's *Taipei* (2013) and Patricia Park's *Re Jane* (2016). Both novels include substantial sojourns to East Asia (Taiwan and South Korea) that advance their respective protagonists' narrative arcs and eventually lead to their return to the United States.

4. Jessica Hagedorn's *Dogeaters* is a notable exception, for it takes place entirely in the Philippines, expanding the definition of Asian America to include postcolonial sites and former US territories.

5. The most salient example of which is discussed in chapter 1 on Younghill Kang's *East Goes West*. See also Choi, *Foreign Student*; Ha Jin, *A Free Life*; Gish Jen, *Typical American*; and David Henry Hwang, *F.O.B.*

6. Examples of spending time abroad abound in Zainichi literature. Yi Yang-ji wrote, in addition to *Yuhi*, a short story, "Koku," about her time abroad in South Korea. The protagonist in Kaneshiro Kazuki's *GO* recounts an extensive period spent in South Korea and a fraught encounter with a taxi driver who berates him for his poor Korean. Lee Hoesung's *Shisha to seisha no ichi* (The market of the living and the dead) chronicles Lee's fictional proxy's return to South Korea and subsequent alienation.

7. See chapter 8 ("Henry James, or the Merchant of Europe") and chapter 9 ("Henry Adams, Traveler") in Stowe, *Going Abroad*.

8. "Once thought of as a privilege for only the predominantly white upper class, students of all ethnic backgrounds and socio-economic classes are increasingly choosing to study abroad." Van Der Meid, "Asian Americans," 71.

9. According to the Institute for International Education, the number of American students studying abroad has grown from 25,464 in 1949 to 903,127 in 2017 (from 1.1 percent to 5.3 percent of the total student population). Institute for International Education, "Enrollment."

10. "Yet even as overall study abroad participation has increased, American students studying abroad have remained disproportionately white in comparison to the racial composition of postsecondary students overall. While 81.8 percent of all study abroad participants in 2007/08 were white, only 64.4 percent of all students

enrolled in postsecondary education in 2007/08 were white." Salisbury, Paulsen, and Pascarella, "Why Do All the Study Abroad Students Look Alike?," 124.

11. Curiously, even as study abroad becomes accessible to the middle class and a wider array of minority students, its cultural representation remains remarkably consistent. While their bourgeois predecessors fret over their nouveau riche outsider status, contemporary study-abroad narratives appear to reflect a similar anxiety regarding the dangers of European culture.

12. In a survey of American students studying abroad in Australia, Nancy Dolby notes that many of them come to recognize a latent national identity that has been internalized to the point of invisibility: "Despite the rhetoric of study abroad, which foregrounds the importance of the 'cross-cultural' experience, for most of the students participating in this study, the critical encounter of study abroad was with the 'American' self." Dolby, "Encountering an American Self," 171.

13. "Additional inquiry has suggested that a combination of family concerns and obligations, familial pressures to move through college quickly and start a career, fears of racism abroad, a lack of minority faculty leading study abroad programs, and a perceived presumption among faculty and administrators that minorities lack an interest in study abroad adds to the propensity among minority students to forego participation." Salisbury, Paulsen, and Pascarella, "Why Do All the Study Abroad Students Look Alike?," 124–25.

14. "Because the plurality of Asian Americans opt to study abroad in Asian countries, more emphasis should be placed on creating study abroad opportunities in this region. The students' desire to learn about a new culture, improve their language skills and learn about their cultural heritage would support these options. In addition, it is important to offer programs of differing lengths so that students have options in terms of how long they wish to be away from the United States." Salisbury, Paulsen, and Pascarella, "Why Do All the Study Abroad Students Look Alike?," 105.

15. J. Kang and Abelmann, "Domestication of South Korean Pre-college Study," 89–118.

16. Indeed, the first president (and dictator) of the People's Republic of Korea, Syngman Rhee, was an international student at several American universities and earned a doctorate at Princeton University before returning to Korea under the stewardship and approval of the international security apparatus of the United States.

17. Terasima and Koike, "Zainichi kankokuchōsenjin no kankokuryūgaku," 23, 27–28, 44.

18. The tendency, Wang notes, is for the field of Asian American studies to primarily define migration and mobilization through the figure of the laborer.

That, unfortunately, tends to elide the importance of the international student as a participant in the formation and projection of Asian America.

> While the important role of U.S.-educated students in Asia has been noted in respective national histories, Asian American studies thus far has paid only scant attention to the figure of the foreign student and his or her activities in the United States. The foreign student lurks at the edges of Asian American history and representation, sometimes acknowledged but oftentimes unrecognized. When this figure does appear, as in Yuji Ichioka's *The Issei* and Rose Hum Lee's *The Chinese in the U.S.A.*, it is often presented as a contrast to the labor migrant, who is posited as the proper subject of Asian American history. (Wang, *Transpacific Articulations*, 4)

19. Wang, *Transpacific Articulations*, 14.
20. Ong, *Flexible Citizenship*, 6.
21. Wang, *Transpacific Articulations*, 112.

22. "Beneath our keen interest in Ethnic Studies including African, Native, Hispanic, and Asian American studies there lies a complex feeling toward the 'America' that has disappeared and the 'America' that is yet to come. Our efforts in Asian American studies may be phrased as follows: It is the act of liberating ourselves from a Euro-centric or Anglo-centric vision and relocating the image of America in a multi-ethnic, multicultural perspective. It is the act of rediscovering the histories and cultures of Asian Americans and those of their ancestral lands as well. It is the act of finding ourselves and our relationships with Asia, which has been so near to Japan in geography but so far in recognition." Quoted in Ueki, "Past, Present, and Future," 131.

23. The one exception may be the series of Korean adoptee annual conventions that bring together Koreans who have been adopted abroad by families in various countries. See Nelson, *Invisible Asians*; Eleana Kim, "Wedding Citizenship and Culture."

24. To be fair, Wang gestures at how Asian American studies benefits from the presence of international students in a pedagogical anecdote from King-Kok Cheung, who recounts in "Pedagogies of Resonance: Teaching African American and Asian American Literature and Culture in Asia" how Burmese students in her classes brought to bear their experiences with an oppressive regime in ways that enriched discussions of Asian American texts. Wang, *Transpacific Articulations*, 131–32.

25. Lee Hoesung was the first Zainichi author to win the Akutagawa Prize in 1972 for *Kinuta wo utsu onna* (The cloth fuller).

26. Upon its publication, Japanese critics hailed Yi's work as a landmark work of

minority literature. Yet others criticized Yi for the same reasons: for example, Kuruko Kazuo, who objected to Yi's work for not centering ethnicity. Wender, *Lamentation as History*, 127. Yi herself bristled at the notion of her work being representative of Zainichi culture writ large. In an interview with Kawamura Minato, she responds, "Your reading is too schematic . . . ; it's too general; I think that Zainichi Koreans are a diverse bunch; I do not feel able to represent them; I can speak only for myself or my characters." Quoted in Wender, *Lamentation as History*, 129.

27. Yi, "Watashi wa chōsenjin," 584–85.

28. An English translation of "Koku" is available in *Into the Light*. Wender, *Into the Light*, 132–41.

29. Yi wrote a precursor to *Yuhi* in "Koku" (Country), in which a Zainichi character dwells upon similar modes of alienation in South Korea.

30. Kawamura, "Intabyu taidan," 270.

31. "She is what I would term an 'exophone' narrator—a narrator who is in the state of 'exophony,' that is, 'being outside of one's mother tongue.'" "What is extraordinary about this exophone narrator is that she does not possess any Japanese language skills, despite the fact that she tells her story in Japanese. Through this narrator's storytelling, the reader is thus forced to encounter and experience an alternate linguistic reality in which an assumed relation between national language and national identity turns into a logical and linguistic knot." C. Ryu, "Beyond Language," 316.

32. Ueda, "'Moji' to iu 'kotoba,'" 128–29.

33. Yokota-Murakami writes,

> In contrast, Lee's *Yuhi*, although largely written in implicit bilingualism (in the large part of the work the readers are exposed only to the Japanese text and the Korean text is hidden), the readers are constantly pressured to imagine the concealed source language, regardless of whether they know some Korean and can imagine the original passage or they do not know Korean and, thus, have no clue. Even without a clue, the "Japanese" text of *Yuhi* encourages, or compels, the readers to imagine the unknown alien language hidden behind it. The monolingual pages of *Yuhi* are, thus, superbly bilingual. (Yokota-Murakami, *Mother-Tongue*, 98–99)

34. In a discussion of Yan Sogiru (referred to as "Yang Sokil" by Yokota-Murakami), Yokota-Murakami outlines the generations' difference in attitude toward Japanese as their primary writing language, and the transition of "mother-tongue" from Korean to Japanese.

> Nonetheless, the feeling of the linguistic discrepancy that tormented the "second and the third generation" writers appears to be quite insignificant among the contemporary Korean-Japanese literati in general. Yang Sokil, an

author of the "third generation" (b. 1936), that is, the so-called "half-Korean, half-Japanese" generation, differentiates himself from the "enfants terribles" of contemporary Korean-Japanese writers . . .

To the embarrassment of the writers of the "third generation" such as Yang, the young literati compose works in Japanese without apparent problematic political consciousness. The problem of "political identity" does not appear to be tormenting them. . . .

. . . The trouble for those generations was that they had to write in Japanese, not in their "mother-tongue" (*bokoku-go*; the language of their motherland, that is, Korea). Now Yang describes the younger generation composing without any problem consciousness in Japanese, which is their "mother-tongue" (*bo-go*, that is, Japanese). (Yokota-Murakami, *Mother-Tongue*, 23–24)

35. Field, "Beyond Envy," 653–54.

36. Wender, *Lamentation as History*, 130.

37. Hayes, "Cultural Identity," 137.

38. Yi, *Yuhi*, 266. Subsequent page citations are given parenthetically in the text. All translations are mine.

39. Onni describes Yuhi's undefinable and ambiguous appearance: "She looked like a high school student. Although I could somewhat tell she was a girl, because of her short hair and glasses it wouldn't have been a stretch to say she resembled an effeminate boy" (271).

40. Ryang, "Denationalized Have No Class," 162.

41. In *An Absent Presence*, Caroline Chung Simpson discusses the absence of Japanese Americans as a presence in the national imaginary; they were systematically interred and removed from the American landscape, in addition to being wiped from its history, but that stark absence simultaneously and paradoxically produces a ghostly presence. Similarly, I capitalize on an absent presence in *Yuhi* to articulate how Yuhi disrupts the Korea-Japan binary and unsettles the conventional narrative of return. See Simpson, *Absent Presence*.

42. Also, he was fluent in Japanese:

"My husband was, well, forced to learn it during the occupation, so he was fluent. But I only heard a little bit as a child, so can't understand a thing today. Ari-ga-to go-zai-mas and go-men na-sai is about the extent of it."

"*Ajumoni*, your pronunciation is pretty good," said Yuhi, laughing for the first time. (280–81)

43. Moreover, he was sympathetic to the plight of the Zainichi: "I heard that our Korean brothers and sisters living there face a lot of discrimination. My husband was upset about that, and you often see it in the newspapers and on T.V." (281).

44. "Despite my having already climbed a few steps up the stairs, Auntie made no attempt to end the conversation. As if talking to my deceased uncle who had reappeared in the room, her voice had taken on a somehow otherworldly dimension. She probably continued to absentmindedly talk to him, even after I made it upstairs" (262).

45. Kwon, *Intimate Empire*, 199.

46. The fictional encounter is made all the more poignant by the fact that the director, Benson Lee, based the fight on a real incident between Korean American and Zainichi Koreans during summer camp in South Korea. B. Lee, "Interview."

Chapter 5: Los Angeles and Osaka Are Burning
Epigraph: Said, *Humanism and Democratic Criticism*, 49.

1. Barack Obama, Facebook post, May 6, 2019, https://www.facebook.com/barackobama/posts/10156674704661749.

2. Chang, "On the First Asian-American President"; Cooper and Fackler, "Obama Says."

3. Min Jin Lee's first novel, *Free Food for Millionaires* (2006), centers on investment banking and Korean American characters in New York City. Her in-progress third book, *American Hagwon*, apparently returns to a Korean American context.

4. Lionnet and Shih, introduction to *Minor Transnationalism*, 7.

5. The central problem in American studies is that despite "its interdisciplinarity and openness to multiculturalism . . . the field of American studies has nonetheless maintained a monolingual and nationalist approach to literary studies, an approach that has been enabled and perpetuated by the exceptionalist thesis." Behdad, "What Can American Studies and Comparative Literature Learn," 613. That is, there is a totalizing predilection extending outward from American studies that precludes a comparative approach. Conversely, comparative literature tends to turn inward to "posit a universalist, unifying view of literature without any reference to the sociohistorical forces in which it is inscribed," for "early scholars of comparative literature viewed the literary text as self-contained, disregarding any other disciplines for its interpretation or understanding, let alone considering its political or ideological implications." Behdad, "What Can American Studies and Comparative Literature Learn," 609–10.

6. Lye, "Introduction," 6.

7. Sohn, Lai, and Goellnicht, "Theorizing Asian American Fiction," 4–5.

8. Sohn, Lai, and Goellnicht, "Theorizing Asian American Fiction," 5.

9. Vazquez, *Triangulations*, 3.

10. C. Kim, "Racial Triangulation," 129.

11. See Gilroy, *Black Atlantic*; Edwards, *Practice of Diaspora*; Daut, *Tropics of Haiti*

12. In *Transpacific Antiracism*, Yuichiro Onishi shows how Black intellectuals looked abroad to reconceptualize Black identity beyond the White American paradigm: "The dynamism of the culture of liberation was such that by stepping into this space, the participants of Afro-Asian solidarity projects began moving in a 'racial groove,' as Du Bois so aptly put it, and changing the groove itself, they made connections across multiple efforts to revise the blueprint of Black radicalism to present a meaning of human liberation that exceeded the boundaries of nations and modern political thought." Onishi, *Transpacific Antiracism*, 11.

13. Yang, "Asian-Owned Store," 173.

14. Relevant Zainichi intellectuals who have discussed the third way at length include Kim Tong Myung, Yoon Kun Hum, and Kim Tae Young. See Kim Tong Myung, "Zainichi chōsenjin no daisan michi"; Yoon, *"Zainichi" o ikiru to wa*; Kim Tae Young, *Aidentiti poritikusu o koete*.

15. See Manzenreiter, "Time, Space and Money."

16. According to Bumsoo Kim, the pachinko industry is dominated by ethnic Koreans in Japan, exceeding 30 trillion yen per year (~275 billion USD) in 1994, with 60–70 percent of the market share. B. Kim, "Bringing Class Back In," 880–82.

17. M. Lee, *Pachinko*, 296–97. Subsequent page citations are given parenthetically in the text.

18. From 1960 to 1962, seventy thousand Zainichi repatriated to North Korea, but that project swiftly came to an end. Many Zainichi Koreans who repatriated to North Korea found themselves returning to less-than-optimal conditions that contradicted North Korean promises of paradise on earth. Additionally, those who returned were looked upon with suspicion and found themselves being accused of espionage for Japan or South Korea. Lie, *Zainichi*, 46–47.

19. Soble, "Novelist Confronts."

20. The prevailing narrative against Korean-owned convenience stores in the 1990s was that Koreans operated them in primarily Black neighborhoods but were not members of, or contributors to, the local community. See K. Kim, *Koreans in the Hood.*, chaps. 2–5, for a more in-depth discussion.

21. M. Kim, "Moeru Sōka," 115. Subsequent page citations are given parenthetically in the text. All translations are mine.

22. For example, she either mishears or misremembers the title of Willie Nelson's performance of "Georgia on My Mind" (written as "Georgia Oh My Town" in the text).

Coda: Zainichi, Korean, American
Epigraph: Stephenson, *Snow Crash*, 20.
1. Wignot, "Unfamiliar Kin."

2. Ever in search for the metropole (first Tokyo, then Berlin), Kuni later immigrated to the United States, where he was a faculty member in the dance department at California State University, Fullerton. He died in California in 2007 at the age of ninety-nine. For an extensive discussion of Kuni's travels, questionable claims, and complicated legacy, see Hoffmann, *Berlin Koreans*, 106–27.

3. A cursory glance shows francophone studies scholars working on Vietnamese French writers and their works, but I have yet to encounter a conscious bridging between Vietnamese American and Vietnamese French fictions through a comparative ethnic studies framework. For a somewhat related study discussing transnational Vietnamese and Vietnamese American film, see Duong, *Treacherous Subjects*.

4. Otterson, "'Pachinko' Ordered."

Bibliography

Barlow, Tani E., ed. *Formations of Colonial Modernity in East Asia*. Durham, NC: Duke University Press, 1997.

Bascara, Victor. *Model-Minority Imperialism*. Minneapolis: University of Minnesota Press, 2006.

Behdad, Ali. "What Can American Studies and Comparative Literature Learn from Each Other." *American Literary History* 24, no. 3 (September 1, 2012): 608–17. https://doi.org/10.1093/alh/ajs033.

Benitez, J. Francisco, and Laurie J. Sears. "Passionate Attachments to Area Studies and Asian American Studies Subjectivity and Diaspora in the Transpacific." In *Transpacific Studies: Framing an Emerging Field*, edited by Viet Thanh Nguyen and Janet Hoskins, 151–77. Intersections: Asian and Pacific American Transcultural Studies. Honolulu: University of Hawaii Press, 2014.

Bhabha, Homi K. *The Location of Culture*. London: Routledge, 2004.

Brasor, Philip. "Korean Wave May Help Erode Discrimination." *Japan Times Online*, June 27, 2004. https://www.japantimes.co.jp/news/2004/06/27/national/media-national/korean-wave-may-help-erode-discrimination/.

Caprio, Mark E. *Japanese Assimilation Policies in Colonial Korea, 1910–1945*. Seattle: University of Washington Press, 2009.

Carroll, Hamilton. "Traumatic Patriarchy: Reading Gendered Nationalisms in Chang-Rae Lee's *A Gesture Life*." *MFS Modern Fiction Studies* 51, no. 3 (2005): 592–616. https://doi.org/10.1353/mfs.2005.0055.

Caruth, Cathy, ed. *Trauma: Explorations in Memory*. Baltimore: Johns Hopkins University Press, 1995.

Chan, Sucheng. *Asian Americans: An Interpretive History*. New York: Twayne, 1991.

Chang, Eric. "On the First Asian-American President." *Vogue*, December 21, 2016. https://www.vogue.com/article/barack-obama-first-asian-american-president.

Chapman, David. "Beyond the Colonised and the Colonisers: Intellectual Discourse and the Inclusion of Korean-Japanese Women's Voices." *Japanese Studies* 26, no. 3 (December 1, 2006): 353–63. https://doi.org/10.1080/10371390600986710.

Chapman, David. "The Third Way and Beyond: Zainichi Korean Identity and the Politics of Belonging." *Japanese Studies* 24, no. 1 (May 1, 2004): 29–44. https://doi.org/10.1080/1037139041000168697.

Cheung, King-Kok. *Chinese American Literature without Borders: Gender, Genre, and Form*. New York: Palgrave Macmillan, 2017.

Ching, Leo T. S. *Becoming Japanese: Colonial Taiwan and the Politics of Identity Formation*. Berkeley: University of California Press, 2001.

Choi, Susan. *The Foreign Student: A Novel*. New York: Harper Perennial, 2004.

Chu, Patricia P. *Assimilating Asians: Gendered Strategies of Authorship in Asian America*. Durham, NC: Duke University Press, 2000.

Chuh, Kandice. "Discomforting Knowledge: Or, Korean 'Comfort Women' and Asian Americanist Critical Practice." *Journal of Asian American Studies* 6, no. 1 (2003): 5–23. https://doi.org/10.1353/jaas.2003.0025.

Chuh, Kandice. "Imaginary Borders." In *Orientations: Mapping Studies in the Asian Diaspora*, edited by Kandice Chuh and Karen Shimakawa, 278–93. Durham, NC: Duke University Press, 2001.

Chuh, Kandice. *Imagine Otherwise: On Asian Americanist Critique*. Durham, NC: Duke University Press, 2003.

Chuh, Kandice, and Karen Shimakawa. "Introduction: Mapping Studies in the Asian Diaspora." In *Orientations: Mapping Studies in the Asian Diaspora*, edited by Kandice Chuh and Karen Shimakawa, 1–24. Durham, NC: Duke University Press, 2001.

Chuh, Kandice, and Karen Shimakawa, eds. *Orientations: Mapping Studies in the Asian Diaspora*. Durham, NC: Duke University Press, 2001.

Chung, Erin Aeran. "The Politics of Contingent Citizenship: Korean Political Engagement in Japan and the United States." In *Diaspora without Homeland: Being Korean in Japan*, edited by Sonia Ryang and John Lie, 147–67. Berkeley: University of California Press, 2009.

Cooper, Helene, and Martin Fackler. "Obama Says U.S. Seeks to Build Stronger Ties to China." *New York Times*, November 13, 2009, sec. Asia Pacific. https://www.nytimes.com/2009/11/14/world/asia/14prexy.html.

Cowie, Jefferson R., and Lauren Boehm. "Dead Man's Town: 'Born in the U.S.A.,'

Social History, and Working-Class Identity." *American Quarterly* 58, no. 2 (2006): 353–78. https://doi.org/10.1353/aq.2006.0040.

Cruz, Denise. *Transpacific Femininities: The Making of the Modern Filipina*. Durham, NC: Duke University Press, 2012.

Daut, Marlene L. *Tropics of Haiti: Race and the Literary History of the Haitian Revolution in the Atlantic World, 1789–1865*. Liverpool: Liverpool University Press, 2015.

Dolby, Nadine. "Encountering an American Self: Study Abroad and National Identity." *Comparative Education Review* 48, no. 2 (2004): 150–73. https://doi.org/10.1086/382620.

Du Bois, W. E. B. *The Souls of Black Folk*. New York: Penguin Classics, 1996.

Duong, Lan P. *Treacherous Subjects: Gender, Culture, and Trans-Vietnamese Feminism*. American Literatures Initiative edition. Philadelphia: Temple University Press, 2012.

Edwards, Brent Hayes. *The Practice of Diaspora: Literature, Translation, and the Rise of Black Internationalism*. Cambridge, MA: Harvard University Press, 2003.

Espiritu, Yen. *Asian American Panethnicity: Bridging Institutions and Identities*. Philadelphia: Temple University Press, 1993.

Fanon, Frantz. *The Wretched of the Earth*. New York: Grove Press, 1965.

Far, Sui Sin [Edith Maude Eaton]. "Leaves from the Mental Portfolio of an Eurasian." In *The Big Aiiieeeee! An Anthology of Chinese American and Japanese American Literature*, edited by Jeffery Paul Chan, Frank Chin, Lawson Fusao Inada, and Shawn Wong, 111–23. New York: Meridian, 1991.

Field, Norma. "Beyond Envy, Boredom, and Suffering: Toward an Emancipatory Politics for Resident Koreans and Other Japanese." *Positions* 1, no. 3 (December 21, 1993): 640–70. https://doi.org/10.1215/10679847-1-3-640.

Finkelstein, Norman G. *The Holocaust Industry: Reflections on the Exploitation of Jewish Suffering*. 2003. Reprint, London: Verso, 2015.

Foucault, Michel. *The History of Sexuality*. Translated by Robert Hurley. Vol. 1. New York: Vintage Books, 1980.

Fujitani, Takashi. *Race for Empire: Koreans as Japanese and Japanese as Americans during World War II*. 2011. Reprint, Berkeley: University of California Press, 2013.

Fukuoka, Yasunori. *Lives of Young Koreans in Japan*. Melbourne: Trans Pacific Press, 2000.

Gilroy, Paul. *The Black Atlantic: Modernity and Double-Consciousness*. 2007. Reprint, Cambridge, MA: Harvard University Press, 1993.

Gluck, Carol. *Japan's Modern Myths*. Princeton, NJ: Princeton University Press, 1985.

Hagedorn, Jessica. *Dogeaters*. New York: Penguin Books, 1991.

Han, Woo Sung. *Unsung Hero: The Story of Colonel Young Oak Kim*. Translated by Edward T. Chang. Riverside, CA: Young Oak Kim Center for Korean American Studies, 2011.

Hanaki, Toru, Arvind Singhal, Min Wha Han, Do Kyun Kim, and Ketan Chitnis. "*Hanryu* Sweeps East Asia: How *Winter Sonata* Is Gripping Japan." *International Communication Gazette* 69, no. 3 (June 1, 2007): 281–94. https://doi.org/10.1177/1748048507076581.

Hanscom, Christopher P., and Dennis Washburn, eds. *The Affect of Difference: Representations of Race in East Asian Empire*. Honolulu: University of Hawaii Press, 2016.

Hayes, Carol. "Cultural Identity in the Work of Yi Yang-Ji." In *Koreans in Japan: Critical Voices from the Margin*, edited by Sonia Ryang, 119–39. London: Routledge, 2005.

Hester, Jeffry T. "Datsu Zainichi-Ron: An Emerging Discourse on Belonging among Ethnic Koreans in Japan." In *Multiculturalism in the New Japan: Crossing the Boundaries Within*, edited by Nelson H. H. Graburn, John Ertl, and R. Kenji Tierney, 139–50. New York: Berghahn Books, 2008.

Hoffmann, Frank. *Berlin Koreans and Pictured Koreans*. Vienna: Praesens, 2015.

Holt, Thomas C. *The Problem of Race in the Twenty-First Century*. Cambridge, MA: Harvard University Press, 2000.

Honda, Michael. "H.Res.121—110th Congress (2007–2008): A Resolution Expressing the Sense of the House of Representatives That the Government of Japan Should Formally Acknowledge, Apologize, and Accept Historical Responsibility in a Clear and Unequivocal Manner for Its Imperial Armed Forces' Coercion of Young Women into Sexual Slavery, Known to the World as 'Comfort Women,' during Its Colonial and Wartime Occupation of Asia and the Pacific Islands from the 1930s through the Duration of World War II." July 30, 2007. https://www.congress.gov/bill/110th-congress/house-resolution/121.

Honda, Michael. "Time for Abe to Apologize, Properly." Opinion CNN, April 29, 2015. http://www.cnn.com/2015/04/28/opinions/honda-abe-comfort-women-issue/index.html.

Hori, Kazuō. *Chōsen kōgyōka no shiteki bunseki: Nihon shihonshugi to shokuminchi keizai* [A historical analysis of Korean industrialization: Japanese capitalism and the colonial economy]. Tokyo: Yubikaku, 1995.

Hoskins, Janet Alison, and Viet Thanh Nguyen, eds. *Transpacific Studies: Framing an Emerging Field*. Honolulu: University of Hawaii Press, 2014.

Hounshell, David. *From the American System to Mass Production, 1800–1932*. Baltimore: Johns Hopkins University Press, 1985.

Howells, William Dean. *A Hazard of New Fortunes*. New York: Penguin Books, 2001.

Huang, Yunte. *Transpacific Displacement: Ethnography, Translation, and Intertextual Travel in Twentieth-Century American Literature*. Berkeley: University of California Press, 2002.

Hurh, Won Moo, and Kwang Chung Kim. *Korean Immigrants in America: A Structural Analysis of Ethnic Confinement and Adhesive Adaptation*. Rutherford, NJ: Fairleigh Dickinson University Press, 1984.

Institute for International Education. "Enrollment." December 21, 2018. https://www.iie.org:443/Research-and-Insights/Open-Doors/Data/International-Students/Enrollment.

Isogai, Jirō. *Zainichi bungaku ron* [A theory of Zainichi literature]. 1937. Reprint, Tokyo: Sinkansha, 2004.

Jansen, Marius B. *The Making of Modern Japan*. Cambridge, MA: Belknap Press, 2000.

Jeon, Joseph Jonghyun. "Koreans in Exile: Younghill Kang and Richard E. Kim." In *The Cambridge History of Asian American Literature*, edited by Rajini Srikanth and Min Hyoung Song, 123–38. Cambridge: Cambridge University Press, 2015. https://doi.org/10.1017/CHO9781107284289.007.

Jerng, Mark C. "Recognizing the Transracial Adoptee: Adoption Life Stories and Chang-Rae Lee's 'A Gesture Life.'" *MELUS* 31, no. 2 (2006): 41–67.

Jo, Moon H. *Korean Immigrants and the Challenge of Adjustment*. Westport, CT: Greenwood Press, 1999.

Kaneshiro, Kazuki. *GO*. Tokyo: Kodansha, 1996.

Kang, Jiyeon, and Nancy Abelmann. "The Domestication of South Korean Precollege Study Abroad in the First Decade of the Millennium." *Journal of Korean Studies* 16, no. 1 (2011): 89–118.

Kang, Sang-jung. "Memories of a Zainichi Korean Childhood." Translated by Robin Fletcher. *Asia-Pacific Journal: Japan Focus* 5, no. 2 (February 2, 2007). http://apjjf.org/-Kang-Sang-Jung/2343/article.html.

Kang, Younghill. "China Is Different." *New Republic*, July 1, 1931.

Kang, Younghill. "Japan's Secret Plans." *Picture Scoop*, December 1942.

Kang, Younghill. "Prelude to Korean Independence." *Travel Magazine*, September 1946.

Kang, Younghill. "The Japanese Mind Is Sick." *Tomorrow*, May 1945.

Kang, Younghill. "When the Japs March In." *American Magazine*, August 1942.

Kang, Younghill. *East Goes West*. New York: Kaya Production, 1997.

Kauanui, J. Kēhaulani. "Asian American Studies and the 'Pacific Question.'" In *Asian American Studies after Critical Mass*, edited by Kent A. Ono, 121–43. New York: Wiley-Blackwell, 2008. https://doi.org/10.1002/9780470774892.ch7.

Kawamura, Minato. "Intabyu taidan—'Zainichi bungaku' o koete: Yi Yang-Ji" [An interview—Getting past "Zainichi literature": Yi Yang-Ji]. *Bungakkai* 43 (March 1989): 264–84.

Kim, Bumsoo. "Bringing Class Back In: The Changing Basis of Inequality and the Korean Minority in Japan." *Ethnic and Racial Studies* 31, no. 5 (July 1, 2008): 871–98. https://doi.org/10.1080/01419870701682279.

Kim, Claire Jean. "The Racial Triangulation of Asian Americans." *Politics and Society* 27, no. 1 (March 1, 1999): 105–38. https://doi.org/10.1177/0032329 299027001005.

Kim, Elaine H. "Searching for a Door to America: Younghill Kang, Korean-American Writer." *Korea Journal* 17, no. 4 (April 1977): 38–47.

Kim, Eleana. "Wedding Citizenship and Culture: Korean Adoptees and the Global Family of Korea." *Social Text* 21, no. 1 (April 25, 2003): 57–81.

Kim, Joanne H. "Mediating Selves: Younghill Kang's Balancing Act." *Hitting Critical Mass* 6 (1999): 51–59.

Kim, Kwang Chung, ed. *Koreans in the Hood: Conflict with African Americans.* Baltimore: Johns Hopkins University Press, 1999.

Kim, Masumi. "Moeru Sōka." In *Nason no sora*, 97–186. Tokyo: Sofukan, 2005.

Kim, Ronyoung. *Clay Walls*. Sag Harbor, NY: Permanent Press, 1996.

Kim, Sok-pom. "Kyomutan ['A Tale of Empty Dreams']." In *Seiji to kakumei* [Politics and revolution], 187–225. Tokyo: Kodansha bungee bunco, 2002.

Kim, Sok-pom. *Zainichi no shisō* [Thoughts on Zainichi]. Tokyo: Chikuma Shobō, 1981.

Kim, Tae Young. *Aidentiti poritikusu o koete* [Beyond identity politics]. Kyoto: Sekai Shishōsha, 1999.

Kim, Tong Myung. "Zainichi chōsenjin no daisan michi" [The third way of resident Koreans]." In *Zainichi kankoku chōsenjin: Sono nihon ni okeru sonzaikachi* [Resident Koreans: The value of their existence in Japan], 21–86. Osaka: Kaifūsha, 1988.

Kitano, Beat. "Chunen josei ga nekkyō suru 'Yon-sama bumu' wa 'Aoyama no motsu nabeya' mitaina mon datte no" [The middle-aged-fueled Yon-Sama fad Is like Aoyama's hot pot boom]. *Sapio* 16, no. 14 (August 18, 2004): 78–79.

Knadler, Stephen P. *The Fugitive Race: Minority Writers Resisting Whiteness.* Jackson: University Press of Mississippi, 2002.

Koizumi, Kenkichiro. "In Search of Wakon." *Technology and Culture* 43, no. 1 (2002): 29–49.

Koshy, Susan. "The Fiction of Asian American Literature." *Yale Journal of Criticism* 9, no. 2 (1996): 315–46. https://doi.org/10.1353/yale.1996.0017.

Kuo, Karen J. *East Is West and West Is East: Gender, Culture, and Interwar Encounters between Asia and America*. Philadelphia: Temple University Press, 2013.

Kuraishi, Ichiro. "*Pacchigi!* and *GO*: Representing Zainichi in Recent Cinema." In *Diaspora without Homeland: Being Korean in Japan*, edited by Sonia Ryang and John Lie, 107–20. Berkeley: University of California Press, 2009.

Kwon, Nayoung Aimee. *Intimate Empire: Collaboration and Colonial Modernity in Korea and Japan*. Durham, NC: Duke University Press, 2015.

Lee, Ana Paulina. *Mandarin Brazil: Race, Representation, and Memory*. Stanford, CA: Stanford University Press, 2018.

Lee, Benson. "Interview with 'Seoul Searching' Director Benson Lee." Conducted by Timothy Tau. *Hyphen* magazine, March 10, 2015. https://hyphenmagazine.com/blog/2015/03/interview-seoul-searching-director-benson-lee.

Lee, Benson, dir. *Seoul Searching*. Netflix, 2015.

Lee, Chang-rae. *A Gesture Life: A Novel*. New York: Riverhead Books, 2000.

Lee, Julia H. *Interracial Encounters: Reciprocal Representations in African American and Asian American Literatures, 1896–1937*. New York: New York University Press, 2011.

Lee, Kun Jong. "The African-American Presence in Younghill Kang's *East Goes West*." *CLA Journal* 57, no. 3 (2014): 224–46.

Lee, Kyhan. "Younghill Kang and the Genesis of Korean-American Literature." *Korea Journal* 31, no. 4 (Winter 1991): 63–78.

Lee, Min Jin. *Pachinko*. New York: Grand Central, 2017.

Lee, Young-Oak. "Transcending Ethnicity: Diasporicity in *A Gesture Life*." *Journal of Asian American Studies* 12, no. 1 (2009): 65–81. https://doi.org/10.1353/jaas.0.0029.

Leong, Andrew. "The Pocket and the Watch: A Collective Individualist Reading of Japanese American Literature." *Verge: Studies in Global Asias* 1, no. 2 (2015): 76–114. https://doi.org/10.5749/vergstudglobasia.1.2.0076.

Lew, Walter. "Grafts, Transplants, Translation: The Americanizing of Younghill Kang." In *Modernism, Inc*, edited by Jani Scandura and Michael Thurston, 171–90. New York: New York University Press, 2001.

Lie, John. *Zainichi*. Berkeley: University of California Press, 2008.

Lim, Shirley Geok-lin. "Feminist and Ethnic Literary Theories in Asian American Literature." *Feminist Studies* 19, no. 3 (1993): 571–95. https://doi.org/10.2307/3178101.

Lionnet, Françoise, and Shu-mei Shih. "Introduction: Thinking through the Minor, Transnationally." In *Minor Transnationalism*, edited by Françoise Lionnet and Shih Shu-mei Shih, 1–26. Durham, NC: Duke University Press, 2005.

Lionnet, Françoise, and Shu-mei Shih, eds. *Minor Transnationalism*. Durham, NC: Duke University Press, 2005.

Lowe, Lisa. *Immigrant Acts: On Asian American Cultural Politics*. Durham, NC: Duke University Press, 1996.

Lowe, Lisa. *The Intimacies of Four Continents*. Durham, NC: Duke University Press, 2015.

Lye, Colleen. "Introduction: In Dialogue with Asian American Studies." *Representations* 99, no. 1 (August 1, 2007): 1–12. https://doi.org/10.1525/rep.2007.99.1.1.

Macmillan, Michael E. "Unwanted Allies: Koreans as Enemy Aliens in World War II." *Hawaiian Journal of History* 19 (1985): 179–203. http://evols.library.manoa.hawaii.edu/handle/10524/571.

Man, Simeon. *Soldiering through Empire: Race and the Making of the Decolonizing Pacific*. Oakland: University of California Press, 2018.

Mitchell, Richard H. *The Korean Minority in Japan*. Berkeley: University of California Press, 1967.

Manzenreiter, Wolfram. "Time, Space and Money: Cultural Dimension of the Pachinko Game." In *The Culture of Japan as Seen through Its Leisure*, edited by Sepp Linhart and Sabine Fruhstuck, 359–82. Albany: SUNY Press, 1998.

Montgomery, David. *The Fall of the House of Labor*. Cambridge: Cambridge University Press, 1987.

Nakamura, Rika. "What Asian American Studies Can Learn from Asia? Towards a Project of Comparative Minority Studies." *Inter-Asia Cultural Studies* 13, no. 2 (June 1, 2012): 251–66. https://doi.org/10.1080/14649373.2012.659812.

"Neither South, North, nor Japan, Korean Resident Writers Mull Allegiance." *Japan Times*, December 27, 2002.

Nelson, Kim Park. *Invisible Asians: Korean American Adoptees, Asian American Experiences, and Racial Exceptionalism*. New Brunswick, NJ: Rutgers University Press, 2016.

Nevins, Allan, and Frank E. Hill. *Ford: The Times, the Man, and the Company*. New York: Scribner's, 1954.

Nguyen, Andy. "Supreme Court Declines Case over Glendale's Controversial 'Comfort Women' Statue." *Los Angeles Times*, March 31, 2017. http://www.latimes.com/socal/glendale-news-press/news/tn-gnp-me-comfort-statue-20170331-story.html.

Nguyen, Viet Thanh, and Janet Alison Hoskins. "Introduction: Transpacific Studies: Critical Perspectives on an Emerging Field." In *Transpacific Studies: Framing an Emerging Field*. Honolulu: University of Hawaii Press, 2014.

Nie, Jing Bao, Nanyan Guo, Mark Selden, and Arthur Kleinman, eds. *Japan's*

Wartime Medical Atrocities: Comparative Inquiries in Science, History, and Ethics. London: Routledge, 2011.

Oh, Sae-a. "'Precious Possessions Hidden': A Cultural Background to Ronyoung Kim's 'Clay Walls.'" *MELUS* 26, no. 3 (2001): 31–49. https://doi.org/10.2307/3185556.

Oh, Seiwoong. "Cross-cultural Reading versus Textual Accessibility in Multicultural Literature." *MELUS* 18, no. 2 (June 1, 1993): 3–16. https://doi.org/10.2307/467930.

Omi, Michael, and Howard Winant. *Racial Formation in the United States.* New York: Routledge, 1986.

Ong, Aihwa. *Flexible Citizenship: The Cultural Logics of Transnationality.* Durham, NC: Duke University Press, 1999.

Onishi, Yuichiro. *Transpacific Antiracism: Afro-Asian Solidarity in 20th-Century Black America, Japan, and Okinawa.* 2013. Reprint, New York: NYU Press, 2014.

Otterson, Joe. "'Pachinko' Ordered to Series at Apple." *Variety* (blog), March 14, 2019. https://variety.com/2019/tv/news/pachinko-series-apple-1203163934/.

Palumbo-Liu, David. *Asian/American: Historical Crossings of a Racial Frontier.* Stanford, CA: Stanford University Press, 1999.

Park, Josephine. *Apparitions of Asia: Modernist Form and Asian American Poetics.* New York: Oxford University Press, 2008.

Park, Soon-Won. *Colonial Industrialization and Labor in Korea: The Onoda Cement Factory.* Cambridge, MA: Harvard University Press, 1999.

Patterson, Wayne. *The Korean Frontier in America: Immigration to Hawaii, 1896–1910.* Honolulu: University of Hawaii Press, 1994.

Patterson, Wayne, and Hyung-chan Kim. *The Koreans in America.* Minneapolis, MN: Lerner Publications, 1977.

Pew Research Center's Social and Demographic Trends Project. "Koreans in the U.S. Fact Sheet." September 8, 2017. https://www.pewsocialtrends.org/fact-sheet/asian-americans-koreans-in-the-u-s/.

Phillips, Jane. "'We'd Be Rich in Korea': Value and Contingency in *Clay Walls* by Ronyoung Kim." *MELUS* 23, no. 2 (1998): 173–87. https://doi.org/10.2307/468018.

Rhee, Suk Koo. "Consumable Bodies and Ethnic (Hi)Stories: Strategies and Risks of Representation in 'A Gesture Life.'" *Discourse* 34, no. 1 (2012): 93–112.

Ryang, Sonia. "The Denationalized Have No Class: The Banishment of Japan's Korean Minority—A Polemic." *CR: The New Centennial Review* 12, no. 1 (November 13, 2012): 159–87. https://doi.org/10.1353/ncr.2012.0030.

Ryang, Sonia. *Koreans in Japan: Critical Voices from the Margin.* London: Routledge, 2005.

Ryang, Sonia. "Introduction: Between the Nations: Diaspora and Koreans in Japan." In *Diaspora without Homeland: Being Korean in Japan*, edited by Sonia Ryang and John Lie, 1–20. Berkeley: University of California Press, 2009.

Ryang, Sonia. "Introduction: Resident Koreans in Japan." In *Koreans in Japan: Critical Voices from the Margin*, edited by Sonia Ryang, 1–12. London: Routledge, 2005.

Ryang, Sonia, and John Lie, eds. *Diaspora without Homeland: Being Korean in Japan*. Berkeley: University of California Press, 2009.

Ryu, Catherine. "Beyond Language: Embracing the Figure of 'The Other' in Yi Yang-Ji's *Yuhi*." In *Representing the Other in Modern Japanese Literature: A Critical Approach*, edited by Rachael Hutchinson and Mark Williams, 312–31. New York: Routledge, 2006.

Said, E. *Humanism and Democratic Criticism*. New York: Palgrave Macmillan, 2004.

Salisbury, Mark H., Michael B. Paulsen, and Ernest T. Pascarella. "Why Do All the Study Abroad Students Look Alike? Applying an Integrated Student Choice Model to Explore Differences in the Factors That Influence White and Minority Students' Intent to Study Abroad." *Research in Higher Education* 52, no. 2 (March 2011): 123–50. https://doi.org/10.1007/s11162-010-9191-2.

Scott, Christopher Donal. "Invisible Men: The Zainichi Korean Presence in Postwar Japanese Culture." PhD diss., Stanford University, 2006.

Shin, Duckhee. "Class and Self-Identity in 'Clay Walls.'" *MELUS* 24, no. 4 (December 22, 1999): 125–36.

Simpson, Caroline Chung. *An Absent Presence: Japanese Americans in Postwar American Culture, 1945–1960*. Durham, NC: Duke University Press, 2002.

Sminkey, Paul. "Korean-Japanese Identity in Kaneshiro Kazuki's *GO*." *Gakujuukenkyukiyou*, no. 28 (2002): 11–22.

Smith, Merrit Roe. *Harpers Ferry Armory and the New Technology: The Challenge of Change*. Ithaca, NY: Cornell University Press, 1977.

Soble, Jonathan. "A Novelist Confronts the Complex Relationship between Japan and Korea." *New York Times*, November 6, 2017, sec. World. https://www.nytimes.com/2017/11/06/books/book-pachinko-min-jin-lee-japan-korea.html.

Sohn, Stephen Hong, Paul Lai, and Donald C. Goellnicht. "Theorizing Asian American Fiction." *MFS: Modern Fiction Studies* 56, no. 1 (March 17, 2010): 1–18. https://doi.org/10.1353/mfs.0.1661.

Son, Elizabeth. *Embodied Reckonings: "Comfort Women," Performance, and Transpacific Redress*. Ann Arbor: University of Michigan Press, 2018.

Sorensen, Leif. *Ethnic Modernism and the Making of US Literary Multiculturalism*. New York: Palgrave Macmillan, 2016.

Stephenson, Neal. *Snow Crash*. New York: Del Rey, 2000.

Stowe, William W. *Going Abroad: European Travel in Nineteenth-Century American Culture*. Princeton, NJ: Princeton University Press, 1994.

Supreme Command for Allied Powers. "Status of Koreans in Japan." n.d. National Archives and Records Administration, RG 331.47, Records of the SCAP Civil Intelligence Section 1945–49.

Takaki, Ronald. *Strangers from a Different Shore: A History of Asian Americans*. New York: Penguin Books, 1989.

Taylor, Frederick Winslow. "The Principles of Scientific Management." In *Scientific Management*. New York: Harper and Row, 1947.

Terasima, Takayosi, and Miyako Koike. "Zainichi kankokuchōsenjin no kankokuryūgaku" [Study abroad in Korea by Koreans born and living in Japan]. *Gifu Daigaku Kyouiku Gakubu Kenkyuu Houkoku* 9, no. 3 (2007): 94–117.

Thoma, Pamela. "Representing Korean American Female Subjects, Negotiating Multiple Americas, and Reading beyond the Ending in Ronyoung Kim's *Clay Walls*." In *Recovered Legacies: Authority and Identity in Early Asian American Literature*, edited by Keith Lawrence and Floyd Cheung, 265–94. Philadelphia, PA: Temple University Press, 2005. http://www.jstor.org/stable/j.ctt14bt1rj.

Tölölyan, Khachig. "The Contemporary Discourse of Diaspora Studies." *Comparative Studies of South Asia, Africa and the Middle East* 27, no. 3 (2007): 647–55.

Tomonari, Noboru. "Configuring Bodies: Self-Identity in the Works of Kaneshiro Kazuki and Yan Sogiru." *Japanese Studies* 25, no. 3 (December 1, 2005): 257–69. https://doi.org/10.1080/10371390500342758.

Tsutsui, William. *Manufacturing Ideology: Scientific Management in Twentieth-Century Japan*. Princeton, NJ: Princeton University Press, 1998.

Ueda, Atsuko. "'Moji' to iu 'kotoba'—I Yanji 'Yuhi' o megutte" [The 'Language' Called 'Writing': On Yi Yang-Ji's *Yuhi*]. *Nihon Kindai Bungaku* 62 (May 2000): 128–43.

Ueki, Teruyo. "Past, Present, and Future of Asian American Studies." *AALA Journal* (Asian American Literature Association), no. 6 (2000): 53–64.

Ueno, Yōichi. *Ueno Yōichi den*. Edited by Ed Misawa Hitoshi. Tokyo: Sangyo Noritsu Tanki Daigaku Shuppanbu, 1967.

US Census Bureau. "The Asian Population: 2010." United States Census Report Number C2010BR-11. March 2012. https://www.census.gov/library/publications/2012/dec/c2010br-11.html.

Van Der Meid, J. Scott. "Asian Americans: Factors Influencing the Decision to Study Abroad." *Frontiers Journal: The Interdisciplinary Journal of Study Abroad* 9 (January 2003): 71–110.

Vazquez, David J. *Triangulations: Narrative Strategies for Navigating Latino Identity.* Minneapolis: University of Minnesota Press, 2011.

Wang, Chih-ming. *Transpacific Articulations: Student Migration and the Remaking of Asian America.* Honolulu: University of Hawaii Press, 2013.

Watanna, Onoto [Winnifred Eaton]. *The Heart of Hyacinth.* New York: Harper, 1903.

Watanna, Onoto. *The Wooing of Wistaria.* New York: Harper, 1902.

Wender, Melissa L. *Into the Light: An Anthology of Literature by Koreans in Japan.* Honolulu: University of Hawaii Press, 2010.

Wender, Melissa. *Lamentation as History: Narratives by Koreans in Japan, 1965–2000.* Palo Alto, CA: Stanford University Press, 2005.

Wignot, Jamila. "Unfamiliar Kin." *Finding Your Roots,* October 10, 2017. Public Broadcasting Service.

Yamamoto, Hisaye. *Seventeen Syllables and Other Stories. Revised and Updated with Four New Stories.* New Brunswick, NJ: Rutgers University Press, 2001.

Yang, Caroline H. "The Asian-Owned Store and the Incommensurable Histories of War in Narratives of the City." *MELUS* 43, no. 2 (June 1, 2018): 172–95. https://doi.org/10.1093/melus/mly012.

Yi, Yang-ji. "Watashi wa chōsenjin" [I am Korean]. In *Yi Yang-Ji zenshū* [The collected works of Yi Yang-Ji], 579–91. Tokyo: Kōdansha, 1993.

Yi, Yang-ji. *Yuhi.* Tokyo: Kōdansha, 1989.

Yokota-Murakami, Takayuki. *Mother-Tongue in Modern Japanese Literature and Criticism: Toward a New Polylingual Poetics.* Singapore: Palgrave Macmillan, 2018. www.palgrave.com/us/book/9789811085116.

Yoneyama, Lisa. *Cold War Ruins: Transpacific Critique of American Justice and Japanese War Crimes.* Durham, NC: Duke University Press Books, 2016.

Yoneyama, Lisa. *Hiroshima Traces: Time, Space, and the Dialectics of Memory.* Berkeley: University of California Press, 1999.

Yoon, Kun Hum. *"Zainichi" o ikiru to wa* [Living as a resident Korean]. Tokyo: Iwanami Shoten, 1992.

Yoshida, Reiji, and Kazuaki Nagata. "Self-Censorship Is Biggest Threat to Free Speech in Japan." *Japan Times Online,* January 22, 2015. http://www.japantimes.co.jp/news/2015/01/22/national/self-censorship-biggest-threat-free-speech-japan/.

Index

adoption: in *A Gesture Life*, 88, 90–95, 97; naming and, 93; *yōshi*, 93–94, 179n34

affect, 164n35

American studies, 7; comparative literature and, 126, 185n5; disciplinary boundaries of, 126, 185n5; minority discourse in, 162n29; monolingualism of, 126; transnational, 159n14

American Studies Association of Korea, x

area studies, 7, 51, 166n47; disciplinary boundaries of, 160n20; ethnic studies, relationship with, 161n29; Zainichi literature in, 24–25

Armisen, Fred, 152–55, *153*; passing and, 154

Asian America, xi; diversity of, 127; Japan and, 6, 12–13, 21–24, 78, 169n5; transnationality of, 29, 104–5, 159n16, 180n4, 181n18

Asian American movement, 7, 160n18; anti-imperialism of, 105; civil rights in, 105, 127; identity formation in, 105

Asian Americans: citizenship of, 8; culture and, 53; racialization of, xi, 8, 82, 129, 164n43; study abroad experiences, 103–6, 181n14; subject formation of, 21, 97. *See also* identity, Asian American; subjectivity, Asian American

Asian American studies: Asian studies, dialogue with, 5–8, 51, 72, 105–6, 126, 155, 160n18, 160nn20–21, 161n22; coalition politics of, 127; comfort women in, 78–79, 83; disciplinary boundaries of, 125; essentialist framework of, 127–28; filial relations, 8; heterogeneity and, 8; human rights in, 83, 99; hybridity and, 8, 9, 91; hypermasculinity of, 161n22; immigration in, 160n21; institutionalization of, 10; intergenerational conflict in, 8; international students in, 182n22, 182n24; Japanese imperialism and, 77–78; Japanese studies and, 11–12, 77–78;

in, 112–13, 116, 118; Korean America
in, 116–17; Korean American subjectivity in, 117; Korean identity
in, 111; Koreanness in, 111; language
in, 109, 111–12, 114, 183n31, 183n33;
linguistic displacement of, 108;
linguistic tensions of, 108–9; passing in, 113–14, 119; return, ideology
of, 112, 119–20; scholarship on, 109;
sojournship in, 111, 113–14, 120, 156;
Yuhi as anomalous, 112–13
Yu Miri, 107

Zainichi, 1; American popular culture
and, 66–67; assimilation of, 14,
16, 60, 175n31; citizenship of, x–xi,
15–16, 52, 57–58, 60–61, 67–68, 95,
140–42, 174n18, 174n21, 175n40; collaboration and, 60; criminalization
of, 16, 56, 139; diasporic discourse
of, 52–53; diasporic subjectivity of,

107; discrimination against, 66–67,
69–71; ethnicity and, 60; hybridity of, 95; identity of, 13–14, 16, 60,
71–72; immigration to Japan, 14–15;
independence of, 18; Koreanness of,
141; migration of, 14–15, 91; nationality and, 60; pachinko businesses
of, 131; as perpetual foreigners, 14,
57–58, 138, 140; racialization of,
xi, 17, 53–54, 56, 63, 68, 139, 142;
repatriation of, 15, 186n18; return
to Korea, 1, 118, 119–20; in *Seoul
Searching*, 120–22; sovereignty of,
18; statelessness of, 15, 18, 52, 54–55,
117; as temporary residents, 14, 59;
use of term, 14, 159n13, 166n50. *See
also* subjectivity, Zainichi
Zainichi Korea, dialogue with Korean
America, 124–25
Zainichi studies, Asian studies and,
xi–xii